BELIEFS AND LEADERSHIP
IN WORLD POLITICS

Advances in Foreign Policy Analysis

Series Editor: Alex Mintz

Foreign policy analysis offers rich theoretical perspectives and diverse methodological approaches. Scholars specializing in foreign policy analysis produce a vast output of research Yet, there were only very few specialized outlets for publishing work in the field. Addressing this need is the purpose of **Advances in Foreign Policy Analysis**. The series bridges the gap between academic and policy approaches to foreign policy analysis, integrates across levels of analysis, spans theoretical approaches to the field, and advances research utilizing decision theory, utility theory, and game theory.

Members of the Board of Advisors

Published by Palgrave Macmillan

BELIEFS AND LEADERSHIP IN WORLD POLITICS

METHODS AND APPLICATIONS OF OPERATIONAL CODE ANALYSIS

Edited by
Mark Schafer and Stephen G. Walker

First published in 2006 by
PALGRAVE MACMILLAN™
175 Fifth Avenue, New York, N.Y. 10010 and
Houndmills, Basingstoke, Hampshire, England RG21 6XS
Companies and representatives throughout the world.

PALGRAVE MACMILLAN is the global academic imprint of the Palgrave Macmillan division of St. Martin's Press, LLC and of Palgrave Macmillan Ltd. Macmillan® is a registered trademark in the United States, United Kingdom and other countries. Palgrave is a registered trademark in the European Union and other countries.

ISBN-13: 978–1–4039–7182–1
ISBN-10: 1–4039–7182–X

Library of Congress Cataloging-in-Publication Data

Beliefs and leadership in world politics : methods and applications of operational code analysis / edited by Mark Schafer and Stephen G. Walker.
    p. cm.—(Advances in foreign policy analysis)
Includes bibliographical references and index.
ISBN 1–4039–7182–X
1. International relations. 2. Communication in politics. 3. Security, International. 4. Game theory. 5. Ideaology. I. Schafer, Mark, professor. II. Walker, Stephen G., 1942– III. Series.

JZ1305.B453 2006
327.101'5193—dc22   2006041582

A catalogue record for this book is available from the British Library.

Design by Newgen Imaging Systems (P) Ltd., Chennai, India.

First edition: September 2006

10 9 8 7 6 5 4 3 2 1

Printed in the United States of America.

We dedicate this volume to Alexander George and Ole Holsti, who led the way as scholars and mentors.

CONTENTS

LIST OF TABLES, FIGURES, AND APPENDICES

Tables

Figures

Appendices

PREFACE

The immediate origins of this book are the confluence of three sources of inspiration. One was a remark by Yaacov Vertzberger in a conversation at a professional meeting. He suggested that an edited volume of recent operational code research would be a valuable resource for graduate students who wanted to learn more about this approach to foreign policy and world politics. Another is an exchange with David Pervin at Palgrave Macmillan Press, who insisted that the contributions to such a volume be original work rather than reprints of previous scholarship. A final source of inspiration was the invitation from Colin and Miriam Elman to include the operational code research program as part of their volume assessing scientific progress in international relations theory. This opportunity became the catalyst for organizing the present volume as a progress report for the community of research scholars in the field of international relations as well as a methodological handbook for graduate students.

Our general aims in this book are to publicize the work in this research program and show how it connects to the concerns of foreign policy analysts and international relations theorists. Alexander George and Ole Holsti led by example with their development of the operational code construct as a belief system, inspired by Nathan Leites' prototypical RAND Corporation study of the beliefs of Russian Bolshevik leaders. They also acted as informal mentors to the editors early in their respective careers. One of the editors first applied George's refinement of Leites' operational code construct to a study of Henry Kissinger in the 1970s, and then used Holsti's typology in a study of the operational codes of U.S. presidents and secretaries of state funded by the National Science Foundation in the early 1980s. The other editor benefited from the mentoring provided by Ole Holsti in the 1990s as an NSF (National Science Foundation) fellow in the interdisciplinary research program on individual cognition and collective decision making at Ohio State University's Mershon Center.

Other individuals also influenced the evolution of the operational code research program. At a Washington, DC meeting of academic and government analysts in the 1980s, John Kringen posed a key question about operational code analysis: "How do you identify the operational code of an illiterate sergeant who has just become the new leader of a state in a Third World nation?" Previous operational code studies had focused on U.S. leaders who had left a paper trail of speeches, books, and other texts prior to assuming office. Many of them were on record with reasoned treatises regarding philosophical beliefs about the nature of world politics and instrumental beliefs about the most effective means of political action.

Kringen's question underlined a dual difficulty associated with expanding operational code analysis as a research program. How do you access foreign leaders to study them? How do you extrapolate their operational codes from data sources that do not directly contain information about their general philosophical and instrumental beliefs? The eventual answer to these riddles was to invest in the development of an "at-a-distance" method for inferring general beliefs from attribution patterns contained in the verbal materials of subjects. The Verbs In Context System (VICS) of content analysis evolved in a series of seminars, conferences, and journal articles over the next two decades.

While the motivations for assembling this volume are relatively transparent in the table of contents and in the chapters by the contributors, the sources of support necessary to complete this volume are less obvious. Therefore, we want to acknowledge them explicitly here. Several individuals and institutions have provided guidance, inspiration, and resources over a very long period of time by including us in collaborative ventures, hosting professional conferences, or inviting us to present our research in symposia at their respective institutions.

One of the most important intellectual catalysts for developing VICS was the research community of "at-a-distance" scholars, including Margaret Hermann, David Winter, Walter Weintraub, Peter Suedfeld, Phillip Tetlock, Jerrold Post, and Stanley Renshon. We owe a large intellectual debt as well to Michael Young and Robert Woyach at Social Science Automation who developed the software for an automated version of VICS in collaboration with the editors in the late 1990s. Another important catalyst was the special learning environment for each of us in different ways as members of the invisible college of political scientists and psychologists at Ohio State University's Mershon Center. Assembled by Margaret Hermann with an NSF grant, this five-year program created a forum for scholarly exchange and provided other resources to encourage Ph.D. students from each discipline to write dissertations in political psychology.

One of us was a senior mentor on the board of faculty advisors while the other was an NSF dissertation fellow in this program. These experiences incubated our future collaborative efforts with Michael Young and also fostered professional ties with Ryan Beasley, Matthew Bonham, Paul t'Hart, Julie Kaarbo, Tom Preston, Theodore Raphael, Eric Stern, Bengt Sundelius, Don Sylvan, and others, which remain close to this day.

Several individuals and institutions have funded our travels to present our research before a variety of audiences. They include Willem Saris and Irmtraud Galhofer in the Department of Methods and Techniques at the University of Amsterdam, Paul Stern and William Gamson at the National Research Council of the National Academy of Sciences in Washington, DC, Victor Sergeev, Pavel Parshin, and Nikolai Biryukov at the Institute for the Study of the USA and Canada in Moscow, Charles Hermann in the George Bush School of Government and Public Service at Texas A & M University, Qingmin Zhang and Liu Zhi Yong at the Foreign Affairs University in Beijing, Jerrold Post and Maurice East in the Elliott School of International Affairs at George Washington University, Colin Elman and Miriam Fendius Elman as organizers at Arizona State University of the Scottsdale Conference on Progress in International Relations Theory, and Margaret Hermann as the director of the Summer Institute in Political Psychology at Ohio State University.

Each of us also owes much to the generations of students whose questions and opinions as scholars and work as research assistants have supported our efforts over the years at Arizona State University and Louisiana State University. They include Steven Hoagland, Tim Murphy Janice Thomson, Jody Kent, Loizos Afxentiou, Mari Ishibashi, Joe Bond, Nevzat Soguk, Doug Van Belle, Wendy Theodore, Brian Dille, Eric Strachan, Scott Payne, Bradley Aldrich, Eric Melancon, and the contributors to this volume. Our thanks extend as well to the administration, staff, and faculty at our respective home institutions for research and travel support as well as a collegial working environment in which to teach and write.

The exchange of ideas between the operational code research program and other research programs in international relations has also enriched our efforts. We are especially grateful to Steven Brams for his patience in reading our early efforts at employing sequential game theory in conjunction with VICS to model the implications of a leader's operational code beliefs in strategic interactions with others in the political universe. We are also keenly aware of the less obvious but important influences of other scholars. They include Robert Axelrod, David Baldwin, Francis Beer, Andrew Bennett, Martha Cottam, David Dessler, Charles Doran, Lawrence Falkowski, Ofer Feldman, Nehemiah Geva, Judith Goldstein, Fred

Greenstein, Joe Hagan, Jeff Hart, Charles Hermann, Richard Herrmann, Valerie Hudson, Robert Jervis, Alistair Ian Johnston, Robert Keohane, Yuen Khong, Jacek Kugler, Charles Kupchan, David Lake, Deborah Larson, Russell Leng, Jack Levy, Steve Majeski, Zeev Maoz, Lisa Martin, Charles McClelland, Alex Mintz, Kenneth Organski, Susan Peterson, Jon Pevehouse, Robert Powell, Jerel Rosati, Bruce Russett, Randall Schweller, Harvey Starr, Charles Taber, Linda Valenty, Yaacov Vertzberger, Kenneth Waltz, and Alexander Wendt.

We thank Sam Robison, Kaitlyn Sill, and Roy Bergeron at Louisiana State University for checking, formatting, and indexing the chapters in this volume. We are also grateful to Heather Van Dusen, Elizabeth Sabo, and Maran Elancheran at Palgrave Press for their careful and competent processing of the manuscript during the production process. While acknowledging here our debts to all of these individuals and to any others we may have inadvertently overlooked, we remain responsible for any errors in the book. Finally, we wish to express deep appreciation to our respective families for their forbearance while we completed this volume. Spouses, pets, children, and grandchildren from blended families offered both diversions and support, and sometimes tolerated interludes of benign neglect, especially during the closing days of preparing the book manuscript for submission to Palgrave Press. It is unlikely this book would be a reality without their continuous goodwill.

Mark Schafer
Baton Rouge, Louisiana
September 30, 2005

Stephen G. Walker
Flagstaff, Arizona
September 30, 2005

CHAPTER 1

BELIEF SYSTEMS AS CAUSAL MECHANISMS IN WORLD POLITICS: AN OVERVIEW OF OPERATIONAL CODE ANALYSIS

Stephen G. Walker and Mark Schafer

When we look at the work on operational codes, we are looking at the most widely used concept relating to the link between belief systems and international relations . . .[O]ver two dozen studies have used it in an attempt to explain the foreign policy choices of leaders . . .[and]. . . in virtually every case, tended to find the concept very useful as a research technique.

Smith, *Belief Systems and International Relations*

Introduction

As the quotation from Smith (1988) indicates, research programs in foreign policy analysis have always maintained that who decides matters. Since the end of the cold war, more scholars and policy makers have come to appreciate the need to study belief systems as causal mechanisms in the post–cold war world. Following their failure to anticipate and explain the end of the conflict between the superpowers, rational choice and international relations theorists have also begun to recognize the need to include the analysis of beliefs and norms in their research programs (Bueno De Mesquita and Lalman 1992; Geva and Mintz 1997; Johnston 1995a; Keohane and Martin 2003;

Schweller 2003). The cold war constrained both the foreign policy choices of the superpowers as well as the actions of others within a bipolar system. In its aftermath, the absence of clear external focal points on which to calculate strategies and tactics has forced policy makers to rely more on the internal focal points offered by their own subjective beliefs about the nature of the political universe and the most effective means for realizing political goals.

This renaissance in the study of belief systems as causal mechanisms has created a demand for a book that makes the methods and applications of operational code analysis available to a new generation of faculty and graduate students with research interests in either foreign policy or international relations. In this handbook of operational code analysis we provide a resource for scholars who wish to incorporate beliefs into their explanations of international relations. Operational code analysis is a classic approach to foreign policy and international relations within the general cognitivist research program in world politics (Tetlock 1998; Walker 1977, 1990). The operational code construct is a complex set of elements defined initially by Nathan Leites (1951, 1953) as conceptions of political strategy in Bolshevik ideology, which functioned as expressions of the Bolshevik character. Alexander George (1969) later conceptualized a leader's operational code as a political belief system with some elements (philosophical beliefs) guiding the diagnosis of the context for action and others (instrumental beliefs) prescribing the most effective strategy and tactics for achieving goals.

The core argument in this volume reflects the cognitivist proposition that beliefs as "subjective representations of reality" matter in the explanation of world politics in several ways not addressed very well by general international relations theories (Tetlock 1998, 876; see also Simon 1957). Structural theories within the neorealist, neoliberal, and constructivist research programs assume that leaders' beliefs simply mirror the foreign and domestic realities that they face as they make foreign policy decisions. Each of these approaches identifies different realities located at different levels of analysis as influential sources of foreign policy. Neorealists emphasize the balance of power among states while neoliberals highlight the economic and political institutions in which leaders are situated. Those constructivists who seek causal explanations rather than hermeneutic interpretations focus on international law and cultural norms that govern foreign policy choices (Fearon and Wendt 2002; Little 1991; Ruggie 1998; Smith 2001). While leaders can act to change the balance of power, domestic and international institutions, and cultural norms over the long run, they are viewed as constraints that limit the menu for choice available to leaders in the short run (Baldwin 1993; Katzenstein 1996).

Actor-based theories of rational choice share this attention to external focal points in the environment as the basis for foreign policy decisions along with the assumption that leaders have common goals constrained by these contextual factors. That is, it is rational to live by the limits imposed by power distributions, institutional configurations, or cultural norms. Moreover, they assume that these constraints are relatively transparent to leaders and that leaders will act on this information so as to maximize their gains and minimize their losses (Geva and Mintz 1997). Neorealists assume that it is rational to seek and maintain a power position in the international system favorable to their interests. Neoliberals assume that it is rational to act so as to insure the interests of international and domestic institutions. Constructivists assume that it is rational to reproduce or replace norms in order to insure an international order that enhances and protects cultural values. Beliefs in each case are assumed to mirror realities that leaders have to recognize as constraints or else change in order to attain and maintain their political goals (Baldwin 1993; Keohane 1983; Kowert and Legro 1996; Moravcsik 2003; Wendt 1999; see also Jervis 1994; Schweller 2003).

Cognitive theories differ with rational choice models and structural theories of foreign policy and world politics regarding the role of beliefs as causal mechanisms. Whereas the latter assign to beliefs the endogenous role of transmission belts (Rose 1998, 147), conveying information about the environment at home and abroad, cognitive theories allow for the possibility that beliefs have an exogenous role. That is, they can and often do operate as causal mechanisms independently of the realities that they are assumed to mirror in other theories. Instead of passively reflecting reality, they steer the decisions of leaders by shaping the leaders' perceptions of reality, acting as mechanisms of cognitive and motivated bias that distort, block, and recast incoming information from the environment (Snyder, Bruck, and Sapin 1954; Steinbrunner 1974; Vertzberger 1990). This role for beliefs is particularly likely when the environment is uncertain, that is, when information is scarce, ambiguous, contradictory, or so abundant that it is difficult for leaders to organize and process (Holsti 1976). It is also very likely to occur when new information does not fit with a leader's preexisting beliefs based on old information, stereotypes, or other cognitive biases associated with threats to vested interests, or aroused by strong emotions such as fear, anger, shame, or hate (Fiske and Taylor 1991; Jervis 1976; Stein 1988).

Simon (1985) identified the different roles assigned to beliefs by structural and cognitive theories of decision making as embodying different conceptions of rationality. Structural theories assume a model of *substantive* rationality in which the decision maker makes choices based on goals and knowledge of the external environment as *mirrored* by his/her beliefs.

Different models of substantive rationality may be employed, including instrumental rationality in which leaders calculate costs and benefits of different options available to them, and strategic rationality in which these cost/benefit calculations explicitly include the impact of likely choices made by others in the domestic or international political arenas (Lake and Powell 1999a; Little 1991; Signorino 1999).

Cognitive theories assume a model of *bounded* rationality in which the decision maker is *steered* by his/her system of beliefs in the identification of options, ends/means calculations, and choice of action (Simon 1985). Leaders may engage in biased behavior rather than optimizing behavior in identifying their choices, and choose actions consistent with their beliefs about external realities even when there is information available that contradicts their beliefs (Holsti 1976; Jervis 1976). They may also refuse to *learn*, that is, to revise their existing beliefs when confronted with new information, and thereby continue a course of action that moves them away from their goals rather than toward them (Levy 1994).

During the cold war it may have been more realistic to assume that beliefs performed a mirroring role in the calculus of foreign policy decisions. Structural international relations theorists did not have to look at the microfoundations of their theories to see if the belief systems of leaders reflected realities, because the highly structured, bipolar system of the cold war era provided leaders with a limited range of choices. Each superpower needed only to know that it had the other to fear and that it should balance against this threat (Waltz 1979). Smaller powers needed only to recognize the power disparity between them and the superpowers and calculate ways to stay out of the cold war or else ally with one of the principal protagonists.

However, in the post–cold war world, the logic of power politics is not so simple (Jervis 1994). There are multiple sources of threats to a state's security and a plethora of international institutions and blocs that may provide opportunities to protect or enhance a state's interests. Threats and opportunities engage states at supranational and subnational levels of analysis in new and complex ways (Keohane and Nye 2001). Globalization processes not only affect regional economic welfare but also relations among classes and ethnic groups within societies. Groups and organizations within societies may align with others in different countries to pose threats to the states that supposedly govern them, as illustrated by the activities of international terrorist groups, drug cartels, and multinational corporations (Keohane 2002).

The application of our core argument to the post–cold war world of the 21st century, therefore, is that it is increasingly important to test the merits of these two roles assigned to beliefs as causal mechanisms. Do beliefs passively mirror reality or do they actively steer the decisions of leaders independent of external realities (Goldstein and Keohane 1993; Walker 2002)? We anticipate that beliefs will become more important as causal mechanisms with steering effects in today's complex, interdependent world. Our goal in this book is to demonstrate that it is worthwhile to learn and apply the methods of content analysis associated with operational code analysis to meet this challenge.

Toward this end, the editors have recruited a talented team of young authors evenly divided between foreign policy analysis and broader international relations research programs. Our claim is that operational code analysis, as a psychological approach adaptable to the study of political phenomena at either the actor or systemic levels of analysis in world politics, is a worthwhile investment to make. We offer the contents of this volume as evidence from the cognitivist research program in world politics to a new generation of graduate students in international relations and to rational choice theorists and other scholars in realist, liberal, and constructivist research programs.

The Development of Operational Code Analysis

The model of bounded rationality in operational code analysis has evolved from the psycho-cultural model in Nathan Leites' prototypical studies of the Bolshevik operational code. Leites emphasized the influence of motivated biases in Lenin's personality and norms from the cultural milieu of the intelligentsia and revolutionary underground in Russia at the turn of the 20th century. This combination of psychological and cultural sources created an "operational code" of conceptions about strategy for the Soviet elite, which internalized Lenin's motivated biases stemming from a high need for power and a fear of annihilation along with norms from a cultural milieu of political autocracy and social repression (Leites 1951, 1953).

Sixteen years later Alexander George (1969) attempted to codify the philosophical and instrumental beliefs in the Bolshevik operational code without modeling the influences that shaped them. He argued that they should simply be considered a belief system that filtered incoming information from the environment and influenced the individual's preferences for different ends and means. The individual's belief system in this approach becomes a mechanism that reflects unspecified personality biases and societal influences. It can be extended in this simplified form as a heuristic to analyze any individual by answering the ten research questions that follow regarding specific philosophical and instrumental beliefs. The answers specify a model of instrumental rationality bounded by a belief system (George 1969, 1979).

The Philosophical Beliefs in an Operational Code

P-1. What is the "essential" nature of political life? Is the political universe essentially one of harmony or of conflict? What is the fundamental character of one's political opponents?

P-2. What are the prospects for the eventual realization of one's fundamental values and aspirations? Can one be optimistic, or must one be pessimistic on this score; and in what respects the one and/or the other?

P-3. Is the political future predictable? In what sense and to what extent?

P-4. How much "control" or "mastery" can one have over historical development? What is one's role in "moving" and "shaping" history in the desired direction?

P-5. What is the role of "chance" in human affairs and in historical development?

The Instrumental Beliefs in an Operational Code

I-1. What is the best approach for selecting goals or objectives for political action?

I-2. How are the goals of action pursued most effectively?

I-3. How are the risks of political action calculated, controlled, and accepted?

I-4. What is the best "timing" of action to advance one's interests?

I-5. What is the utility and role of different means for advancing one's interests?

Contemporary operational code analysis uses the Verbs In Context System (VICS) of content analysis to provide quantitative answers to George's ten questions about philosophical and instrumental beliefs. The details for this method are covered in chapter 2 of this volume, including a general overview of the logic of the system, a complete description of the operationalized indexes that provide answers to George's questions, and a step-by-step set of instructions for conducting VICS analysis.

In chapter 2 we also discuss the advantages of having quantitative indicators for the operational code. If we think of the operational code in terms of steering effects associated with bounded rationality, then the quantitative indicators of the operational code are appropriate explanatory variables. There are several examples of this type of work in the literature. Using event data as the dependent variable, Walker, Schafer, and Young (1999) assess the operational codes of U.S. presidents George H.W. Bush and Bill Clinton to model the actions of each leader's administration in post–cold war conflicts. Schafer and Gassler (2000) look at Anwar Sadat's operational code and find that experiential learning caused Sadat's beliefs to change, thus contributing to his decision to initiate the peace process with his historic visit to Israel. Schafer and Crichlow (2000) look at Bill Clinton's changing operational code over time and correlate that with shifts in U.S. behavior during several different foreign policy episodes.

Schafer, Robison, and Aldrich (2006) use some of the quantitative indicators in the operational code as a proxy for frustration levels, and demonstrate how rising frustration levels contributed to aggression by rebel leaders of the 1916 Easter Rising in Ireland. Analyzing public statements and event data, Schafer and Walker (n.d.) show that democratic leaders Bill Clinton and Tony Blair exhibit different operational codes and different patterns of foreign policy behavior toward nondemocratic regimes. They find that the operational code differences are statistically related to differences in their respective states' behavior in the Kosovo conflict. Malici (2005, 2006) and Marfleet and Miller (2005) examine the impact of operational code differences on allies in coordinating their foreign policy efforts in the United Nations Security Council and in dealing with the rogue states of Serbia, Iraq, Kosovo, and Afghanistan. They find that these differences explain fluctuations in the relations among Germany, France, Britain, and the United States as NATO allies in responding to threats posed by terrorists and ethnic violence in the Balkans and in the Middle East.

Quantitative operational code data also allow us to investigate changes in beliefs over time or differences between subjects, thus positioning the operational code as the dependent variable in our models. The first application using VICS looked at Jimmy Carter's operational code during his four years as president. Walker, Schafer, and Young (1998) find that his general beliefs changed notably only during his final year, seemingly as a result of the Soviet invasion of Afghanistan, the Iranian hostage crisis, and events on the Horn of Africa. Walker, Schafer, and Marfleet (2001) analyze the sources of change in the operational code beliefs of British Cabinet members as "experiential learning" (Levy 1994) during the conduct of Britain's appeasement strategy toward Germany prior to World War II. They identify different levels of learning (instrumental and philosophical) by British leaders, as they altered their operational code beliefs but not their strategy of appeasement in response to a series of crises with Germany stimulated by Austrian, Czech, and Polish territorial conflicts between 1937 and 1939. Other studies show that sometimes the behavior but not the beliefs of leaders change in response to significant environmental shifts. Malici and Malici (2005a, b) show that the beliefs of leaders in North Korea and Cuba did not change significantly after the end of the cold war even though behavior patterns by the states did change, thus demonstrating adaptive behavioral responses as opposed to cognitive change.

Finally, some operational code studies employ quantitative indices to differentiate the beliefs of leaders by domain and explain these differences as the contextual effects of adaptation by leaders to different issue areas, policy arenas, and targets. In these studies the beliefs of leaders become intervening variables between environmental conditions and foreign policy behavior. Examples include the study of Carter's operational code, which revealed differences in his beliefs across the issue areas of human rights, U.S.–Soviet relations, and regional conflicts (Walker, Schafer, and Young 1998), the impact of domestic and foreign policy domains on the philosophical beliefs in the operational codes of George H.W. Bush and William Jefferson Clinton (Schafer, Young, and Walker 2002), and the differences in the philosophical and instrumental beliefs of Bill Clinton and Tony Blair in dealing with democracies and nondemocracies as targets of their foreign policies (Schafer and Walker n.d.).

Still other studies show that the policy arena makes a difference. Walker and Schafer (2000) investigate the leader–advisor nexus in the Johnson White House by comparing Johnson's operational code beliefs in his public speeches to those of his key advisors in private memoranda. Marfleet (2000) explores the beliefs in John F. Kennedy's public and private statements during the Cuban Missile crisis. Dille (2000) investigates the differences in prepared speeches versus spontaneous interviews for Presidents Ronald Reagan and George H.W. Bush. The results of all three studies indicate that these leaders (with the exception of Reagan) exhibited more conflict-oriented beliefs in private or spontaneous statements than in public or prepared statements.

In the present volume three chapters use VICS data as explanatory variables in statistical models. Drury (chapter 9) investigates the effect of presidential operational codes on U.S. decisions regarding the use of economic sanctions. Stevenson (chapter 10) uses VICS indices as part of a model explaining U.S. trade dispute initiatives. Thies (chapter 11) investigates the operational codes of central bankers in dealing with the financial crisis in Southeast Asia at the end of the 1990s. Two chapters look primarily at the operational code as a dependent variable. Robison (chapter 5) looks at operational codes in the George W. Bush administration, compares and contrasts different groups of advisors and the President, and looks at differences over time. Lazarevska, Sholl, and Young (chapter 9) use operational code data along with data from Leadership Trait Analysis (Hermann 2003) to model psychological differences in terrorists and non-terrorists.

In short, if statistical models can investigate behavior by actors in international politics, operational code data can be included either as independent or dependent variables. The research thus far in the literature and in the present volume suggests that such data are often important explanatory variables.

Some of our other work uses operational code data in a very different way, one that directly engages the logic and concepts of game theory and formal modeling. Rather than conceptualizing the game as exogenous to a leader (as structuralists and rationalists do), however, our work asks what the nature of the game, as perceived and defined by the leader, is? The operational code is particularly appropriate for this endeavor because it captures the subject's beliefs about self's best approach and strategy *and* self's beliefs about other's likely approach and strategy. These beliefs about self and other constitute the leader's dyadic subjective game. It may be wrong or off target compared to reality, and external observers may be able to identify a game that more directly fits reality. In the end, however, it seems that the subjective beliefs held by a leader are the ones that are most likely to influence his/her choice of moves.

Much of our recent work uses this game-theoretic approach (Malici 2005, 2006; Marfleet and Miller 2005; Walker and Schafer 2003, 2001). In addition, several chapters in the present volume use this approach. Marfleet and Walker (chapter 3) conduct an agent-based computer simulation using 12 possible two-player games derived from a typology of belief systems identified with VICS indices and corresponding inferences about preferences from this typology. Crichlow (chapter 4) employs this typology to analyze the subjective games of Prime Minister Thatcher and several of her key advisors across three different decision-making episodes. Malici (chapter 6) uses sequential game theory to model the effect of Gorbachev's moves on the subjective games in Reagan's belief system at the end of the cold war. Feng (chapter 7) models the operational codes and subjective games of leaders across the Taiwan Straits.

The effort to combine psychological data with formal game-theoretic approaches to foreign policy analysis is relatively new to political psychologists (Larson 1986; Maoz 1990; Maoz and Mor 2002; Walker 1977, 1991, 2004b; Walker and Schafer 2004), and is less common among formal modelers. Yet, it is central to much of our contemporary work using the operational code. For these two reasons, we focus the rest of this chapter on the theoretical and empirical underpinnings of this approach. The next section begins with a brief discussion of the connections among operational code data, motivational analyses, and game-theoretic approaches. We discuss classic and sequential game theory, and provide simple examples that demonstrate how operational code data can be used to model a leader's subjective game. We conclude with an example of an application of this approach—an analysis of the changing subjective games of Yitzak Rabin and Shimon Peres from the 1970s to the 1990s.

Game Theory and Operational Code Analysis

Ole Holsti used George's ten questions about a leader's philosophical and instrumental beliefs to construct a typology of operational code belief systems. He identified six types of operational codes (A,B,C,D,E,F), based on the nature (temporary/ permanent) and source (individual/society/ international system) of conflict in the political universe (Holsti 1977; see also Waltz 1959). These key beliefs implied answers to the remaining questions about philosophical and instrumental beliefs, which were derived by Holsti (1977) and later revised by Walker (1983, 1990). The revised Holsti typology appears in figure 1.1, which collapses three of Holsti's six types into a single DEF type with shared beliefs except for the belief regarding the source of conflict in the political universe. The revised typology is organized along three motivational axes of power, affiliation, and achievement, and the four types of belief systems are located in quadrants formed by these axes. Their placement reflects the respective combinations of motivational images contained in their philosophical and instrumental beliefs (Walker 1983, 1990).

The quantitative answers to George's ten questions about philosophical and instrumental beliefs generated by VICS may be used to locate a leader within quadrants of the revised Holsti typology (Walker, Schafer and Young 1998, 2003; Young 2001). VICS focuses on the verbs in the leader's public statements and their attributions regarding the exercise of power to Self and Others. The VICS indices for three master beliefs, (P-1) Nature of the Political Universe, (I-1) Strategic Approach to Goals, and (P-4) Ability to Control Historical Development, are mapped as dimensions on the vertical (P-1/I-1) and horizontal (P-4) axes in figure 1.1 to locate a leader's images of Self and Other in the four quadrants of the Holsti typology.

The locations for Self (I-1, P-4a) and Other (P-1, P-4b) in their respective quadrants are associated with predictions about the strategic preferences of Self and Other regarding the political outcomes of settlement, submission, domination, and deadlock. For example, in Quadrant A of figure 1.1 the strategic preferences (ranked from $4 =$ highest to $1 =$ lowest) are $4 =$ settle, $3 =$ deadlock, $2 =$ dominate, $1 =$ submit. The combination of preferences

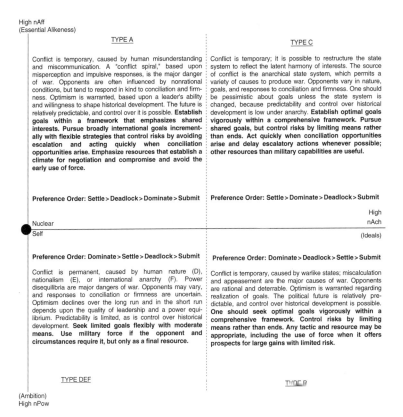

High nAff
(Essential Alikeness)

TYPE A

Conflict is temporary, caused by human misunderstanding and miscommunication. A "conflict spiral," based upon misperception and impulsive responses, is the major danger of war. Opponents are often influenced by nonrational conditions, but tend to respond in kind to conciliation and firmness. Optimism is warranted, based upon a leader's ability and willingness to shape historical development. The future is relatively predictable, and control over it is possible. **Establish goals within a framework that emphasizes shared interests. Pursue broadly international goals incrementally with flexible strategies that control risks by avoiding escalation and acting quickly when conciliation opportunities arise. Emphasize resources that establish a climate for negotiation and compromise and avoid the early use of force.**

Preference Order: Settle > Deadlock > Dominate > Submit

Nuclear

Self

Preference Order: Dominate > Settle > Deadlock > Submit

Conflict is permanent, caused by human nature (D), nationalism (E), or international anarchy (F). Power disequilibria are major dangers of war. Opponents may vary, and responses to conciliation or firmness are uncertain. Optimism declines over the long run and in the short run depends upon the quality of leadership and a power equilibrium. Predictability is limited, as is control over historical development. **Seek limited goals flexibly with moderate means. Use military force if the opponent and circumstances require it, but only as a final resource.**

TYPE DEF

(Ambition)
High nPow

TYPE C

Conflict is temporary; it is possible to restructure the state system to reflect the latent harmony of interests. The source of conflict is the anarchical state system, which permits a variety of causes to produce war. Opponents vary in nature, goals, and responses to conciliation and firmness. One should be pessimistic about goals unless the state system is changed, because predictability and control over historical development is low under anarchy. **Establish optimal goals vigorously within a comprehensive framework. Pursue shared goals, but control risks by limiting means rather than ends. Act quickly when conciliation opportunities arise and delay escalatory actions whenever possible; other resources than military capabilities are useful.**

Preference Order: Settle > Dominate > Deadlock > Submit

High
nAch

(Ideals)

Preference Order: Dominate > Deadlock > Settle > Submit

Conflict is temporary, caused by warlike states; miscalculation and appeasement are the major causes of war. Opponents are rational and deterrable. Optimism is warranted regarding realization of goals. The political future is relatively predictable, and control over historical development is possible. **One should seek optimal goals vigorously within a comprehensive framework. Control risks by limiting means rather than ends. Any tactic and resource may be appropriate, including the use of force when it offers prospects for large gains with limited risk.**

TYPE B

Figure 1.1 Contents of the Revised Holsti Operational Code Typology.

Note: (Instrumental beliefs are in bold, and philosophical beliefs are not.)
Source: Walker 1983, 1990.

for Self and Other model the "subjective game" in Self's operational code belief system as a 2 × 2 game matrix (Maoz 1990; Walker 2004b), which describes Self's possible choices toward Other and the corresponding choices of Other toward Self. In figure 1.2, the 2 × 2 game matrix shows a Type A identity for Self and a Type DEF identity for Other. Each player has two strategies: Cooperate (CO) and Conflict (CF). The intersection of strategies by Self and Other leading to a stable outcome for the subjective game, that is, an equilibrium is either settlement (4,3) or deadlock (3,2). Which one is the more likely outcome depends on the rules of play.

Classical game theory's rules of play make the assumptions that each player *simultaneously* moves without any pre-play communication between them and without repeated plays of the game, which leads to deadlock

Type A/Type DEF Subjective Game

		OTHER				OTHER				OTHER	
		CO	CF			CO	CF			CO	CF
SELF	CO	4,3	1,4	SELF	CO	S & O Settle	S Submits/ O Dominates	SELF	CO	4,3	1,4
	CF	2,1	3,2*		CF	S Dominates/ O Submits	S & O Deadlock		CF	2,1	3,2*

Self's Strategy: CF	Possible Outcomes	Other's Strategy: CF

Self = Type A and Other = Type DEF. The myopic Nash equilibrium from classical game theory for this game is asterisked. The non-myopic equilibrium for this game from sequential game theory is underlined (see Brams 1994, appendix, p. 217, game 27).

Backward Induction Steps for Self to Choose "Stay" *

		Alter CO CF		Alter CO CF		Alter CO CF		Alter CO CF
Ego	CO	4,3 1,4	CO	4,3 1,4	CO	4,3←1,4	CO	4,3←1,4
			Ego	⊥	Ego	⊥	Ego	⊥ ⊤
	CF	2,1→"3,2"	CF	2,1→"3,2"	CF	2,1→"3,2"	CF	2,1→"3,2"
		Step (1)		Step (2)		Step (3)		Step (4)

Backward Induction Steps for Other to Choose "Move"*

		Alter CO CF		Alter CO CF		Alter CO CF		Alter CO CF
Ego	CO	4,3 1,4	CO	4,3→|1,4	CO	4,3→|1,4	CO	4,3→|1,4
			Ego	↓	Ego	↑ ↓	Ego	↑ ↓
	CF	2,1 "3,2"	CF	2,1 "3,2"	CF	2,1 "3,2"	CF	2,1←"3,2"
		Step (1)		Step (2)		Step (3)		Step (4)

Figure 1.2   Myopic and Non-myopic Solutions to a Leader's Subjective Game.

Note: * The initial state is in quotation marks, and the nonmyopic equilibrium is underlined. The symbols "→" and "→|" indicate the respective strategic choices of "move" or "stay" by the player with the next move (Self) given the initial state (Brams 1994).

(3,2) as the final state (Rapoport and Guyer 1966). It is a myopic Nash equilibrium in which neither player can move immediately to a better outcome. Deadlock is also the logical outcome under these rules of play because a Conflict strategy is best single-play strategy for both players in the absence of pre-play communication between them.

Other's unconditional best (dominant) strategy is (CF), because it is the better strategy no matter what strategy Self chooses. If Self chooses (CO), then by choosing (CF) Other gets his/her highest-ranked outcome (1,4). If Self chooses (CF), then Other avoids his/her lowest-ranked outcome (2,1) by choosing (CF). Self's conditional best strategy is also (CF), because Self knows (CF) is Other's dominant strategy and assumes that it will be Other's choice. Therefore, Self chooses the better of the two strategies for Self on the condition that Other will choose (CF). By choosing (CF), Self avoids his/her lowest-ranked outcome and gets the next-highest outcome.

The sequential game theory known as the Theory of Moves (TOM) developed by Brams (1994) makes the assumption that each player *alternates* moves until the game terminates when neither player chooses to make another move. Under TOM's rules of play allowing alternating moves, prior (pre-play) communication, and repeated plays of the game, settlement is the final state for this game when deadlock is the initial state. Although settlement (4,3) is a superior outcome for both players compared to (3,2), in other words, both players are better off at (4,3) than at (3,2), it is not a Nash equilibrium because Other can defect to (1,4) and achieve a better outcome than at (4,3).

However, settlement is a non-myopic equilibrium because of the rule of play in TOM that allows alternating moves, creating a mutual incentive for both players to look ahead more than one move. The assumption is that each player knows under this rule of play that if Other defects to (1,4), then Self will move to (3,2), which is a worse outcome for both players. The same "look ahead" logic implies further that Other would then move to (2,1) followed by Self's move to (4,3). Thinking ahead through this sequence of moves, therefore, should lead to a decision by Other to "stay" at (4,3), because that is where he/she would return as a result of an initial decision to "move." Moreover, Self has no incentive to choose move from (4,3) because a decision to stay results in Self's highest-ranked outcome (Brams 1994, 2002).

The logic of "thinking ahead" to the non-myopic equilibrium of (4,3) from the Nash equilibrium initial state of (3,2) is depicted in the other game matrices in figure 1.2 via the process of "backward induction" by considering (3,2) as a final state and reasoning backward in four steps to it as an initial state (Brams 1994, 2002). The symbols connecting the cells of the game summarize this reasoning process, in which an arrow ($\rightarrow$) indicates that a player would choose move because it would improve his/her final outcome and a blocked arrow ($\rightarrow|$) indicates that a player would choose stay because moving would not lead to a better final outcome. The prediction for this strategic interaction game is that Self will choose stay while Other will choose move as strategies that will lead to settlement as the final outcome.

The demonstration of this prediction takes the form of calculating the logic of each player's process of thinking ahead regarding the consequences of choosing stay or move from the initial state of (3,2) under TOM's assumption that both players will follow this logic. If Self has the next move and thinks ahead, then in this example Self will choose stay based on the following steps of backward induction clockwise for Self in figure 1.2's game matrices. Although Other (Step 1) would choose to move from (2,1) to (3,2), Self (Step 2) would not choose to move from (4,3) to (2,1). Moreover, Other (Step 3) would not choose to move from (1,4) to (4,3) and, therefore, Self (Step 4) would not choose to move from (3,2) to (1,4). In each instance except for the move from (2,1) to (3,2), the other alternating moves do not improve a player's final outcome (see figure 1.2).

However, Self thinks that Other will choose move rather than stay because, thinking ahead, it is clear that the ensuing sequence of moves leads to (4,3) as the final outcome. Reasoning backward counterclockwise in the game matrices for Other in figure 1.2, Self (Step 1) will choose to move from (1,4) to (3,2), but Other (Step 2) will not move from (4,3) to (1,4) knowing that Self will then move to (3,2). Other also knows that Self (Step 3) will move to (4,3) from (2,1), which gives Other (Step 4) the incentive to move from (3,2) to (2,1) on the assumption that Self will both move to (4,3) and stay there (see figure 1.2).

Since Smith's (1988) assessment of previous operational code studies, the methodological and theoretical innovations represented by VICS and TOM have extended the scope and significance of operational code analysis. While remaining an approach that focuses on the psychological dynamics of decision making by a political leader, it has expanded its scope to include explicit attention to social–psychological and strategic interactions within and between states. It has thereby become more interactive and dynamic, that is, the emphasis has expanded to include two-sided analyses of relations between decision-making units and toward the analysis of foreign policy change (Walker 2003, 2004b; Walker and Schafer n.d.).

Levy (1994) has identified several mechanisms associated with foreign policy change. *Experiential learning* is the alteration of beliefs that leads to foreign policy change. *Structural adaptation* is a change of behavior in response to a change in context occasioned by an alteration in the balance of power between states over time, a shift in the leader's attention from one policy domain to another, or a change from one state to another as a target of foreign policy. *Social learning* is a change in behavior in response to a stimulus in the form of actions by another state. Neither of the latter two processes of behavioral change require a change in beliefs, in other words, experiential learning, but both processes may account for alterations in a leader's beliefs over time or the differentiation of a leader's operational code beliefs by target.

The following examples show how operational code analysis can be applied to the explanation of leader–advisor relations inside a single state and to the analysis of dyadic relations between pairs of states over time. The beliefs of leaders in these cases act as causal mechanisms that can simply mirror the external environment, compete with external stimuli and conditions to steer foreign policy decisions, or account for changes in foreign policy decisions via the alteration of beliefs in a process of experiential learning over time.

Methodological Applications and Substantive Contributions

The Arab–Israeli conflict has lasted over a half century since the creation of the state of Israel in 1948. There have been several wars since its independence became a contested political fact between Israel and its neighbors. Depending on the historical context, the belief systems of Israeli leaders have varied regarding their diagnosis of the political universe and the best strategies and tactics for Israel to pursue in order to maintain its independence. These belief changes reflect processes of structural adaptation and social learning in response to changes in the external environment. Crichlow's (1998) comparison of Knesset speeches by two prominent Israeli leaders whose political lives spanned two different decades shows that they exhibited divergent operational codes from each other during the 1974–1977 period following the Yom Kippur War and later moved toward convergence during 1992–1995 following the Oslo agreements.

Prime Minister Yitzak Rabin and Cabinet Minister Shimon Peres showed sharp differences in key philosophical and instrumental beliefs during the first period. Both leaders viewed the political universe as definitely hostile with different degrees of pessimism in the early 1970s. However, Peres was significantly less confident about his ability to control historical development and much less cooperative in his strategic and tactical choice propensities. The differences in their Self (I-1, P-4a) and Other (P-1, P-4b) master beliefs during the 1970s generated different subjective games for their respective operational codes in figure 1.3.

Rabin's Self coordinates placed Israel in the Type C (I-1 = Cooperative, P-4a = High Control) quadrant with preferences ranked as {settle > dominate > deadlock > submit}. The coordinates for Other in his operational code are located in the Type DEF (P-1 = Hostile, P-4b = Low Control) quadrant with preferences ranked as {dominate > settle >

18

Subjective Games of Rabin and Peres in the 1970s

	G28 OTHER				OTHER				G28 OTHER	
	CO	CF			CO	CF			CO	CF
CO	<u>4,3</u>|←	1,4		CO	Settle	Submit		CO	<u>4,3</u> →|	1,4
ISRAEL	↓	‾↑	**ISRAEL**				**ISRAEL**		↑	↓
CF	3,1 →	"2,2"*		CF	Dominate	Deadlock	CF	3,1 ←	"2,2"*

RABIN STRATEGY: STAY   **ISRAEL OUTCOMES**   **OTHER STRATEGY: MOVE**

	G24 OTHER				OTHER				G24 OTHER	
	CO	CF			CO	CF			CO	CF
CO	4,2 |←	1,4		CO	Settle	Submit		CO	4,2 →	1,4
ISRAEL	↓	‾↑	**ISRAEL**				**ISRAEL**		↑	↓
CF	2,1 →	"<u>3,3</u>"*		CF	Dominate	Deadlock	CF	2,1 |←	"<u>3,3</u>"*

PERES STRATEGY: STAY   **ISRAEL OUTCOMES**   **OTHER STRATEGY: STAY**

Strategies for Israel and Other in the 1990s

	OTHER				OTHER				OTHER	
	CO	CF			CO	CF			CO	CF
CO	<u>4,4</u> →|	1,2		CO	Settle	Submit		CO	<u>4,4</u> ←|	1,2
ISRAEL	↑	↓	**ISRAEL**				**ISRAEL**		↓	↑
CF	"3,1" |←	2,3*		CF	Dominate	Deadlock	CF	"3,1" ←	2,3*

RABIN STRATEGY: MOVE   **ISRAEL OUTCOMES**   **OTHER STRATEGY: MOVE**

	OTHER				OTHER				OTHER	
	CO	CF			CO	CF			CO	CF
CO	<u>4,3</u> →|	1,4		CO	Settle	Dominate		CO	4,3 |←	1,4
ISRAEL	↑	↓	**ISRAEL**				**ISRAEL**	↓	‾↑
CF	"3,1" |←	2,2*		CF	Submit	Deadlock	CF	"3,1" →	2,2*

PERES STRATEGY: MOVE   **OTHER OUTCOMES**   **OTHER STRATEGY: MOVE**

Figure 1.3   Israeli Subjective Games and Strategies in 1970s and 1990s.

Note: * The initial state is in quotation marks, and the final state is underlined for each game. Nash equilibria are asterisked. The symbols "→" and "→|" indicate the respective strategic choices of "move" or "stay" by the player with the next move (Self or Other) given the initial state (Brams 1994).

deadlock > submit}. The Self coordinates for Peres placed Israel in the Type A (I-1 = Cooperation, P-4a = Low Control) quadrant with preferences ranked as {settle > deadlock > dominate > submit}. The coordinates for Other in his operational code are in the Type B (P-1 = Hostile, P-4b = High Control) quadrant with preferences ranked as {dominate > deadlock > settle > submit}.

These differences suggest that the two leaders disagreed about the immediate prospects for a peace settlement between Arabs and Jews. Rabin's subjective game of the 1970s in figure 1.3 has a non-myopic equilibrium of (4,3) settlement while Peres' subjective game of the 1970s has (3,3) deadlock as both a Brams non-myopic equilibrium and a Nash equilibrium (Brams 1994). Do these different subjective games lead to significant differences in preferences regarding Israeli strategies and to divergent expectations about Other's strategies? Rabin's assessment of the optimal strategies for Self and Other depend on his definition of the situation as a starting point in his subjective game.

With deadlock as the initial state, Israel's optimal strategy is to stay at (2,2) with a conflict (CF) strategy in the expectation that Other will choose to move by changing from a strategy of conflict (CF) to a strategy of cooperation (CO), which is what the Egyptian leader Anwar Sadat chose to do shortly after Menachem Begin replaced Rabin as the prime minister of Israel (Barnett 1998; Brams 1997, 2002; Maoz and Mor 2002). In order for Israel to have maintained the strategic initiative in this subjective game, the "initial state" would need to be domination (3,1), which may have been the case in the immediate aftermath of the Yom Kippur War after the superpowers intervened to prevent Israeli forces from rolling into Cairo after the entrapment of Egyptian forces in the Sinai east of the Suez canal (Barnett 1998).

From an initial state of (3,1) following the cease-fire, TOM prescribes for Israel a strategy of magnanimity in the form of a move to settlement (4,3) in order to avoid a move to deadlock (2,3) by Other (Brams 1994, 75–84). Following the cease-fire imposed by the superpowers, however, the situation evolved very quickly from military victory to diplomatic deadlock between Israel and Egypt as Secretary of State Henry Kissinger began a mediator strategy of shuttle diplomacy between Tel Aviv and Cairo (Barnett 1998; Kissinger 1982).

A magnanimity strategy would have been very difficult to implement in the 1970s, given the intervention of the two superpowers and the disagreement over strategy between Rabin and other Cabinet members such as Shimon Peres. The strategies in Peres's 1970s subjective game for Self and Other appear in figure 1.3. TOM prescribes a stay strategy for both Self and Other, because deadlock is both the Nash equilibrium and TOM's non-myopic equilibrium for this game. Since deadlock is the most plausible definition of the situation following the Yom Kippur War, the prospects for a move toward settlement were low if Peres represented the prevailing view within the Isracli Cabinet. If domination (2,1) is defined as the initial state in the Peres game, the Israeli strategy would also be stay at (2,1) with the expectation that Other will move from its worst (lowest-ranked) outcome to deadlock (3,3). Unlike Rabin, Mr. Peres expected that a move by Israel from domination (2,1) to settlement (4,2) would be an unstable outcome, because he believed that Other ranks deadlock (3,3) higher than settlement (4,2) and will move to (1,4) even if Israel then moves to (3,3) to avoid its worst outcome.

The comparative study of Rabin and Peres by Crichlow (1998) also illustrates experiential learning by both leaders accompanying structural adaptation to changes in the Middle East. By the early 1990s, Israel's power position had increased in the Middle East so that Peres and Rabin attributed the same Type C strategic orientation to Self. Their images of Other also changed, but the convergence was only partial. Rabin now attributed a Type A orientation to Other while Peres shifted from a Type B to Rabin's former Type DEF image of Other.

The two leaders shared a common prescription for Israel of move from an initial state of domination to settlement as a final outcome, as the comparison of their 1990s subjective games shows in figure 1.3. They also anticipated that Other will move toward settlement, though along different paths. Peres believes that if Other moves to deadlock, Israel should choose stay in anticipation that Other will then move from this new initial state toward settlement to break the deadlock. This non-myopic reasoning is the position that Rabin held in the 1970s, as Peres' subjective game of the 1990s is identical to Rabin's game of the 1970s. If Israel does not take the strategic initiative and Other moves from domination to deadlock, Rabin believes that either Israel or Other should shift to a CO strategy with the expectation that both would then move to settlement (CO, CO), because both parties have the incentive to move toward their highest ranked outcome (4,4) of mutual cooperation (Brams 1994, 215). The partial congruence between the operational codes of the two Israeli leaders is consistent with the moves toward peace by Israel symbolized by the Oslo accords during the 1990s.

The overview in this chapter of the evolution of operational code analysis during the past ten years identifies and illustrates the various ways that beliefs can matter in explaining foreign policy choices and strategic interactions in world politics. They show how recent methodological innovations in measuring beliefs and modeling their behavioral implications allow scholars to retrieve and analyze the belief systems of leaders from public statements and link them statistically to behavior with more precision and greater sophistication. The ability to link beliefs and actions with models of 2×2 games extracted from the VICS indices for key philosophical and instrumental beliefs opens up further opportunities to study strategic interactions in world politics as well as foreign policy decisions by a single state. The rigor of game theory models specifies both actions by states and outcomes between them.

Plan of the Book

In part II, we investigate in more detail the methodological problems and solutions associated with the application of these developments in the study of beliefs and foreign policy decisions. Chapter 2 is a primer on the use of the VICS to do content analysis by hand and by machine in order to retrieve and classify a leader's beliefs. Chapter 3 presents an expanded Theory of Inferences about Preferences (TIP), which identifies a taxonomy of subjective games derived from a leader's key beliefs about the nature of the political universe, the relative control over historical development by self and other, and the attribution of strategies to self and other. In the remainder of this volume, we address three domains of inquiry regarding how beliefs matter in world politics and employ VICS to link beliefs with foreign policy behavior and strategic interaction between states.

In part III, the focus is the application of the VICS indices to the analysis of leader–advisor relations within the governments of Margaret Thatcher and George W. Bush. The Thatcher Cabinet study in chapter 4 analyzes the impact of structural adaptation across different geographical and policy domains by comparing and contrasting the contents and the influence of beliefs held by the Prime Minister and her key advisors during both security and economic decision-making episodes. It also assesses the insights into Cabinet cohesion provided by an analysis of the definitions of the situation associated with different Cabinet members and the steering effects of beliefs on the positions taken by different leaders in the policy debates within the Thatcher Cabinet.

The Bush administration study in chapter 5 compares and contrasts the operational code beliefs of the President and his advisors in the defense and state departments before and after the 9/11 terrorist attacks on the Pentagon and the World Trade Center. In addition to a focus on the dynamics of the advisory process within the White House, there is an assessment of the experiential learning effects of these attacks on the beliefs of the President and his key advisors. Whereas beliefs in the Thatcher study are independent variables that explain differences in decision-making behavior, beliefs in the Bush study are dependent variables that change in response to stimuli from the external environment. By extension these changes in beliefs become causal mechanisms that may explain changes in the Bush administration's foreign policy following the 9/11 terrorist attacks.

In part IV, we present applications of operational code analysis to research puzzles in the domain of security studies. A dyadic analysis of Soviet–American relations in chapter 6 illustrates the application of subjective games analysis to the dynamics between Gorbachev and Reagan that ended the cold war and assesses the experiential learning effects of external stimuli on a leader's belief system and choice propensities. A case study of strategic relations between Beijing and Taipei after the cold war in chapter 7 shows how to identify the strategic implications of differences and similarities between the images of self and other held by protagonists during an international crisis. The personality profiles of terrorist leaders and how their operational code beliefs and underlying personality traits differ from other types of leaders is the focus of chapter 8 in this part of the volume.

In part V, we extend the tools of operational code analysis to the domain of international political economy. The use of economic sanctions by U.S. presidents in chapter 9, the initiation of trade disputes by U.S. presidents with Canada in chapter 10, and the role of central bankers in handling the financial crisis in Southeast Asia in chapter 11 are analyzed with the aid of VICS to identify the impact of operational code beliefs on the foreign policy behavior of these states and institutions.

Finally, in chapter 12, the editors discuss the findings from the previous chapters in this volume, project the future of operational code analysis as a research program, and identify types of fruitful theoretical links between actor-centered and structure-oriented research programs that may develop in the study of world politics.

PART II

METHODS: CONTENT ANALYSIS AND FORMAL MODELS

CHAPTER 2

OPERATIONAL CODE ANALYSIS AT A DISTANCE: THE VERBS IN CONTEXT SYSTEM OF CONTENT ANALYSIS

Mark Schafer and Stephen G. Walker

Introduction

Snyder, Bruck, and Sapin (1962) argued many years ago that those of us interested in understanding foreign policy decisions needed to get inside the "black box" of the decision-making process. Doing so, they pointed out, required a focus on the agents involved in the process. This agent-centered approach differed significantly from the broader, structural approaches that had marked the study of global politics prior to their revolutionary work. At an intuitive level it makes sense to focus on the process and the agents involved, and indeed, most of our casual conversations about international politics and foreign policy center around individuals and small decision-making groups. Many of the major subfields in international politics are nonetheless populated by structural or systems-level approaches, which either ignore individuals altogether or make simplified assumptions about agent-centered or micro-level processes that are under-theorized or not tested.

We speculate that perhaps this gap stems in part from a perceived difficulty in incorporating individual agents in ways that contribute rigorously to causal analyses of foreign policy decisions. A rigorous approach to understanding agents requires that we identify generalizable constructs that produce probabilistic, patterned behavior across agents. While the types and forms of possible constructs vary significantly, inevitably many are psychological in nature. Therefore, they require not only some knowledge of psychology, which involves the study of the human mind, but also some systematic procedures for measuring psychological characteristics. Immediately, the challenge becomes clear: how can we rigorously assess psychological characteristics of individuals—a large-enough pool of individuals to create meaningful generalizations—when we rarely if ever have direct access to the leaders who interest us as our subjects?

The most common solution in the political psychology literature to this challenge is called "at-a-distance" methodology (Hermann 1980; Post 2003; Schafer 2000; Winter 1980; Winter, Hermann, Weintraub, and Walker 1991; Winter and Stewart 1977), meaning that we assess the psychological characteristics of individuals from a distance without having direct access to them. The fundamental logic informing this method is the assumption that we can infer psychological characteristics based upon the subject's verbal behavior: what an individual says and how he or she says it can tell us important things about his or her "state of mind." While verbal material is not the only indicator of an individual's state of mind, it is certainly an important and valid one. Indeed, most of us use a casual version of this in everyday life: we use verbal cues to understand someone's political ideology, to gauge an individual's general state of happiness or depression, or to learn about his or her beliefs about a topic or issue. Nearly everyone knows the old adage about assessing someone's optimism by listening to his or her description of a glass that is half full (or half empty).

If we can systematically analyze verbal behavior, and if we have constructs that let us theoretically connect the verbal behavior with psychological characteristics, then we can conduct analysis of at least some of the psychology of any subject for whom we have verbal behavior. The good news is that we have access to verbal material for many different agents who are or were involved in foreign policy decision making. Also, researchers in political psychology over the years have developed psychological constructs that can analyze these sources. Some of these constructs use quantitative methods, which raise a couple of questions. Are quantitative indicators of psychology necessary? Don't they leave out what might be important information about a leader's idiosyncratic psychology?

We do not argue that a quantitative approach to at-a-distance measurement is a panacea, or that quantitative indicators produce the only kind of research information that contributes significantly to our knowledge of leaders and the foreign policy decision-making process. Indeed, along the way, we have learned much from more qualitative approaches done by several scholars (Burke and Greenstein 1989; George 1968, 1980, 1991; George and George 1956, 1998; Glad 1973, 1980; Greenstein 1969; Larson 1985; Post 1979, 1980; Purkitt 1998; Renshon 1996; Runyon 1983; Tucker 1965; Vertzberger 1997). We only argue here that it can also be valuable to have quantitative data for psychological variables, and note there are several methods and approaches in existence that make such endeavors possible.

Quantitative approaches provide us with specific types of measurements, meaning that we can make direct, meaningful comparisons across our subjects and conduct statistical analyses that allow for probabilistic generalizations. It is one thing to say that a leader is driven by a need for power. It is quite another to say that his or her need for power is higher than all but 5 percent of the population of other leaders and, on average, people with higher needs for power are probabilistically much more likely to initiate war. In addition, quantitative approaches are reproducible and directly cumulative, which contribute to the efficiency and effectiveness of building a research program. It is not the case that quantitative approaches purport to provide insights from holistic depth psychology for each subject, but rather "traits are chosen which have some evident relationship to the behavior under examination" (Hermann 1974, 203) and, therefore, make contributions to a science of political psychology that cannot otherwise be made.

The previous chapter introduced the operational code construct and its important history in foreign policy analysis. It also briefly introduced the Verbs In Context System (VICS), which is the systematic, at-a-distance method that has been developed for quantitative operational code analysis. A major task of this chapter is to provide more information on VICS, what it is, and how it is done. Before we turn to a more extensive discussion of VICS, however, we will discuss briefly some of the different kinds of constructs used in the political psychology literature to assess psychological characteristics at-a-distance.

At-A-Distance Constructs in Political Psychology

There are many terms, definitions, and categories we might use to organize the available number of psychological constructs. Greenstein (1969) pointed out that the term "personality" is the broadest, most inclusive term when referring to any type of mental or behavioral activity. As classically used by psychologists, personality includes such things as attitudes, cognitions, motivations, and other ego-defense mechanisms. However, we have found it helpful to use the distinction made by many political scientists, which separates cognitions and attitudes from other components of personality such as motives and ego-defense mechanisms (Greenstein 1969;

Schafer 2000). Cognitions and attitudes are products of mental functioning that involve relatively *conscious* thinking about a subject or object. Motives, ego-defense mechanisms, and other components of depth psychology are generally considered to be more *unconscious* responses and reactions.

The conscious–unconscious distinction is certainly not perfect. Indeed, though conscious thinking may form cognitions, they often function at a level below our conscious awareness. And, though motives often come from sources outside of our conscious awareness, we may become aware of some of their manifestations. Still, the distinction is helpful in organizing our at-a-distance constructs in political psychology.

Several scholars have developed at-a-distance constructs that operate more on the unconscious side of the divide. David Winter and his colleagues (1980, 1987, 1991, 1993; Winter and Stewart 1977) have an extensive research program on motives that investigates needs for power, affiliation, and achievement. Margaret Hermann and her colleagues (1980, 1984, 1987, 2003) have another major research program investigating several different traits, including conceptual complexity, distrust, need for power, task orientation, control orientation, self confidence, and others. Weintraub (1986) has devised a system for looking systematically at clinical personality profiles of subjects.

Many scholars have also conducted research on the cognitive side of the divide, covering such topics as misperceptions (Holsti 1972; Jervis 1976), images (M. Cottam 1985, 1986, 1992, 1994; R. Cottam 1977; Finlay, Holsti, and Fagen 1967; Herrmann 1984; Larson 1985; Kaplowitz 1990; Herrmann and Fischerkeller 1995; Herrmann et al. 1997; Herrmann and Keller 2004), cognitive maps (Axelrod 1976; Bonham 1993; Bonham and Shapiro 1986; Levi and Tetlock 1980; Maoz and Shayer 1987; Walters 2005; Young 1996), cognitive style (Suedfeld and Tetlock 1977; Tetlock 1983, 1985), belief systems, and operational codes (Bennett 1999; George 1969, 1979; Herrmann, Tetlock, and Visser 1999; Holsti 1970, 1977; Khong 1992; Larson 1994; Rosati 1987; Walker 1977, 1983, 1990, 2003; Walker, Schafer, and Young 1998, 1999).

Our focus on beliefs in the operational code approach prompts us to clarify what we mean by "beliefs" and "belief systems." The simple answer, "beliefs are what you believe," does not get us very far, nor is it particularly useful to stipulate that "belief systems are beliefs that are related to one another." However, these two statements are useful starting points. To believe something is to affirm that you know it, which implies that the believer has acquired some form of knowledge. We call this knowledge *information*, that is, something that has *informed* impressions stored on our brains. Modern cognitive neuroscience is able to detect neurons in which these impressions reside plus how and whether neurons are connected by synapses to others in a particular pattern, creating a more complex impression of knowledge that forms a neural network in the brain.[1]

These neural knowledge networks are not beliefs or belief systems per se, but they are the building blocks for them. Beliefs and belief systems are higher-level circuits and systems of neural network patterns that have been reenforced by stimuli to become stable over time and have been stored in the brain's memory. They can also be altered by other stimuli that deviate from the original pattern of reenforcement. Both reenforcement and alteration are processes of learning.

> Most systems of the brain are *plastic*, that is, modifiable by experience, which means that the synapses involved are changed by experience . . . Learning (synaptic plasticity) is . . .[a]n innate capacity for synapses to record and store information . . .[and]. . . what allows systems to encode experiences. If the synapses of a particular brain system cannot change, this system will not have the ability to be modified by experience and to maintain the modified state. As a result the organism will not be able to learn and remember through the functioning of that system. (LeDoux 2002, 8–9; italics added)

These networks of stored knowledge in one part of the brain are associated closely with other neural networks of feelings in another part of the brain activated by the same stimuli. The different parts of the human brain are capable of constructing and coordinating complex patterns of interrelated systems of cognitions, emotions, and motivations, then using them as guides for responding to stimuli from the environment (LeDoux 2002). We become aware of these linkages and mechanisms in varying degrees through the medium of language, which allows human beings to communicate to others what each of us knows, feels, and wants.

The operational code approach to the study of belief systems asks what the individual knows, feels, and wants regarding the exercise of power in human affairs.[2] What are his or her beliefs about the distribution of power between self and others? The likely exercise of power by others? The most effective exercise of power by self? Because the exercise of power is a *social* phenomenon involving both self and others as either the subject or the object of the exercise of power, operational code analysis identifies a *political* belief system about self and others and how they interact with one another.[3]

While this belief system in principle can be reduced to the information stored in complex systems of beliefs, feelings, and motivations in the brain of an individual, we cannot yet, in practice, trace it to this level of existence. Instead, we access the contents and relationships of a belief system through its effects as manifested in the language of human subjects. We may find that a belief system is explicitly shared by a community of human beings as a cultural phenomenon transmitted by agents of socialization such as educational, religious, or political institutions. We may also find that an individual's belief system is unique in some respects to that person's life experiences. Both societal and individual belief systems may change over time, that is to say, learning may strengthen or weaken beliefs in degree as well as change in kind by acquiring new beliefs and discarding old ones. Belief systems may also be more or less conscious and explicit. It is possible for people to be relatively unaware of their beliefs, as in the case of racial prejudices that are not recognized by believers but detected by an outside observer.

In the following discussion of VICS, the indices for the separate beliefs in the operational code construct are consistent with the principles of reenforcement and alteration that characterize the operation of neural networks. Stimuli from the environment embedded in a subject's rhetoric are weighted for central tendency, variety, and balance in the construction of indices for beliefs about others and weighted by positive $(+)$ and negative $(-)$ valences to reflect corresponding associations of positive and negative affect (feelings). The same principles are followed in the construction of indices for beliefs about the self. Beliefs about self and other are linked subsequently in chapter 3 to motivations regarding the exercise of power with a theory of inferences about preferences regarding the political outcomes of domination, submission, settlement, and deadlock associated with the exercise of power (see also Walker 1983, 1995, 2003, 2004b; Winter and Stewart 1977).

The Verbs In Context System

Our objective with VICS is to develop a content analysis system for verbal material that will let us assess the cognitive beliefs of our subjects in the form of an "operational code."[4] The premise for the system is that the way individuals speak about power relationships in the political universe will tell us much about their beliefs regarding the exercise of power. Many years before the development of VICS, others developed various content analysis systems with a focus on actions in the form of state behavior. Several of these content-analysis event data systems relied on the properties of verbs (Azar 1980; Azar and Ben-Dak 1975; Callahan, Brady, and Hermann 1982; Goldstein 1992; Hermann 1971; Hermann et al. 1973; Hoggard and McClelland 1969; Langois and Langois 1999; McClelland 1968, 1972; Schrodt, Davis, and Weddle 1994).

Some of these event data systems developed scales to code verbs, which measure intensities of conflict, cooperation, and participation in the international system (Azar and Ben-Dak 1975; Callahan, Brady, and Hermann 1982; Goldstein 1992; Leng 1993). Two simple sentences illustrate the logic of this approach: (i) State X attacks State Z; and (ii) State W praises State Y. The two root verbs, *attack* and *praise*, give very different messages about state action. The former by X is conflictual in direction and has a very high level of intensity as a negative *deed*, while the latter by W is cooperative in direction with a relatively modest level of intensity as a positive *word*. In addition to communicating conflict or cooperation, therefore, we maintain that verbs map various forms of the exercise of power as identified by scholars who conceptualize power as a control relationship between self and other (Baldwin 1971, 1978, 1980; Dahl 1957; McClelland 1966). *Deeds* indicate the exercise of power in the form of positive and negative actions. *Words* represent the exercise of power in the form of making threats and promises or in the form of invoking authority to support or oppose actions between states or other agents in world politics.

Since our purpose is to look for manifestations of beliefs about power in relationships, we have built VICS on the logic of the classification systems for event data and their focus on verbs. The key difference is that VICS focuses primarily on verbs in speech acts by our subjects, that is, texts of their private or public statements in the form of diaries, letters, speeches, memoranda, interviews, and press conferences, and not on verbs attributed to our subjects in secondary sources or in reports of state actions by external observers such as journalists, historians, or commentators.

By coding the direction and scaling the intensity of transitive verbs in our subject's rhetoric and then indexing the results, we end up with a broad picture of the way the actor sees the exercise of power in the political universe by self and others. Some may see it as very hostile and use many more conflict-oriented verbs than cooperative ones. Others may see it as quite friendly and use more cooperative-oriented verbs to express their beliefs about the exercise of power. Verbs that are neutral are coded as "0"; they add no information in terms of direction or intensity and are not included in the VICS dictionary of transitive verbs.

As discussed in the previous chapter, the operational code construct includes two broad sets of beliefs. Philosophical beliefs are external attributions that the leader makes about the political universe and other actors in the political universe. Instrumental beliefs are internal attributions that the subject makes regarding his or her own best approaches to political action. It is necessary, therefore, that we distinguish in our content analysis system when the subject is talking about self and when he or she is talking about others. This distinction is relatively simple to make in verbal material by looking at the grammatical subject of the verb: either the speaker is talking about others in the political universe or about self (and other in-group actors with which he or she identifies and over which he or she has some control or influence).

These two linguistic components, the subject and the verb, combine to form the recording unit—called the "utterance"—for the VICS system. Verbs are first coded for direction as cooperative (+) or conflictual (−), and then coded for intensity as words or deeds. Cooperative and conflict *deeds* are the most intense sanctions (rewards and punishments) at the opposite ends of a continuum separated by *words* of lower intensity that communicate as threats, promises, or expressions of authority by the potential or symbolic use of sanctions. These distinctions produce a scale with six values ranging from −3 to +3, which are marked by the following verb signifiers as the exercise of different forms of power: Punish (−3), Threaten (−2), Oppose (−1), Support (+1), Promise (+2), and Reward (+3).[5]

When the utterances are sorted and aggregated, the results provide the foundation of our system, which gives quantitative answers to the operational code questions. When we want to know how an actor sees others exercise power in the political universe—his philosophical beliefs—we aggregate and index his verbs when he is talking about other actors. When we are interested in how our subject thinks self ought to exercise power, we index his verbs when he is talking about himself and his in-groups; these indicate his instrumental beliefs. Taken together, we have a picture of the leader's belief system regarding acts of conflict and cooperation by self and others in the political universe. In short, we have his operational code.

The preceding discussion is a simple overview of the logic of VICS of content analysis. The system actually includes 17 different indices, all of which rest fundamentally on these linguistic components, aggregated in different ways to identify different elements in the operational code construct. The next section explains the calculation of each index and its logic in identifying the elements in the inventory of questions provided by George (1969) to guide the construction of a leader's political belief system.

The VICS Indices

We begin with an explanation of the operational definitions for the philosophical indices—those that provide information about the subject's beliefs regarding the nature of politics and other actors in the political universe. Then we present and discuss the indices for the instrumental beliefs. They are often identified later by their number, for example, P-1 or I-1, which conforms to the corresponding number of the belief in George's questionnaire inventory of philosophical and instrumental beliefs.

The Nature of the Political Universe (P-1): Friendly, Mixed, Hostile
We conceptualize both the first Philosophical and Instrumental beliefs as "master beliefs," meaning that, based upon theories of cognitive consistency, the other beliefs within each category should flow from and be theoretically and empirically linked with them.[6] Our index for this belief is broad and general to capture the *balance* of the leader's views of other actors in the political universe. We assume that the leader's images of other actors' policies and actions reflect the leader's beliefs about politics, political conflict, and the nature of other actors. We compute a simple ratio of the frequency of positive to negative utterances the leader makes when talking about others in the political universe. The index varies between −1 and +1 with low scores indicating that, on average, the leader sees others as more hostile in the political universe while a high score indicates that the leader sees others as more friendly.[7] The specific formula for the P-1 index is the percentage of positive utterances about others minus the percentage of negative utterances about others.

Prospects for Realizing Fundamental Values (P-2): Optimism versus Pessimism
This index and the ones for the remaining philosophical beliefs are related in part to P-1 as a master belief. A leader who sees a friendly, positive world is going to be more optimistic about realizing his fundamental values, and a leader who sees a hostile world of other actors trying to block the realization of his objectives is going to be more pessimistic. With this index we go beyond the balance of cooperative and conflictual utterances to include the way the subject perceives the *intensity* of others' actions. A leader might see the political universe as balanced between good and evil (P-1), but if he sees the evil side in much more intense terms—as engaging in more hostile deeds—then he is less optimistic about his prospects for success. To calculate this index, we weight each verb according to the intensity value of its coding category (−3 to +3) and divide the result by the total number of coded verbs. This index varies from −1 at the pessimistic end of the continuum to +1 at the optimistic end. The formula for the P-2 index is the mean intensity of utterances about others divided by three.[8]

Predictability of the Political Universe (P-3): Low to High
With this index we examine whether the subject sees others acting in consistent, predictable ways. Our measure for this index is informed by the literature on information theory (Garner 1962; McClelland 1968, 1972), which suggests that uncertainty corresponds to a distribution pattern of

total variety for a set of observations across a set of categories while certainty corresponds to a distribution pattern of total uniformity within one category in a set of categories. Therefore, we assess predictability by using a *dispersion* measure that calculates the variation in the distribution of observations across our scale of six verb categories when the subject is talking about other actors. The logic is that the wider the variety of actions the subject attributes to others, the less predictable are their actions. If the subject sees others engaging primarily in one or two categories of action, then he believes others' actions are more consistent and, therefore, more predictable.

As with all of the indices, this is not necessarily an assessment of reality—in this case an accurate prediction about others' actions—but rather an assessment of the subject's underlying belief about predictability. An actor could live in a world where others are pursuing a full variety of cooperative and conflictual actions, but if the actor only perceives others as pursuing threats and punishments, then he believes others' next moves are more predictable. The dispersion measure we use is the Index of Qualitative Variation (IQV; Watson and McGaw 1980, 88). The formula for the P-3 index is one minus the IQV, which varies between 0 and 1 with lower scores indicating that the subject sees less predictability in the political universe and higher scores indicating perceptions of more predictability.[9]

Control Over Historical Development (P-4): Low to High

This index is the only one that includes utterances the subject makes about both self and other. Here we are interested in assessing the subject's views of how much he sees self as being in control. Building on the locus-of-control literature (Kaplowitz 1978; Langer 1983; Lefcourt 1976; Phares 1976), we investigate who the actor sees as taking the most action in the political universe—self or others. If the subject's rhetoric indicates that self is taking most of the action, then self sees self as more in control. On the other hand, if the rhetoric indicates that others are the ones who act more frequently, then self is attributing control to others. To measure this, we compute a simple ratio of the number of self attributions to the number of actions that self attributes to others. The index varies between 0 and 1. Low scores indicate that the subject sees the locus of control residing more with others while higher scores indicate that the subjects sees self as having more control.[10] The formula for the P-4 index is the number of *self* utterances divided by the sum of *self* utterances plus *other* utterances.

Role of Chance (P-5): Low to High

We surmise that the role of chance is logically related to the two previously mentioned philosophical beliefs (P-3 and P-4). The more predictable the political universe and the more self has control over events in the political universe, the lower is the role of chance. To calculate an index for this belief, we simply multiplied P-3 by P-4. The greater the product of P-3 x P-4, the lesser the role of chance. We transform this interaction term to make the direction of the index vary so that higher scores indicate a higher role assigned to chance and lower scores indicate a lower role. The role of chance index can range from 0 to 1. The specific formula for P-5 is one minus the product of the Predictability Index (P-3) times the Control Index (P-4).

We turn now to a discussion of the indices for instrumental beliefs. We have deliberately created some parallels between the philosophical and the instrumental indices, because we are interested in the same kinds of information; only here the information comes from the subject talking about self. The first two instrumental beliefs deal with the subject's views on goals, objectives, strategies, and tactics for the self in the political universe. We do not identify specific goals or objectives for the subject, which would require qualitative research beyond the scope of VICS. We do investigate the subject's beliefs about the utility of cooperative and conflictual actions as indicated in his or her rhetoric. We separate these out into two broad categories of actions: strategies and tactics (Leng 1993; Snyder and Diesing 1977). Strategies vary in direction while tactics vary in intensity.

Direction of Strategy (I-1): Cooperative Mixed, Conflictual
We compute an index that gauges the leader's beliefs about the best strategic direction for actions. This index parallels P-1 by investigating the general balance of cooperative and conflictual utterances the subject makes, except that this index aggregates utterances when the subject is talking about self and self's in-groups. The logic is that the more self talks about taking cooperative action, the more cooperatively he or she defines the direction of his or her strategy, and vice versa. This index varies from -1 to $+1$. Lower scores indicate that the subject attributes more utility to conflict actions; higher scores indicate that a cooperative strategy is more useful. The formula for I-1 is the percentage of cooperative $(+)$ utterances made when talking about self minus the percentage of conflictual $(-)$ utterances regarding self.

Intensity of Tactics (I-2)
Going beyond the directional balance of the leader's beliefs about self's actions found in I-1, here we are interested in the leader's beliefs about intensity when pursuing tactics. This index parallels P-2 mentioned earlier, and once again we weight the verbs according to our six-point intensity scale: Punish -3, Threaten -2, Oppose -1, Support $+1$, Promise $+2$, and Reward $+3$. By weighting each verb when the subject is talking about

self and then dividing by the total number of self utterances, we end up with the average level of cooperative or conflictual intensity the subject demonstrates in his rhetoric. The intensity of tactics index ranges from -1 to $+1$, with lower scores indicating self's belief about the utility of hostile tactics, and higher scores indicating a belief in the utility of cooperative tactics. The formula for I-2 is the mean intensity of utterances made when talking about self divided by three.[11]

Risk Orientation (I-3): Averse to Acceptant

Here we are interested in how risk aversive or risk acceptant the subject is. Risk levels can be related to the distribution of choices the actor makes: higher levels of diversity in action mean that the risk associated with any one action is diminished. Lower levels of diversity result in exposure to a higher level of risk if that type of action fails (see Milburn and Billings 1976; Morrow 1987; Snyder and Diesing 1977). In economic terms, a diversified portfolio of securities reduces risk exposure, whereas a nondiversified portfolio runs great risk if the underlying security goes bad. To use the old adage, putting all of your eggs in one basket is quite risky.

To assess diversity in choice of tactics, we turn again to the IQV as a measure of dispersion. Here we look at the dispersion of the subject's utterances regarding the self across the six different verb categories. The risk orientation index can vary from 0 to 1. Scores at the lower end of the continuum indicate that the subject's rhetoric is well diversified across the six verb categories and, therefore, the subject is risk averse. Higher scores indicate less diversity and therefore higher levels of risk acceptance. The formula for the I-3 index is one minus the IQV.[12]

Importance of Timing of Actions (I-4): Low to High Flexibility

The fourth instrumental belief pertains to the timing of self's actions. We use two indices here that continue our investigation of the diversity of actions in the leader's rhetoric. The idea is that diversity levels provide insight into the relative frequency and, therefore, the flexibility of actions. The first index (I-4a) investigates the diversity of the leader's choices in terms of cooperation and conflict actions. The second index (I-4b) measures the diversity of the leader's actions in terms of the distribution of words and deeds. Both indices range between 0 and 1 with higher values indicating greater flexibility. The formula for I-4a is one minus the absolute value of [the percentage of cooperative self utterances minus the percentage of conflictual self utterances]. The formula for the I-4b index is one minus the absolute value of [the percentage of *word* self utterances minus the percentage of *deed* self utterances].

We use the absolute value of the percentage differences in brackets here because we are *not* interested, in this case, in the direction of the subject's tactics (that shows up in I-1), but rather in the absolute level of diversity as marked by the variation in the percentage differences from one. For example, if the subject is perfectly diversified between cooperation and conflict with his rhetoric, it would mean that half his self attributions were cooperative and half conflictual. When we subtract the latter from the former, we end up with zero ($.50 - .50 = 0$). On the other hand, if a leader used only conflict rhetoric when talking about self's actions, we would end up with an absolute value of one ($|0 - 1| = 1$), showing no diversity.

When we subtract these absolute values from one, it maintains the logical direction of the index. Higher scores (as in the first example earlier, $1 - |0| = 1$) indicate greater diversity in cooperative and conflictual tactics, and lower scores (as in the second example earlier, $1 - |-1| = 0$) indicate lower diversity. Using the same logic, we can consider the extent to which the leader diversifies his tactics across word and deed categories with the formula for the I-4b index. Therefore, the scores for I-4a and I-4b also indicate how the subject manages two kinds of risk, which help to interpret more specifically the subject's risk orientation (I-3). The first one balances the risk of domination by others against the risk associated with deadlock as an outcome. The other one balances the risk of doing too much against the risk of not doing enough.

Utility of Means (I-5): Low to High
Here we are interested in the leader's beliefs about the utility of different tactics that mark the exercise of political power. Does the leader find utility in cooperative deeds? Or does he or she see value in conflictual words? Perhaps it is a combination of two or three different categories of action that are most useful. To operationalize this belief, we have created six different indices, each of which corresponds to one of the six verb categories found in VICS. We simply compute the use of each separate verb category as a percentage of total verbs coded when the subject is talking about self. Each index varies from 0 to 1, with lower scores indicating less utility and higher scores indicating more utility for each form of the exercise of power. The six formulae are as follows:

I-5 Punish: The sum of all self utterances coded as "Punish" divided by the sum of all self utterances.

I-5 Threaten: The sum of all self utterances coded as "Threaten" divided by the sum of all self utterances.

I-5 Oppose: The sum of all self utterances coded as "Oppose" divided by the sum of all self utterances.

I-5 Support: The sum of all self utterances coded as "Support" divided by the sum of all self utterances.

I-5 Promise: The sum of all self utterances coded as "Promise" divided by the sum of all self utterances.

I-5 Reward: The sum of all self utterances coded as "Reward" divided by the sum of all self utterances.

In the next two sections we discuss specific procedures for VICS coding and cover several other issues pertaining to VICS research designs, many of which are also relevant to other at-a-distance approaches. These topics include unit of analysis and aggregation issues, volume of material, comparison data, and the endogeneity problem.

Coding Procedures

It is possible to do VICS coding either by hand or with a computer. Our own initial work using VICS was all coded by hand (Crichlow 1998; Schafer and Walker 2001b, n.d.; Schafer, Young, and Walker 2002; Walker, Schafer, and Young 1998, 1999), which is very labor intensive and time consuming. In addition, human error will always be present and perhaps act as a confounding factor in the statistical models. Several years ago, Social Science Automation (www.socialscienceautomation.com) developed an automated, full-language parser software program for personal computers (*Profiler Plus*), which was intended particularly for at-a-distance, psychological assessments of subjects. We have worked extensively with the company to develop very large dictionaries specifically intended for VICS.[13]

The two most obvious advantages to using an automated coding system are that it is fast and efficient. Automated coding can help move us past the "coding bottleneck" that has slowed research in at-a-distance programs since their inception. Computer-based coding also essentially eliminates human biases and error. As with human coders, it is not the case that the computer codes everything perfectly. However, it is the case that if the computer makes an error, it will make the exact same error every time across that particular text and across all texts where it encounters the same verbal construction, meaning that the errors should generally not bias the data. The same cannot be said for human coders who may suffer from fatigue effects, personal political biases, learning effects, and other idiosyncratic stylistic differences. In each of these cases, the pattern of human errors may directionally bias the data. Put somewhat differently, automated coding gives us 100 percent coding reliability—a critically important advancement over human coding. Since the development of the Profiler Plus platform for VICS, most of our research has used that software for our operational code analyses (Malici 2005, 2006; Malici and Malici 2005a; Marfleet and Miller 2005; Walker and Schafer 2003, 2004; Walker, Schafer, and Marfleet 2001). Indeed, all but one of the articles in this volume use Profiler Plus.

In spite of the advantages of automated coding, some researchers may find it useful to conduct coding by hand. Scott Crichlow's chapter in this volume is a fine example of the kind of research that can be conducted this way. Regardless of the coding method selected, there is an important caveat. Although the underlying logic of hand coding and automated coding for VICS is the same, the two systems rely on quite different approaches to coding. They may produce significantly different results across texts, because each system has some strengths and weaknesses that will produce different kinds of results. Automated coding results in 100 percent reliability, but it is limited by the number of verbs and rules in the coding system and cannot subjectively interpret obscure phrases. Human coding can sometimes subjectively interpret obscure phrases, but it suffers from potential bias, fatigue, and idiosyncratic differences in coders. Therefore, it is usually inappropriate to compare data coded by hand to that coded by a computer. We discuss here in some detail the procedures used for both coding approaches.

Hand Coding

The logic of VICS coding was presented earlier in the section entitled "The Verbs In Context System." VICS is built upon the transitive verbs in a speaker's rhetoric. The other essential coding information needed by the system is the verb's grammatical subject. Coding begins with gathering appropriate texts relevant to the research question at hand. Once gathered, the text may be marked up, beginning with underlining or highlighting the verbs in the texts. Then the coder must make decisions and apply the appropriate code to each verb following the rules specified later. This is followed by identifying the subject as self or other, and adding other contextual information as appropriate to the research question. Coders should follow these procedures, literally moving through the text one verb-based utterance at a time, and specifying a data line for each verb.

The following is a list of the steps to be followed for coding texts by hand using VICS. Before beginning to code, make note of the speaker, date, audience, occasion for the speech act, and other situation variables that might be of interest for your research question.

1. Identify the verb-based utterance

The recording unit for this content analysis system is the verb-based utterance, which requires at a minimum a verb or verb phrase and a subject. The sentence does not always work as a recording unit because many sentences have multiple verb-based utterances.

2. Code the verb

   A. Clearly identify the transitive verb or verb-based phrase.
   B. Specify the positive or negative valence of the verb: is its direction cooperative (+) or conflictual (−)? If it is neutral, discard the verb and move onto the next one.
   C. Specify whether the verb is a word or deed. Deeds are actions that have been done. Words are promises or threats of future action or symbolic declarations of support or opposition. Note that all future-tense constructions should be coded as words. For example, the phrase "we will attack . . ." is not an actual attack but an indication that an attack will take place in the future; therefore it is not a deed but a threat of future action.
   D. Specify the appropriate final coding category for the verb from the six possibilities: Punish (−3), Threaten (−2), Oppose (−1), Support (+1), Promise (+2), and Reward (+3). Note that deeds are always −3 or +3, depending upon direction, and that words always go into the remaining four categories, −2, −1, +1, and +2. A helpful and short-hand way to specify this on a code sheet is by simply using the numeric value for each category. Although you should go through all four of these verb-coding stages and make shorthand notes along the way in the text of the document, the final data line requires only the numeric code for the verb category.

3. Specify the subject of the verb

Is the speaker himself or herself (or one of his or her identified in-groups) the subject for the verb? Or is it some actor external to the speaker? The final coding values for the subject of the utterance are either *self* or *other*.

4. Identify any additional information from the context of the utterance or broader parts of the speech act that might be relevant to your specific research question

You may wish to specify a contextual domain for the utterance, such as whether it pertains to an international issue or a domestic one. You may be interested in the target or direct object of the verb. We have coded such things as the general topic or subject area the speaker is talking about (Walker, Schafer, and Young 1998), and the regime type (democratic or nondemocratic) of *other* in each utterance (both when *other* is subject and object) (Schafer and Walker n.d.). There are many possibilities that may be of interest.

An Example

Here is a quote taken from President Carter's January 4, 1980 address to the nation: "Massive Soviet military forces have invaded the small, non-aligned, sovereign nation of Afghanistan . . ."

1. Identify the verb-based utterance

In this case the whole phrase is one utterance.

2. Code the verb

    A. The verb phrase is "have invaded."
    B. The direction of the verb is conflictual ($-$).
    C. The verb is a deed.
    D. Conflict deeds are coded as -3.

3. Specify the subject of the verb

The subject is "Massive Soviet military forces." Jimmy Carter is the speaker and is clearly not referring to himself or any of his in groups. Therefore, subject is coded as *other*.

4. Additional contextual information

Depending upon the research question, we may wish to record that the subject area is the cold war, or U.S.–Soviet relations, or Afghanistan. Or we may record that *other* is a nondemocracy. Or we may specify that the domain is *foreign*. The complete data line for this utterance would look something like the following, depending on your choice of contextual variables: -3 *other foreign nondemocracy*.

Automated Coding

Specific instructions for automated coding with Profiler Plus as a general software program are available from Social Science Automation, Inc. However, there are some procedures specific to VICS that are appropriate to pass along here. As with hand coding, the process begins with collecting speech acts that are appropriate for the research question. In order to be read by the software program the texts must be in digital format. Today many speech acts are already available in digital format, either through government websites or elsewhere on the Internet, or through CD-ROM digital collections (and perhaps other formats as well). If texts are not in digital format, we have either manually typed them into word processors or scanned and edited the originals to convert them to digital format.

Once in digital format, we use Profiler Plus's document preparation component to mark up the text and embed certain contextual information. Mark-up is necessary to tell Profiler Plus to "ignore" such things as questions from the press, headers and footers, nonpolitical comments, and other material that we do not want coded but do want preserved to maintain context. Other contextual information we embed in each file always includes the name of the speaker and the date of the speech act. We may include additional information, depending upon our research question, such as audience, type of speech act, level of spontaneity, and others.

Profiler Plus currently differentiates self and other automatically by relying on self-referential pronouns (I, me, we, us, etc.) in each verb-based utterance. If Profiler Plus does not identify a self pronoun in an utterance, it concludes that the speaker is referring to others. Self-referential pronouns account for a large number of utterances that speakers make regarding self. For example, if Jimmy Carter had responded to the Soviet invasion of Afghanistan, "We strongly oppose this act of aggression against the sovereign state of Afghanistan," Profiler Plus would have coded it as a −1 (oppose) *self*. However, subjects also sometimes use other, non-pronoun references when talking about *self*. Jimmy Carter might instead have said, "The U.S. strongly opposes . . . ," in which case Profiler Plus would, by default, code the utterance as *other*.

Because so many self references are pronouns, some research projects ignore this problem and still produce beneficial insights. However, many of us working with VICS have also adopted a fix that captures a larger percentage of self references. We manually go through samples of speech acts by the individual subject and note the non-pronouns that he or she uses with frequency to refer to self and self's in-groups. We develop subject-specific "self" dictionaries that tell Profiler Plus to code the utterance as self when it sees one of those references as the subject of the verb. Thus, for each U.S. president we would include such self references as "America," "United States," "White House," "U.S. Military," and others, including ones that are idiosyncratic for each president.

Research Design Issues

Once the data have been coded, it must be aggregated at some level so that the indices can be computed. Although the recording unit for VICS is the verb-based utterance, this unit does not suffice as the unit of analysis. The indices require more than a single value in order to be meaningful. What are the possibilities for the unit of analysis using VICS? The first possibility is the speech act itself, which may be a complete speech, a press conference, an interview, or virtually any other verbal expression that has a natural beginning and end. Once all of the verbs and subjects are coded for any single speech act, these utterances can be disaggregated, that is, separated into self and other utterances and then summed in each of the separate six verb categories, resulting in 12 values per speech act. These are used to calculate the indices noted earlier, and thus produce operational code scores for that speech act.

Once we have index values for each speech act in our design, we may use the speech act as the unit of analysis to conduct statistical analyses. These may include such things as: computing mean scores to profile the subject using a norming group as the basis for comparison; comparing mean scores across different leaders; comparing means of one leader for one or more time periods; comparing means of different types of leaders, such as first versus third world, democratic versus nondemocratic, or capitalist versus communist; or using the data as independent variables in regression models.

With virtually all of our research we at least initially aggregate the data to the level of the speech act. However, it is not always the case that this becomes the final unit of analysis. This is the case primarily because of two possible issues associated with aggregation. First, sometimes the research design favors a larger unit of analysis than the speech act itself. For instance, in some of our work we have aggregated to the year as our unit of analysis (Dille and Young 2000; Schafer and Crichlow 2000; Schafer, Robison, and Aldrich 2006; Walker, Schafer, and Young, 1998). This can be done simply by summing all of the verbs in each of the six verb categories (separated by self and other) for the entire year and then computing the VICS indices.

The difference between a summed score and a mean score for the year (using speech acts as the unit) is that by summing the year, we weight each verb-based utterance equally, whereas if the speech is the unit of analysis, a mean score gives greater weight to verbs in shorter speeches. The disadvantage is that by aggregating the data to the year, we can no longer run some statistical analyses, such as t-tests or ANOVA, that would use the year as a cell in the design. This is so because we end up with one score for the year, as opposed to several scores, and we cannot compute variance based upon one score. These aggregated data may still be compared, however, by using the mean and standard deviation of a broadly sampled group, which we call a norming group (discussed in more detail later), as the basis for comparison. Individual research designs should specify which strategy is most valid given the research question at hand.

The other occasion for aggregation has to do with those speech acts that are too short to produce meaningful values on the VICS indices. For example, if a speech act produced only two or three coded verbs, then it might be impossible to compute some of the index scores because there would be no denominator, or some indices might be extreme scores such as ones, zeros, or negative ones simply because of scarcity of data. These speech acts, by themselves, simply cannot be used. One option would be to discard any speech act that produces fewer than a minimally acceptable cutoff point. In our research this cutoff point has been between 15 and 20 coded verbs.[14] Of course, discarding such speech acts has the effect of losing data, and one can argue that all data are valuable and should be used.

In some cases our research design has allowed us to aggregate the verbs from these smaller speech acts with the verbs from another speech act that has a date close to the original. For example, if Jimmy Carter's speech on January 4, 1980 produced only ten coded verbs, we could, depending upon the research design, combine those verbs with another speech coded a few days later. Some research designs might require or allow the data to be aggregated to the month, quarter, or some other time frame. As with the possibilities noted earlier, there are pros and cons with each choice, and there is no substitute for the researcher's judgment and insight regarding the particular project.

An immediate, corollary question that we are often asked is: how much verbal material is enough? There is no perfect answer. One speech act that produces 15 coded verbs will not give us a profile in which we have a lot of confidence. But it is also not necessary to code every speech in a subject's career to construct a good profile. We recommend to students that they collect about ten randomly selected speech acts for a basic profile after identifying the sample frame (for instance, foreign policy speeches or speeches from a particular time period).

The answer for more sophisticated analyses depends in large part upon the particulars of the research design. For instance, ANOVA will require multiple units of analysis for each cell in the design. Sophisticated statistical power analysis can provide an approximate indication of the minimum number of units per cell necessary to find possible statistical differences. In addition, degrees of freedom and the number of factors in the design also affect statistical analyses. Some ANOVA designs can get by with as few as ten units per cell, or perhaps even fewer. Similar kinds of limits and restrictions also apply to OLS regression and other statistical modeling techniques.

Over the years we have gathered a large number of speech acts by many different leaders across different eras and locales in international politics. We have computed means and standard deviations for the VICS indices in this sample and use this "norming" data for comparison purposes in several of our research projects. Since the sample is large and diverse, it functions as a proxy for "the average leader." Profiling a new subject then is simply a matter of aggregating the raw data and computing VICS indices for the subject, and then comparing those scores to the norming sample's scores. We compute z-scores for the subject for each VICS index, thus showing how many standard deviations the subject is away from the sample score.

The logic of using the sample data can be extended to more complicated research designs as well; however, some cautions are in order. Our sample is built entirely from speech acts coded with Profiler Plus; thus, its statistics cannot be compared to hand-coded material. In addition, we have constructed self dictionaries for each subject in the sample base, meaning that the values should not be compared to research projects that have not developed self dictionaries or have done so in a manner significantly different from our approach. We have found that having data from a norming group is extremely helpful for our analyses. The data is archived at Louisiana State University and is publicly available. But we urge caution in its use if the underlying approach to coding is different from ours.

The final issues we discuss here are the endogeneity problem, circular reasoning, and temporal issues in general. Our general causal model is that a subject's operational code has an effect on the state's policy actions. That model is elaborated upon in the previous chapter. Here, we address an issue that frequently comes up: isn't it tautological, or at least an endogeneity problem that you code what a leader says to derive his operational code and then correlate it with what he does? Isn't the act of saying something tantamount to doing it? Aren't you coding the same thing on the independent and dependent variable sides of the equation? The short answer is no, we are not coding the same things on each side of the equation. That requires some explanation, which we provide later. Nonetheless, we find it helpful with some designs to make certain that we explicitly avoid the endogeneity problem, which we also discuss later.

While it is true that some state actions come first in the form of a leader's public statement, such a single specific action is only a very small part of a leader's rhetoric. In a recent project investigating Teddy Roosevelt as a realist archetype, we coded nearly 500 verbs per speech. At most, one or two of those verbs might show up using standard methods for collecting event data. While an event-generating verb might be present in VICS coded material, it is generally swamped by the other material in the speech act. In other words, each speech act produces a generalized picture of a subject's broad belief system, as opposed to a specific act of foreign policy.

In addition, with our research, we carefully use different methods and approaches for the independent variables and the dependent variable. VICS is almost always on the independent side of the equation. On the dependent side, we often include event data that is gathered from the leads of articles in major newspapers (Schafer and Walker n.d.; Walker, Schafer, and Young 1999). These data may include an event that is derived directly from a speech by the leader, but they also include events from many different sources such as the military, other key actors in the foreign policy process, allies, IGOs, and others. Both conceptually and in practice, operational code data are very different from event data. Nonetheless, we are generally sensitive to the endogeneity problem when we construct our research designs. Where possible, we separate VICS data temporally from data collected for the dependent variable. This step can be done in a number of ways, such as lagging the dependent variable by collecting VICS data in a period immediately preceding the onset of the decision episode, and by changing the identity of the dependent variable from the frequency of actions to the sequence of actions.

Other Issues in At-A-Distance Assessments

There are a number of other issues and potential problems associated with at-a-distance research, some of which have been raised and discussed elsewhere (Schafer 2000). Although an extensive discussion of these topics is beyond the scope of this chapter, in this section we mention a few of them briefly.

Authorship

One issue of concern is authorship of the verbal material that we code with VICS, which is often related to the issue of the type of source material one should use. If a speechwriter wrote the speech, then are we not capturing the speechwriter's operational code as opposed to the leader's? If the data we were gathering dealt with the unconscious characteristics of the leader, we would be more concerned about speechwriter effects. Indeed, some of the at-a-distance research programs on unconscious characteristics do not use prepared speeches by their subjects. Instead, they use verbal material that is more spontaneous, such as interviews or press conferences.

However, VICS gathers cognitive information—information that has been consciously processed—and is, therefore, more transparent. Put differently, while a leader may not know his or her unconscious need for power (and a speech writer seems unlikely to somehow build it into speech patterns), the same cannot be said about more transparent cognitive information. A speech writer is likely to know the leader's views on specific policy issues and general cooperative and conflictual tendencies. Speechwriters do not generally write speeches that belie the leader's general positions and policy preferences.

In addition, speeches are often the product of several key players in an administration. There may be bureaucratic wrangling over terms and positions, and the phrasing is often discussed in decision-making meetings at the highest level of the state. In other words, formal speeches by leaders are generally the product of the state's decision-making apparatus, and, therefore, represent the official views of the state. We often refer to the data we gather from formal speeches as the "state's" operational code. VICS has been used with both spontaneous and prepared materials and seems to provide insight in both cases. Our research has shown that there are some interesting differences in VICS indices between prepared and spontaneous comments by a leader (Dille 2000; Marfleet 2000; Schafer and Crichlow 2000). This topic is an area where more research needs to be done and where individual researchers need to make their own informed decisions based upon their particular research designs.

Deception

What if leaders intentionally deceive? What if they engage in "impression management" (Tetlock and Manstead 1985)? Doesn't that skew VICS results? Our response is related to the one mentioned earlier regarding the endogeneity problem. Intentional deception or impression management may affect a very small number of verbs, but the large numbers of utterances we code per subject generally swamp these few intentional deceptions. It may be possible to deceive the public or other actors in international politics with a few brief phrases, but it is an entirely different matter to deceive VICS indices calculated from whole speech acts that include large numbers of utterances. It is also the case, as Rosati (1987, 191) points out, that speech acts—even deceptive ones—often have the effect of locking leaders into courses of action; otherwise they can be accused of lying.

Leaders and Advisors

Finally, there is the issue of leaders and advisors: whose operational code do we need for effective yet efficient explanations? Were data costs not a concern, our answer would be that we need the operational codes for everyone involved! Of course, data is not free, so individual research designs need to focus and manage the scope of their projects. In theory, operational codes of advisors feed into the operational code of the leader and the state. The focus of most of our research has been the leader of the state, because his or her speeches are more likely the product of the whole state, he or she speaks on behalf of the state, and is generally the most important decision maker for the state. Some research that focuses on leaders and advisors has been conducted (Walker and Schafer 2000), and more is reported in the chapters by Crichlow and Robison for this volume. The more data we are able to gather regarding leaders and advisors, the more complete will be our modeling. We hope to see more research on the leader–advisor nexus in the future.

A related issue is the linkage among beliefs, preferences, decisions, and outcomes. George (1979) has argued that beliefs influence policy preferences directly, but the linkage between beliefs and decisions is indirect and subject to the influence of intervening causal mechanisms such as cognitive shortcuts, decision heuristics, cognitive and motivational biases within the individual, small group and bureaucratic processes within the government, and external stimuli in the form of actions by other states (Farnham 1994, 1997; George 1980; Hermann 2001; Janis 1982; Lake and Powell 1999a; Levy 1997; Mintz 2004). However, we contend that beliefs also act as causal mechanisms to constrain and specify a state's foreign policy at different levels of decision: preferences, strategies, tactics, and moves (see George 1969, 1979; Larson 1994; Walker 1983, 1995, 2003, 2004b).

It is an empirical question whether the bounded rationality of belief systems as schemata or the effects of other decision heuristics and biases offer a more robust explanation of behavior. If beliefs do shape preferences and if we can infer a leader's preferences from his beliefs, then we may be able to predict and explain choices at the strategic level of decision, which will also constrain tactics and moves as a form of bounded rationality (Simon 1957; Tetlock 1998). Over time, the test is whether the intensity and sequence of a state's behavior conforms statistically and formally to the strategic and tactical orientations of the state's operational code and to our theory of inferences about preferences in chapter 3.[15]

Lake and Powell (1999a) maintain that a state's actions are the outcome of bargaining and strategic interaction processes inside the state between players with preferences about different decisions on the menu for choice, which aggregate as outcomes to become a state's foreign policy decisions. In turn, foreign policy decisions by states intersect as strategic choices to generate international outcomes between dyads. We contend that operational code analysis is well-suited to investigate both the strategic interactions between leaders and advisors within states and the strategic interactions between states that aggregate beliefs, preferences, decisions, and outcomes at different levels of decision and analysis. The elaboration of this claim is the focus of the next chapter, informed by a theory of inferences about preferences from belief systems and a theory of moves about strategic interactions within and between states.

Notes

1. Neural networks are brain cells (called neurons) that are separated by synapses (small gaps between neurons) through which electrochemical processes operate to transmit signals and messages. These communication patterns are capable of higher-order patterns of divergent and convergent connectivity called circuits and systems, distinguished by different electrical signals and chemical messages acting as transmitters of impressions of external stimuli and expressions of internal responses. The messages may be cognitions containing information, emotions expressing feelings, or motivations directing action (LeDoux 2002).

2. LeDoux (2002) argues that the study of the mind is a trilogy that includes the study of cognition, emotion, and motivation. Historically, each of these mental processes has received varying amounts of attention in the discipline of psychology without really addressing how the brain actually operates to generate these processes. More recently, cognitive science has developed as a discipline that focuses almost exclusively on cognition, influenced by apparent parallels between computers and mental processes such as memory and the transmission of information. Most recently, cognitive neuroscience has expanded the focus of cognitive science to include emotion and motivation, and focus explicitly on how the brain operates as integrated physiological systems to generate cognitions, emotions, and motivations (see also LeDoux and Hirst 1986). Operational code analysis addresses this trilogy by focusing on beliefs (cognitions) with valences of positive and negative affect (emotion) associated with needs for power, achievement, and affiliation (motivations). See Walker (1983, 1990, 1995, 2003) for an elaboration of the different elements of this trilogy in operational code analysis.

3. A political belief system conceptualized as beliefs about the exercise of power is consistent with theorists who conceptualize politics as a social

process that involves "a struggle for power" (Morgenthau 1985), "who gets what, when, and how" (Lasswell 1958), and the "authoritative allocation of values" (Easton 1953). Leites (1951, 1953) also emphasized the social dimension of a leader's operational code as a psycho-cultural construct similar to the conception of strategic culture in contemporary international relations theory (see also Johnston 1995a; Katzenstein 1996; Walker 2003, 2004b).

4. The operational code construct was defined initially by Leites (1953, 15) as "the conceptions of political 'strategy' " regarding the exercise of power in Bolshevik ideology, which included as ontological statements, causal attributions, and prescriptive norms under the umbrella label of "beliefs." George (1969) refined this conceptualization by distinguishing between philosophical beliefs about the nature of the political universe and instrumental beliefs about the most effective means of political action, which were linked together as a political belief system. Holsti (1977) developed a typology of such belief systems, which Walker (1983, 1995, 2004b) refined and linked to different images of self and other with corresponding differences in motivations and preferences. Walker, Schafer and Young (1998, 2003) developed the VICS to differentiate images of self and other in these belief systems.

5. The word/deed distinction appears explicitly in WEIS and CREON event scales (see Hermann 1971; Hermann et al. 1973; McClelland and Hoggard 1969). Three position scales on each side of a zero point include the semantic differential scale (Osgood, Suci, and Tannenbaum, 1957) employed by Holsti (1967) and Starr (1984) and the event data scales in Callahan et al. (1982) and Leng (1993). More extensive scales with several positions include Goldstein's WEIS scale (1992) and Azar's COPDAB scale (1980). Critics of these more extensive scales include the founder of the WEIS scheme (McClelland 1983) and Beer et al. (1992).

6. George (1969) made the first reference to a "master belief," suggesting that the first philosophical belief would be the schematic basis for the remaining beliefs. Our empirical work using VICS suggests that instrumental beliefs may vary significantly from philosophical beliefs, thus leading us to conceptualize two, not one, master beliefs in the operational code.

7. The definitions of high score and low score are relative and depend upon such things as the method of coding (hand vs. machine), the comparison population, the statistical model, and other factors. This point is discussed in greater depth later.

8. This index is divided by three simply to make its values consistent with the other balance indices, which take a maximum value of $+1$. Because the intensity scale for the coded verbs ranges from -3 to $+3$, without this divisor the index would also range from -3 to $+3$.

9. "The Index of Qualitative Variation is a ratio of the number of different pairs of observations in a distribution to the maximum possible number of different pairs for a distribution with the same N [number of cases] and the

same number of variable classifications" (Watson and McGaw 1980, 88). We subtract the IQV from one to maintain the directional logic of the index, making higher scores indicate more predictability and lower scores indicate less predictability.

10. In the game-theoretic models discussed extensively in the introduction to this volume, we are interested in the subject's views of others' level of control also (which contributes to our understanding of the strategy that the subject sees others playing). Logically, this is simply the inverse of P-4. To differentiate these two values in our models we generally refer to self's level of control as P-4a and to others' level of control as P-4b.

11. Once again we divide this index by three to get an index with a maximum value of $+1$, the same as the other indices.

12. IQV is defined earlier in the discussion on P-3. We subtract the IQV from one to maintain the logical direction of the index.

13. At press time the dictionary included 781 core verbs and 14,871 application rules.

14. In earlier work we specified a minimum length of 1500 words for a speech act. While this criteria often works, the value that matters most for computing VICS indices is the number of utterances in the speech act that are coded by VICS.

15. We also want to acknowledge explicitly here the potential influence of other processes and the advisability of controlling for them where we can in our attempts to link beliefs and behavior. Some of our other related research on foreign policy decision-making processes has, in fact, focused on these kinds of causal mechanisms located inside and outside the state (see Schafer 1996, 1997, 1999; Schafer and Crichlow 1996, 2002; Walker and Watson 1989, 1992, 1994).

CHAPTER 3

A WORLD OF BELIEFS: MODELING INTERACTIONS AMONG AGENTS WITH DIFFERENT OPERATIONAL CODES

B. Gregory Marfleet and Stephen G. Walker

Introduction

The organization of the operational code research program spans levels of analysis as well as levels of foreign policy decisions. It has an "inside-out" structure in which the beliefs of individuals are at the core of the research program. Its focus then expands across leaders, advisors, and groups within the state in order to aggregate a prevailing set of shared beliefs or identify differences that require resolution in order to generate an operational code for the state (Malici 2005; Marfleet 2000; Walker and Schafer 2000). The resolution of contending beliefs held by the leaders of a government are strategic decision-making episodes with the results appearing in the public statements accompanying a foreign policy decision (Lake and Powell 1999b).

Foreign policy decisions are organized at several levels from the "bottom up." At the most basic level they are conceptualized as the words and deeds that represent the exercise of political power by the state. Combinations of words and deeds are aggregated into moves, which are bounded by the words and deeds of another state in a sequence of behavioral exchanges between members of a dyad. Different sequences of moves over time form different tactics. For example, if State A (Ego) threatens (words), State B (Alter) responds with a counterthreat (words), State A mobilizes naval forces (deeds), the tactical sequence of three moves is Punish for Ego (conflict words by Ego, conflict words by Alter, conflict deeds for Ego). If the fourth move in this sequence is Alter's actions (deeds) in compliance with Ego's initial threat, then the tactical sequence for Alter is Bluff, in other words, conflict words by Alter, conflict deeds by Ego, cooperative deeds by Alter (Snyder and Diesing 1977; Walker 2004a).

It is also possible to classify each actor's move in a tactical sequence by reference to its previous move in the series as an escalatory (E) or de-escalatory (D) move so that the Punish sequence becomes (EEE) and the Bluff sequence becomes (EED). The expansion of the logical possibilities in this classification scheme appears in figure 3.1. Together combinations of tactical sequences exchanged between members of a dyad become strategies of interaction within a strategic interaction episode that form the context for its final outcome at the systemic level of analysis (Walker 2004a).

For example, a Punish/Bluff sequence between Ego and Alter (EEED) ends with an escalatory (E) move by Ego and a de-escalatory (D) move by Alter, which aggregates to an outcome of (E,D) defined as domination by Ego and submission by Alter. Other possible outcomes include: (D,D) mutual cooperation between Ego and Alter, (E,E) mutual conflict between them, and (D,E) submission by Ego and domination by Alter. If these tactical outcomes stabilize the interactions between the two states and thereby represent an equilibrium between them, then they also represent the interaction of strategic choices directed toward that equilibrium by each actor and form the boundaries of a strategic interaction episode.

Aggregating across these levels of moves, tactics, and strategies also spans the conventional divide between foreign policy and international relations by shifting the unit of analysis from the monadic (state) level to the dyadic (systemic) level, as the unit of decision shifts from a state's exercise of power by words and deeds to the interplay of power between states exhibited by their strategic interactions (Lake and Powell 1999b). Put more succinctly, foreign policy decisions generate processes of world politics. Beginning with an inside-out focus on leaders, that is to say, "the world in their minds," (Vertzberger 1990), the operational code research program extends its scope from beliefs through actions to interactions in order to trace how and why "anarchy is what states make of it" (Wendt 1992).

Type A Quadrant		(I-1/P-1)		Type C Quadrant	
		+2.0			
P1				**P3**	
Appease				Exploit	
DED		+1.5		DDE	
(+ <)				(+ >)	
		+1.0			
	P2			**P2**	
	Reward			Deter	
	DDD	+0.5		DEE	
	(+ =)			(+ =)	

(P-4) −2.0 −1.5 −1.0 −0.5 ±0.0   +0.5 +1.0 +1.5 +2.0 **(P-4)**

	P5			**P5**	
	Compel	−0.5		Punish	
	EDD			EEE	
	(− =)	−1.0		(− =)	
P4				**P6**	
Bluff		−1.5		Bully	
EED				EDE	
(− <)		−2.0		(− >)	
		(I-1/P-1)			

Type DEF Quadrant   **Type B Quadrant**

Figure 3.1   VICS★ Prediction Template for Tactics and Strategies.★★

Note:

★ I-1 and P-1 indices are scaled along the vertical axis, and P-4 indices for Ego and Alter are scaled along the horizontal axis with VICS scores expressed as standard deviations from the mean for a norming group of leaders from different eras and regions.

★★ Reward, Deter, Punish, and Compel tactics around the midpoint of the horizontal axis are variants of reciprocity tactics in which Ego initiates either an escalatory (E) move or de-escalatory (D) move and then responds in kind when Alter escalates (E) or de-escalates (D) in response to Ego's initial move. Appease, Bluff, Exploit, and Bully tactics at the extremes of the horizontal axis are variants of unconditional conflict or cooperation tactics in which Ego initiates either an escalatory (E) move or de-escalatory (D) move and then does not reciprocate after Alter escalates (E) or de-escalates (D) in response to Ego's initial move. These tactics are associated with the six strategic propositions in TIP, as indicated by the P1 . . . P6 notations.

Although the initial puzzles are the behaviors and relations between states, the operational code research program also analyzes feedback over time from behavioral interactions back to beliefs and takes into account the context in which strategic choices are made by states. The processes of social learning, experiential learning, and structural adaptation complete an "outside-in" feedback loop linking information from the environment with the beliefs and behaviors of leaders (Leng 2000; Levy 1994; see also Walker, Schafer, and Marfleet 2001; Walker, Schafer, and Young 1998).

Operational code analysis also links conceptually different levels of decision from the "top down" after operationalizing them empirically from the "bottom up." While the operational definitions of moves, tactics, and strategies are from the lowest level of decision up to the highest level of decision, their conceptualization also orders them from strategies down to moves in strategic interaction episodes. The assumption is that moves and tactics may be guided by the strategies for the subjective games embedded in a leader's belief system, which are defined by different combinations of "master beliefs" and a theory of inferences about strategic preferences.

According to the theory, these master beliefs are (P-1) the image of Other in the political universe, (I-1) the image of Self in the political universe, and (P-4) the leader's belief regarding his or her relative ability to control events between Self and Other in the political universe. A deductive Theory of Inferences about Preferences (TIP) associates the types of belief systems in Holsti's revised typology of operational codes with different preference rankings for the strategic interaction outcomes of settlement, domination, deadlock, and submission (Walker 2004b). In a given strategic interaction episode, there are two different subjective games constructed from each player's belief system regarding the outcomes of domination, submission, settlement, or deadlock, which may be the same homogeneous game.

However, the possibility of slippage among them makes it desirable to consider heterogeneous combinations in order to explain fully the strategies and outcomes of interactions between dyads (Walker 2004b). It is possible that the subjective games in the belief systems of Ego and Alter are different, but their subsequent interactions based on those games lead to a mutually expected outcome. Conversely, the belief systems might appear compatible while the outcome is unexpected. In this account, both the outcomes of peace (D,D) and war (E,E) at the end of a strategic interaction episode may be the product of misperceptions and miscalculations (Brams 1994, 157–182; Stein 1990). The stability of this equilibrium is also likely to vary, depending on the degree of congruence between the subjective games of each leader. Each leader may draw different lessons from their strategic interactions. Their reflections upon why the equilibrium between them occurred may undermine it and influence their interactions in subsequent episodes (Brams 1994; Maoz and Mor 2002; Marfleet and Miller 2005; Stein 1990).

Research designs for linking master beliefs and different levels of decision via TIP in figure 3.2 may proceed either deductively (top-down) from

A Top-Down Deductive Theory of Inferences Based on Beliefs

Self/Other Attributions*	Signs	Propositions
Cooperative, Low	(+, <)	1
Cooperative, Equal	(+, =)	2
Cooperative, High	(+, >)	3
Conflictual, Low	(−, <)	4
Conflictual, Equal	(−, =)	5
Conflictual, High	(−, >)	6

*VICS Indices for (I-1, P-4a) Self's strategic orientation and locus of control or (P-1, P-4b) Other's strategic orientation and locus of control.

A Bottom-Up Inductive Theory of Inferences Based on Tactics

Propositions:	1	2	2	3	4	5	5	6
Beliefs:	(+, <)	(+, =)	(+, =)	(+, >)	(−, <)	(−, =)	(−, =)	(−, >)
Tactics:	Appease	Reward	Deter	Exploit	Bluff	Compel	Punish	Bully
Moves:	DED	DDD	DEE	DDE	EED	EDD	EEE	EDE

Propositions Based on Inferences from Beliefs or Tactics

(1) If (+, <), then Settle > Deadlock > Submit > Dominate.

(2) If (+, =), then Settle > Deadlock > Dominate > Submit.

(3) If (+, >), then Settle > Dominate > Deadlock > Submit.

(4) If (−, <), then Dominate > Settle > Submit > Deadlock.

(5) If (−, =), then Dominate > Settle > Deadlock > Submit.

(6) If (−, >), then Dominate > Deadlock > Settle > Submit.

Figure 3.2 A Theory of Inferences about Preferences (TIP) from Beliefs or Tactics.

beliefs to moves or inductively (bottom–up) from moves to beliefs. In the first instance, we ask what beliefs and strategic preferences imply different strategies, tactics, and moves. In the second instance, we ask what a particular sequence of moves (tactics) reveals about antecedent beliefs and strategies (Walker and Schafer 2004). These two designs can also be linked dynamically over time by asking: if Other's decisions do not correspond to the expectations in Self's subjective game, do they act as communications tactics that alter the link between Self's beliefs and behavior (social learning) and/or alter Self's beliefs (experiential learning)? The tactics identified in figure 3.2 may alter the link between beliefs and behavior via the processes of social and experiential learning by revealing strategic preferences (Walker and Schafer 2004; Walker, Schafer, and Marfleet 2001).

A World of Beliefs

In this chapter we incorporate elements from both research designs to explore the mirroring, steering, and learning effects of beliefs (Walker 2002; Walker and Schafer 2004). Beginning from the top down with the identification of a world of beliefs from the possible combinations of subjective games specified in the deductive TIP, we model the strategies and corresponding equilibria constructed for these subjective games with the strategies, tactics, and moves specified by the sequential game models in Brams's Theory of Moves (TOM). Together these two theories (TIP and TOM) predict and explain the links among beliefs, strategies, and outcomes between the dyads.

With the models of strategic interaction from TIP and TOM, we can answer several substantive research questions with hypotheses about how agents in the real world are likely to exercise power and what kind of political world the interplay of the exercise of power is likely to produce between them (Walker 2004b; see also Wendt 1999). What happens when beliefs have mirroring effects (when the subjective games within each agent's world of beliefs are congruent)? What happens when the subjective games of Self and Other are the same, but the identities of Ego and Alter are switched around? What happens when the subjective games for Self and Other are not the same (when the strategies attributed to Ego and Alter are not the same and beliefs exercise exogenous steering effects instead of endogenous mirroring effects)?

The answers to these questions lead to still more research questions and hypotheses about the answers. What happens when the differences in subjective games lead to unexpected outcomes—what does each player "learn" from this gap between expected and actual outcomes? Which operational codes (strategies) are the most effective against the others, that is to say, when the subjective games of dyad members are not congruent, which strategy is most effective? Which kinds of strategies are effective against which other kinds of strategies, for example, with cooperative versus coercive strategies? If a particular strategy for Self is not effective against Other's strategy, what strategy would be more effective? These are just some of the substantive problems solved by a "theory complex" or alliance between TIP and TOM, which we will answer with solutions in the form of hypotheses about solving empirical puzzles between agents in the real world (Laudan 1977).

Using the six preference orderings delineated in the propositions in figure 3.2, we begin our analysis by first identifying the 12 possible subjective games that these propositions allow. The number of possible games is restricted by the nature of the operational code indices on which they are based. To identify a particular agent's subjective game, we must know how the agent defines his or her image of Self (cooperative or conflictual), how the agent perceives the image of Other (again, cooperative or conflictual) and how the agent perceives his or her relative ability to control events between Self and Other.

Cooperative (+) or conflictual (−) orientations for Self and Other images are independent assessments with four possible combinations (+,+), (+,−), (−,+), or (−,−). In contrast, control is a relational measure that can be distributed in three ways: more or less equally (=, =), to the advantage of Self over Other (>, <), or the reverse (<, >). The combination of the four image orientations and three perceptions of control distribution define the twelve possible games. Since the six preference rankings that define a player's possible strategies are already associated with specific combinations of self image (+ or −) and sense of control (<, =, >) the variant factor in defining the subjective game is whether the agent perceives the other as essentially friendly or hostile.

For each tactical orientation suggested in figure 3.2, we can identify two possible opponents. The subjective games depicted in figure 3.3 were created by combining the preference ordering for Self with those of the *perceived* Other. For example, for an agent with an "Appease" orientation—one with a cooperative self image but with a perception of relative control deficiency—the possible opponent will always be perceived as relatively more in control of events. However, the opponent could be either cooperative (Exploit) or conflictual (Bully) in orientation. Combining these sets of preferences yields two subjective games, one for "Appease +" (vs. Exploit) and the other for "Appease −" (vs. Bully).

Figure 3.3 marks out all of the possible combinations of preferences implied in TIP in normal game form. In some instances the preferences of Other are identical to Self, for example, Reward/Deter (+, =) versus Reward/Deter (+, =) and paired Compel/Punish (−, =) strategies, and have symmetrical payoffs. More often, asymmetrical subjective games are the result. It should be emphasized that the ordering of payoffs across quadrants provides a formal representation only of Ego's perception of his/her strategic

(1) Appease (+, <) vs. Exploit (+, >) or Bully (−, >)

		Exploit						Bully		
	CO	**4,4**	2,3				CO	4,2	**2,4**	
SELF				[0100]		SELF				[0010]
	CF	1,1	3,2				CF	1,1	**3,3**	
		(0,1,2,3 / 0)						*(1 / 1 & 0,2,3 / 2)*		

(2) Reward/Deter (+, =) vs. Reward/Deter (+, =) or Compel/Punish (−, =)

		Reward/Deter						Compel/Punish		
	CO	**4,4**	1,2				CO	4,3	1,4	
SELF				[0100]		SELF				[0110]
	CF	2,1	3,3				CF	2,1	**3,2**	
		(0,1,2,3 / 0)						*(0 3 / 0 & 1,2 / 2)*		

(3) Exploit (+, >) vs. Appease (+, <) or Bluff (−, <)

		Appease						Bluff		
	CO	**4,4**	1,1				CO	4,3	1,4	
SELF				[0100]		SELF				[0110]
	CF	3,2	2,3				CF	3,2	2,1	
		(0,1,2,3 / 0)						*(1 / 3 & 0,2,3 / 0)*		

(4) Bluff (−, <) vs. Exploit (+, >) or Bully (−, >)

		Exploit						Bully		
	CO	3,4	2,3				CO	3,2	**2,4**	
SELF				[0001]		SELF				[0001]
	CF	4,1	1,2				CF	4,1	1,3	
		(3 / 1 & 0,1,2 / 0)						*(0,1,2,3, / 1)*		

(5) Compel/Punish (−, =) vs. Reward/Deter (+, =) or Compel/Punish (−, =)

		Reward/Deter						Compel/Punish		
	CO	3,4	1,2				CO	3,3	1,4	
SELF				[0101]		SELF				[0111]
	CF	4,1	**2,3**				CF	4,1	**2,2**	
		(0,2 / 0 & 1,3 / 2)						*(0 / 0 & 1,2,3 / 2)*		

(6) Bully (−, >) vs. Appease (+, <) or Bluff (−, <)

		Appease						Bluff		
	CO	2,4	1,1				CO	2,3	1,4	
SELF				[1111]		SELF				[1111]
	CF	4,2	**3,3**				CF	**4,2**	3,1	
		(3 / 3 & 0,1,2 / 2)						*(0,1,2,3 / 3)*		

Figure 3.3 Subjective Games, Expected Outcomes, and Moore Machine Strings for 12 Operational Code Agents.

Note: Expected outcomes in parentheses (S/E) where S indicates the starting quadrant(s) and E is the expected outcome using a TOM solution. TOM non-myopic equilibria are in bold text in the normal game matrices. Nash equilibria are underlined. Quadrants are numbered as $\frac{0|1}{3|2}$. CO = Cooperation, CF = Conflict.

Bracketed numbers indicate Moore machine strings used as agent response sets in the simulation.

environment. As noted, the agent's perception of the opponent's preferences may or may not accurately mirror those of Alter. Regardless of whether or not mirroring occurs, the subjective games provide a framework for choice and action for the agent, thereby acting as steering mechanisms.

To translate these games into action repertoires, we apply Brams's (1994) TOM. Unlike Nash solutions that require participants to simultaneously select a strategy as if they had never interacted prior to meeting in the game, Brams's TOM solutions incorporate both the history of prior interaction and allow for sequential rather than simultaneous choice. Solving a game using TOM requires adherence to a set of rules of play. Paraphrased, they are: (i) the game begins in some quadrant of the normal form depiction (the initial state); (ii) the initiating player has the option of staying at the initial state or changing his or her strategy to move to a new quadrant; (iii) the responding player can likewise switch or not; (iv) players will not move from a state unless it will lead (eventually) to a more preferred outcome; (v) these response opportunities alternate until the player whose turn it is to move chooses not to, or (vi) play returns to the initial state. Two caveats to these rules are: first, should the initiating player choose not to move in the first round, the opponent may "take precedence" and override the player that tried to stay thereby initiating the game; second, backtracking is not allowed and any move that would return the game to a previously occupied quadrant results in termination (Brams 1994, 21–28).

TOM solutions generate an alternative form of equilibrium to the commonly understood Nash solutions. Determining which of the often multiple, TOM-identified, "non-myopic equilibria" (NMEs) hold for any particular game depends on the initial state or starting quadrant. Figure 3.3 depicts all of the potential NMEs for each game by highlighting the payoffs for those quadrants in bold type. Nash solutions are also underlined. In addition, below each game is a list of starting quadrants and associated NME outcome quadrants in italic text. To generate these solutions we assume that the Ego is the row player and is also the initiator. If for some reason these assumptions are inappropriate, it is possible to reorient and place Alter as initiator by referring to the analogous game with the row and column positions switched. For example, Game 2 (Reward/Deter vs. Compel/ Punish) could be reoriented to Game 5 (Compel/Punish vs. Reward/ Deter) if, in fact, Alter was initiating and Ego was responding. According to TOM, who actually moves first is determined endogenously by backward induction or by order power if there is still an indeterminacy (Brams 1994, 121–124).

The identification of these equilibria provides two important pieces of information about an agent's subjective game. First, they indicate at what outcome quadrant the agent anticipates the game will arrive, given some starting state in the game. Second, by generating these solutions we can identify how each agent would respond (move or stay) to being placed in a particular quadrant. The numbers in brackets to the right of each game matrix depict these movement propensities.

To interpret these numerical movement strings, first number the quadrants in a normal form game matrix from 0 to 3 beginning with the top left quadrant and proceeding clockwise. Likewise, mark the string of numbers 0, 1, 2, and 3 starting with the left-most digit and moving right. The strings describe the actions of the agent upon entering a quadrant: 0s indicate that the agent would choose to cooperate, 1s indicate a choice for conflict. In some instances the resulting strategy choice may initiate a change to a new quadrant; in others it will not.

An Agent-Based Computational Model

Agent-based modeling (ABM) is a form of computational modeling that differs from formal, rational-choice techniques commonly found in game theoretic research. Instead of using complex sets of equations, inferred preference utilities, and multivariate differential calculus to find equilibrium outcomes to mathematically defined choice situations, agent-based models employ computational tools to interact programmable agents within a parameterized environment (Parunak, Savit, and Riolo 1998). Because these agents can be as simple or complex as the researcher desires, ABM fits easily within the "bounded-rationality" paradigm of choice research.

Digit strings (or bit strings), such as those in figure 3.3, are common ways to depict the finite computational automata used and are called Moore machines (Hopcraft and Ullman 1979). Each number string defines a computational agent's response to a set of states that encapsulates the range of possible choices it might encounter. At each state, the machine provides the information needed for the agent to act in the given situation and to direct the agent to (perhaps) adopt some new state. The four-character strings provided in the figure are nearly as simple as could be made to play a 2 × 2 game; even simpler game strategies such as "always cooperate" or "always defect" are also possible to depict by a single digit. Because we invoke the logic of TOM to define the agent repertoires and employ a sequential notion of game play, we can rely on the position of the game (quadrant) to provide "state" information and thereby make practical the use of these simple automata.

For our model we created 12 programmed agents corresponding to the games in figure 3.3. Each agent was supplied with a set of rules guiding its game play that reflects the Moore machine strings. The agents were also provided with a set of anticipated outcomes that reflect the NME associated with each starting quadrant. At the termination of the interaction, these expected outcomes for the row player (initiator) were compared to the actual results of the game play. We designed a round-robin tournament where each agent interacted with every other agent (including its own twin), both as initiator and as respondent (column player).

TOM-inspired rules for sequential game play were employed to determine the outcome of each pairing. True TOM rules could not be applied, since neither agent was provided with information about the actual preferences of their opponent. Both agents play the game strictly in accordance with the TOM-derived solutions appropriate for their subjective games, which are preprogrammed as a response set. Although an outside observer with perfect information could construct some kind of "objective" game from a combination of the agent preferences, such a construct is neither epistemologically nor computationally required for this experiment.

To run one paired interaction of agents, an initial state was selected and two agents were chosen. Agent 1 (the row player) was asked to select a move in response to its current position. If that response implied a shift from the current quadrant, then the new quadrant information was provided to the second agent, who could respond. As in the formal rules of TOM, if the row player did not initiate movement then the column player took precedence and was given the chance to continue play by moving. These alternating moves proceeded until one of three terminating events occurred: both players opted not to move from the current quadrant, one player tried to backtrack to a previously occupied quadrant, or they returned to their initial state.

Since returning to the initial state suggests a problem of infinite cycling, this termination rule is consistent with the TOM principle that says that players would anticipate and avoid cycling problems by not moving from the initial state if the resulting sequence would lead them back to the same quadrant. While the agents in the model cannot anticipate cycling the way TOM players could (since they have no knowledge of the objective game that would lead to it), their response to cycling is to prevent second or subsequent iterations of a cycle by stopping when they return to the starting quadrant. Although the process may differ from a pure TOM solution, the end result is the same—cycling problems result in termination of the game at the starting quadrant.

For each run of the computational model, the outcome of the interaction of the two agents was recorded, and then two new agents were selected. This was repeated until all possible combinations of agents and starting quadrants were explored. Since the NMEs for each subjective game are dependent on the initial state, our tournament matched all the agent pairs four times, each with a different starting quadrant for a total of $12 \times 12 \times 4$, or 576 games. As simple as this model was, the sheer number of possible games and outcomes (and the potential for human error in

Table 3.1 Expected Outcomes Versus Simulation-Generated Outcomes for all Possible Pairs of Agents and Starting Quadrants

	APP +	APP −	REW/ DET +	REW/ DET −	EXP +	EXP −	BLUFF +	BLUFF −	COMP/ PUN+	COMP/ PUN−	BULLY +	BULLY −
APP +	0|0 0|0	0|0 0|2	0|0 0|0	0|0 0|2	0|0 0|0	0|0 0|2	0|0 0|0	0|0 0|0	0|0 0|0	0|0 0|2	0|2 0|2	0|2 0|2
APP −	0|0 1|0	0|0 1|0	2|0 1|0	2|0 1|0	2|0 1|0	2|0 1|0	2|0 1|1	2|0 1|1	2|0 1|1	2|0 1|1	2|1 1|1	2|1 1|1
REW/ DET +	2|0 2|0	2|0 2|0	2|0 2|0	2|0 2|0	2|0 2|0	2|0 2|0	2|0 2|0	2|0 2|0	2|0 2|0	2|0 2|0	2|1 2|2	2|1 2|2
REW/ DET −	0|0 0|0	0|0 0|0	0|0 0|0	0|0 0|0	0|0 0|0	0|0 0|0	0|0 0|0	0|0 0|0	0|0 0|0	0|0 0|0	0|2 0|2	0|2 0|2
EXP +	0|0 0|0	0|0 2|2	0|0 2|0	0|0 2|2	0|0 2|0	0|0 2|2	0|0 2|0	0|0 2|0	0|0 2|0	0|0 2|2	0|2 2|2	0|2 2|2
EXP −	0|0 2|0	0|0 2|0	0|0 2|0	0|0 2|0	0|0 2|0	0|0 2|0	0|0 2|0	0|0 2|0	0|0 2|0	0|0 2|0	0|2 2|2	0|2 2|2
EXP +	0|0 0|0	0|0 0|0	0|0 0|0	0|0 0|0	0|0 0|0	0|0 0|0	0|0 0|0	0|0 0|0	0|0 0|0	0|0 0|0	0|2 0|2	0|2 0|2
EXP −	0|0 3|0	0|0 3|0	0|0 3|0	0|0 3|0	3|0 3|0	3|0 3|2	0|0 3|0	0|0 3|0	0|0 3|0	0|0 3|0	0|2 3|2	0|2 3|2
	0|0 0|0	0|0 0|0	0|0 0|0	0|0 0|0	0|0 0|0	0|0 0|2	0|0 0|0	0|0 0|0	0|0 0|0	0|0 0|0	0|2 0|2	0|2 0|2
BLUFF +	1|0 0|0	1|0 0|0	1|0 0|0	1|0 0|0	1|0 0|0	1|0 0|0	1|3 0|1	1|3 0|1	1|1 0|1	1|1 0|1	1|1 0|1	1|1 0|1

BLUFF	1|0	1|0	1|0	1|0	1|0	1|0	1|0	1|0	1|0	1|0	1|0	1|0	1|0	1|0	1|0	1|0	1|0	1|1	1|1	1|1	1|1	1|1	1|1	1|1
–	1|0	1|0	1|3	1|0	1|3	1|0	1|0	1|0	1|0	1|0	1|3	1|3	1|1	1|1	1|1	1|1	1|1	1|1	2|2	0|2	2|2	2|2	0|2	1|1
COMP/	0|0	2|2	0|0	2|2	0|0	2|2	2|2	0|0	0|0	0|0	0|0	0|0	0|0	2|3	2|2	2|2	0|2	0|2	2|2	0|2	0|2	0|1	2|1	0|1
PUN +	2|0	0|0	2|3	0|0	2|3	0|0	0|0	0|0	2|0	2|0	2|3	0|1	2|1	0|1	2|1	0|0	2|1	0|1	2|1	0|1	2|1	0|1	2|1	0|1
COMP/	0|0	2|2	0|0	2|2	0|0	2|2	2|2	0|0	0|0	0|0	0|0	2|3	0|0	2|3	0|0	2|2	0|0	2|2	0|2	0|2	2|2	0|2	0|2	2|2
PUN –	2|3	2|2	2|3	2|2	2|3	2|2	2|2	2|3	2|3	2|3	2|3	2|3	2|3	2|3	2|3	2|3	2|3	2|3	2|2	2|2	2|2	2|2	2|2	2|2
BULLY	2|3	2|2	3|3	2|2	3|3	2|2	2|2	3|3	2|3	2|3	3|3	3|3	3|3	3|3	3|2	3|2	3|2	3|2	3|2	3|2	3|2	3|2	3|2	3|2
+	3|3	3|2	3|3	3|2	3|3	3|2	3|2	3|3	3|3	3|3	3|3	3|3	3|3	3|3	3|2	3|2	3|2	3|2	3|2	3|2	3|2	3|2	3|2	3|2
BULLY	3|3	3|2	3|3	3|2	3|3	3|2	3|2	3|3	3|3	3|3	3|3	3|3	3|3	3|3	3|2	3|2	3|2	3|2	3|2	3|2	3|2	3|2	3|2	3|2
–	3|3	3|2	3|3	3|2	3|3	3|2	3|2	3|3	3|3	3|3	3|3	3|3	3|3	3|3	3|2	3|2	3|2	3|2	3|2	3|2	3|2	3|2	3|2	3|2

Note: Cells indicate expected and actual (E | A) outcome by quadrant (see note for Figure 3.3 for quadrant numbering convention) of the interaction between paired agents moving according to the logic dictated by their subjective games. Cells are grouped into blocks of four representing the four possible starting quadrants in a normal game. Bold text indicates outcomes that deviated from that expected by the row player (first mover). The proportion of outcomes that were correctly anticipated by the row player is 56% over 576 possible configurations of agents and starting quadrants.

generating solutions by hand) precluded anything but a computational approach. Table 3.1 shows the results of the round-robin tournament. Each row of this table depicts the results of the games between the row-designated TIP agent and the column agents. Each block of four cells depicts the expected and actual (simulated) outcomes for the game that began in that quadrant of the 2 × 2 game matrix. When expected and actual outcomes disagree, the cell values are displayed in bold text.

Discussion and Application

At the beginning of this section of the chapter, we raised several additional research questions about the impact of accurate mirroring, incongruent games, and which TIP-based strategies were likely to be successful at predicting outcomes. The following discussion of the simulation results answers some of those questions and points the way to answering others with an application to the Arab–Israeli conflict following the 1973 October War.

Simulation Results

In the computer simulation, 12 agent pairings involved congruent TIP-based strategies, implying that the subjective games of Ego and Alter accurately mirrored one another. For example when an "Exploit+" agent (whose subjective game is defined by the preference interaction of the Exploit strategy with an opponent's Appease strategy) is paired with an "Appease+" agent (whose subjective game is defined by the preference interaction of the Appease strategy with an opponent's Exploit strategy) the games of Ego and Alter are the same (but transposed for row and column positions). These 12 interactions, multiplied by four quadrants, accounted for 48 of the 576 simulated games. For the simulation as a whole, actual outcomes conformed to agent expectations 321 times out of 576 games, or slightly less than 56 percent of the time. The predictive accuracy of outcomes for the subset of congruent pairs was significantly higher with 81.25 percent (39 out of 48) of the outcomes correctly predicted.

When errors in prediction between agents with subjective games that incorporated accurate mirroring occurred, they appeared to result from issues of game asymmetry and the position of the Nash equilibrium. Accurate mirroring does not always mean that the player preferences were symmetrical. Ultimately, perfect predictive accuracy occurred only in those cases where the Nash equilibrium was also the Pareto optimal outcome (the highest possible combined payoff for both agents). This condition is most apparent where quadrant 0 was the (4,4) outcome, but it was also the case in the "Bully $-$" versus "Bluff $-$" interactions, where quadrant 3 (4,2) is both the Nash solution and is Pareto optimal. In other congruence situations where errors were present, the subjective games of the agents lacked any Nash equilibrium and the interactions were subject to cycling. To some extent, the errant predictions in the model were likely a function of the pared-down nature of the four-digit Moore machine play repertoires.

Clearly, even with occasional errors, the mirroring of Alter's preferences in one's own subjective game substantially improves predictive accuracy. In contrast, incongruence between Ego's perceptions and Alter's preferences comes with a cost. After removing the particularly successful subset of cases where congruence was present, the overall level of accuracy for the remaining population was reduced to 278 of 528 interactions or just over 52 percent.

Mirroring may be one way to achieve success at least in anticipating outcomes (Wendt 1999). The results of the simulation suggest some alternate approaches. Table 3.2 provides information about the relative performance of the TIP-based agents according to three criteria. The first criterion is accuracy. The least accurate player in anticipating the outcomes of paired interactions with all other agents was the "Appease $-$" player who was correct only 25 percent of the time. In contrast, the highest level of overall accuracy was almost 73 percent, which was achieved by the "Compel/Punish $-$" player.

When predictive accuracy is further broken down to examine separately the games between each agent and the subsets of agents with either cooperative (Appease, Reward/Deter, Exploit) or conflictual (Bluff, Compel/Punish, Bully) orientations, the relative positions of the high and low performers appears to be reinforced. The "Appease $-$" player exhibits the second lowest rank for each subcategory. Its meager 13 percent accuracy when matched with a cooperative player is lower than the level that could be achieved through random guessing. "Appease $-$" is surpassed in ineptitude only by the completely inaccurate "Bluff $-$" player, who scored no correct predictions.

In contrast to these low performers, the "Compel/Punish $-$" player achieved a level of accuracy among the cooperative players that exceeds the level displayed among the mirroring group. This strategy was also the second best (after "Bluff $-$" with 75 percent) at predicting outcomes with conflictually oriented opponents as well. The source of this strategy's success may be attributable to the particular subjective game of this agent. "Compel/Punish $-$" possesses a symmetrical subjective game that conforms to the commonly seen Prisoner's Dilemma payoff structure.

Moreover, the strategy of moves [0111] defined for this agent's Moore machine from the TOM solutions indicates that, when presented with a

Table 3.2 Three Performance Indicators for 12 TIP-Based Agents by Opponent

Tip-based Agent	Correct Predictions (% of Total)			Payoffs as a Percentage of Maximum Possible			Frequency of Quadrant 0 or 3 Outcomes (as a % of total)		
	All	Coop.	Conf.	All	Coop.	Conf.	All	Coop.	Conf.
Appease −	12 (25.0)	3 (12.5)	9 (37.5)	86.5	96.9	76.0	32–0 (67.7)	21–0 (43.8)	11–0 (22.9)
Bluff −	18 (37.5)	0 (0.00)	18 (75.0)	67.2	76.0	58.3	27–3 (62.5)	23–1 (50.0)	4–2 (12.5)
Bully −	18 (37.5)	8 (33.3)	10 (41.6)	84.4	83.3	85.4	0–18 (37.5)	0–8 (16.7)	0–10 (20.8)
Exploit −	26 (54.1)	15 (62.5)	11 (45.8)	83.3	87.5	79.2	32–0 (67.7)	21–0 (43.8)	14–0 (29.2)
Bluff+	26 (54.1)	18 (75.0)	8 (33.3)	67.2	76.0	58.3	27–3 (62.5)	23–1 (50.0)	4–2 (12.5)
Compel/Punish +	26 (54.1)	18 (75.0)	8 (33.3)	60.9	69.8	52.1	10–11 (43.8)	12–1 (37.5)	4–4 (16.7)
Appease+	32 (66.7)	21 (87.5)	11 (45.8)	88.5	96.9	80.2	32–0 (67.7)	21–0 (43.8)	11–0 (22.9)
Reward/Deter +	32 (66.7)	21 (87.5)	11 (45.8)	85.4	96.9	73.9	32–0 (67.7)	21–0 (43.8)	11–0 (22.9)
Reward/Deter −	32 (66.7)	18 (75.0)	14 (58.3)	91.6	93.8	89.6	32–0 (67.7)	18–0 (37.5)	14–0 (29.2)
Exploit +	32 (66.7)	21 (87.5)	11 (45.8)	80.2	93.8	66.7	32–0 (67.7)	21–0 (43.8)	11–0 (22.9)
Bully +	32 (66.7)	18 (75.0)	14 (58.3)	84.4	83.3	85.4	0–18 (37.5)	0–8 (16.7)	0–10 (20.8)
Compel/Punish −	35 (72.9)	20 (83.3)	15 (62.5)	66.7	64.6	68.8	21–5 (54.2)	6–4 (20.8)	4–7 (22.9)

cooperative opponent and a game that begins in quadrant 0, mutual cooperation will be anticipated and achieved. In all other instances, this strategy
reverts to pure defection. Ironically, its high level of success in prediction
may arise from its insistence on forcing deadlock outcomes against
noncooperative opponents.

Assuming one's opponent is equal in ability to control events and prone
toward conflict leads to a strategy that seemingly reduces unanticipated
outcomes. This result is consistent with Leng's (1993) finding that a "firm-
but-fair" strategy is the optimum strategy to avoid an agent's worst outcome. Interestingly, the ability that some agents had for predicting
outcomes when they were the initiator did not translate into predictability
of outcomes when that strategy was the responding column player. No significant correlation existed between the ability to predict and the predictability of outcomes when a particular agent was the responding player.
This suggests that the successful predictors were the agents whose own
moves brought about their expected outcomes.

Beyond individual success or failure among TIP-based strategies,
table 3.2 suggests a broader pattern for classes of agents. Of the six highest
performing strategies with regard to accuracy, five are agents that perceived
their level of control over events to be superior or equal to their opponent's. In addition, four of the six were cooperative in their self orientation
and half of the top performing strategies in terms of outcome accuracy held
both cooperative Self and Other images. No strategies in the bottom half
displayed this type of orientation. Conversely, half of the poor predictors
were low control agents ($<$) with a majority of them manifesting hostile
impressions of the other.

Empirical evidence from studies of bargaining and negotiation suggests
that, among human agents, these patterns might be self-reinforcing (Leng
2000). Agents with high control who correctly anticipated outcomes will
tend to have their faith in their own efficacy reinforced. The result of this
reinforcement may be a tendency to persist with similar strategies in future
interactions. Conversely, low-control agents who fail to predict outcomes
may find their sense of powerlessness to be reinforced. Though failure
might suggest that such agents would be more likely to adjust their strategies
in response, their low control scores coupled with their belief in the hostility
of opponents may leave them convinced that adaptation would be fruitless
(Peterson, Marie, and Seligman 1993).

The success of an interaction strategy must be judged by more than its
capacity to anticipate (or force) certain outcomes. To evaluate which
strategies were most successful, we must also investigate the types of
outcomes achieved and the payoffs associated with them. Two approaches to

evaluation may be relevant depending upon how one identifies the goals of interaction. Leng (2000), for example, observed two distinct approaches to interstate bargaining and negotiation episodes. The "hawk" approach, rooted in a *realpolitik* worldview, conceives of dyadic interactions as contests to be won or lost. The "dove" approach, derived from social psychology, sees conflict as a social pathology that can be ameliorated through the building of trust and eventually cooperation. Adopting a hawk orientation toward success, we evaluate the strategies according to their ability to accumulate maximum payoffs (to regularly achieve their most preferred outcome). Following the dove logic, we assess the degree to which initiating agents (row players) can induce cooperative behavior from the opponent by ending the interaction in either quadrant 0 or 3.

Table 3.2 also shows the accumulated payoff for each agent. This was calculated using the outcome data and the payoff structure information from figure 3.3. The percentages indicate the proportion of the maximum achievable payoff that was earned by that strategy (100 percent would imply that every interaction earned a "4" payoff). The table suggests that evaluating strategies based solely on accuracy may be missing an important dimension. Several of the approaches that we deemed unsuccessful at prediction (e.g., "Appease −") appear to be quite successful at generating favorable payoffs. Others that were highly accurate earn relatively lower scores. These results suggest that, as we surmised, the high level of predictive accuracy earned by strategies like "Compel/Punish −" resulted from the acceptance of frequent deadlocks, effectively trading off potential gains for a lower risk of unexpected outcomes.

As in the accuracy prediction table, the results depicted suggest a broader pattern about the TIP agents. Again, four of the six top performing agents and six of the eight with 80 percent or better scores are those with a cooperative Self orientation. Unlike the prediction results, high-control agents do not dominate the group of high performers and there appears to be no relationship between control and overall scoring. The single most outstanding performance by one of the strategies is certainly that of the "Reward/Deter −" agent, who achieved nearly 90 percent of maximum payoffs against both cooperative and conflictual opponents.

Turning to our dovish criteria of evaluation, the final performance indicator in Table 3.2 exhibits an even stronger relationship between a positive self orientation and success. All of the top performing agents in inducing cooperation from opponents had cooperative Self strategies. Importantly, though much of the success of these strategies results from their cooperative interactions with other cooperative agents, all six of these agents outperformed five of the six noncooperative agents in inducing quadrant

0 or 3 outcomes (several tied with the top performing conflictual agent with 22.9 percent success).

Again, the "Reward/Deter $-$" agent merits special attention having tied for the highest score in achieving Q0 or Q3 outcomes for cooperative *and* conflictual opponents. Considering this agent's high level of overall scoring performance and the solid level of predictive accuracy (66.7 percent or second overall), the strategy defined by a cooperative Self paired against an Other that is perceived to be hostile and to have equal control over events appears to be the clear candidate for overall performer. Examining the Moore machine strategy [0110] of this agent will immediately suggest the basis for this player's success. The responses match cooperation with cooperation and conflict with conflict thereby manifesting the tit-for-tat logic of reciprocity that has often been shown to be effective in iterated games and crisis situations (Axelrod 1984; Leng and Walker 1982).

Egyptian–Israeli Case Study

A case study that illustrates several of these results and points the way to answering other research questions is the analysis by Walker (2004b) of the subjective games for Sadat and Rabin following the 1973 October War between Israel and Egypt. The analysis is based on an earlier version of TIP and the VICS indices calculated for the P-1, I-1, and P-4 master beliefs in separate operational code analyses of Rabin by Crichlow (1998) and Sadat by Schafer and Glasser (2000). Locating the two leaders in figure 3.3 with the latest version of TIP and the indices of the master beliefs from these earlier studies reveals that Sadat's subjective game after the October War attributed a Compel/Punish $(-, =)$ strategy to both Self and Other. The indices for Rabin's master beliefs defined a subjective game that attributes a Reward/Deter $(+, =)$ strategy to Self and a Compel/Punish $(-, =)$ strategy to Other (Walker 2004b, 97).

These subjective games in figure 3.3 are partly congruent by attributing the same strategy to Alter, but they differ in the strategy they attribute to Ego. The differences in the strategic preferences attributed to Egypt and Israel, however, lead to the same prescription for Ego in deciding whether to "stay" or "move" from an initial state of deadlock following the October War. Conversely, the lack of full congruence between the two subjective games leads to different predictions about whether Alter will choose to stay or move. Sadat's subjective game prescribes that Egypt should choose stay and predicts that Israel will also choose stay. Rabin's subjective game prescribes that Israel should choose stay but predicts that Egypt will choose move. Both players were actually correct in predicting the Other's choice.

Rabin chose to stay at the deadlock outcome until Sadat chose to move toward settlement. The Egyptian leader signaled his intent to move away from deadlock in his famous decision to go to Jerusalem and address the Israeli parliament (Walker 2004b).

What caused Sadat to change his strategy? Schafer and Glasser (2000) do not provide data that show a change in his master beliefs leading to a change in his subjective game; however, it appears likely that his I-1 belief about the best strategic orientation switched to become cooperative. Sadat's VICS index of $-.07$ score was at a "tipping" point (Walker 2004b; Wendt 1999). Although the valence of the Egyptian leader's I-1 score was conflictual, the magnitude was so close to 0 ($-.07$) that it would not take much experiential learning by Sadat to cause a shift to a cooperative strategic orientation toward Israel in response to the experience of continued deadlock. This shift in beliefs would then make the subjective games of both leaders more congruent. Now Sadat as well as Rabin would expect Other to choose move and be ready to reciprocate or respond to the efforts of third parties to mediate the conflict (Walker 2004b).

Henry Kissinger's mediating role in the conflict helped Israel and Egypt to reach disengagement and interim Sinai agreements by 1976. Following elections in Israel, the new Israeli prime minister Menachem Begin impressed Sadat as "some one who could deliver," and Sadat decided in the summer of 1977 to launch a diplomatic initiative toward a full peace agreement with Israel (Maoz and Mor 2002, 155–157). The signal by Sadat that he would be willing to address the Knesset turned out to be sufficient to break the stalemate and pave the road toward the Camp David Settlement (Walker 2004b). Did Sadat's subjective game change sufficiently to explain this shift in strategy? Sequential game theory analyses by other scholars of Sadat's decision to "go to Jerusalem" conclude that it did, though they do not agree on the exact identity of the game (see Brams 1997, 2002, 396–399; Maoz and Mor 2002, 159–165).

Conclusion

This modeling exercise has explored the implications of strategic interaction patterns between leaders with different subjective games based on the master beliefs in their respective operational codes. TIP and TOM link the master beliefs and strategies of leaders through the exercise of political power to the different possible equilibria of settlement, domination, submission, and deadlock in world politics. TOM demonstrates the likely equilibrium reached by different players with agent-based models of subjective games constructed from TIP.

The models of strategic interaction that emerge from the intersection of players with totally congruent, partly congruent, and incongruent subjective games reveal that the degree of congruence makes a difference. Totally congruent games in which each player plays the same game and also assigns the same identities of Ego and Alter to the players are most likely to lead to equilibria that are successful outcomes from the standpoints of both players. Partly congruent games in which each player is playing the same game but assigns the identities of Ego and Alter to Self and Other in reverse order are less likely to produce successful outcomes. The least successful outcomes are associated with players with incongruent subjective games that attribute different preference rankings for each player. TIP and TOM provide theoretical explanations and predictions about the strategies of each player even when the subjective games of two players are not congruent.

PART III

APPLICATIONS: THE DOMAIN OF LEADER–ADVISOR RELATIONS

CHAPTER 4

THE EYES OF KESTEVEN★: HOW THE WORLDVIEWS OF MARGARET THATCHER AND HER CABINET INFLUENCED BRITISH FOREIGN POLICY

Scott Crichlow

Introduction

Operational code analysis has been a useful tool for examining the influential linkages that exist between the fundamental foreign policy beliefs of individual leaders and their behavior in international affairs. This literature has undergone refinements in recent years, and the development of new methods for carrying out this work has enabled much more rigorous and detailed studies to be done in this area. Nonetheless, pertinent research questions remain for those of us interested in the sources of foreign policy, and the recent advances in this research agenda should make it a fertile field of inquiry for some time to come.

One substantive area of inquiry in this line of research that continues to present unanswered questions concerns the degree to which differences between the operational codes of members of the same decision-making team shape the policy splits that occur within administrations. Are these sorts of differences responsible for individuals pursuing different strategies who are ostensibly members of the same decision-making unit? Do such

★ Margaret Thatcher's official title is now Baroness Thatcher of Kesteven.

intra-administration policy divides mirror splits that exist between the operational codes of members of the same decision-making group? If so, do these differences affect which policy stances are adopted at the highest levels of government? I aim to provide answers to these questions through an examination of foreign policy events during Margaret Thatcher's reign atop the British government that featured marked differences of opinion within her cabinet.

This project deals with prominent and controversial moments in British foreign policy during the 1980s. I examine whether or not the strategies pursued by the primary members of the government regarding key international problems were consistent with what one would expect on the basis of their operational codes. I examine these connections through an examination of decision making in the 1982 Falklands War, the 1986 South Africa sanctions debate, and policy debates relating to economic ties with Europe in the last years of the decade. Through these investigations I hope to add to our knowledge of how leaders choose their favored strategies, the origins of intra-administration policy disputes, and their effects on government policy.

Operational Codes and Strategic Choices in International Affairs

One use for operational code analysis is to employ it as the basis for predictions about the strategies leaders will favor and pursue in their interactions with other international actors. A particularly useful template for such analyses has been reported by Marfleet and Walker in chapter 3 of this volume. Building upon earlier work by Holsti (1977), Walker (1983, 2004b), and Walker, Schafer, and Young (2003), the Theory of Inferences about Preferences (TIP) identifies indices that specify whether a leader is generally oriented toward strategies involving conflict or cooperation (I-1), and the degree to which that individual believes that the self controls historical development (P-4). Taken together, these variables point to a leader's subjective game that predicts strategies and tactics of escalation and de-escalation in self/other dyads. More generally, they point to the types of strategies leaders may engage in that differ from the norm of reciprocity. For example, leaders who believe in cooperative strategies and also believe that they have little control in shaping the world around them are more like to engage in appeasement tactics than other leaders.

This template offers a new strain of operational code research. While knowing a leader's basic beliefs about the nature of the political universe and generally preferred types of behavior can provide a great deal of useful information, international interactions tend to be dyadic relationships. And beyond providing us solely with the general behavioral tendencies toward cooperation or conflict behavior of particular actors, this template of strategies offers the possibility of predicting sequences of moves between Self and Other. Substituting P-1 for I-1 and calculating a P-4 index for Other identifies Self's view of Other's choice propensities for strategies and tactics. From this information it is possible to infer the preferences of both Self and Other for the political outcomes of settlement, domination, deadlock, and submission.

Operational Code Indices

The key independent variables in this study, the operational code scores of members of the British government, were measured on the basis of quantitative content analyses consistent with the protocols developed by Walker, Schafer, and Young (1998, 2003). I coded comments made by these leaders in time frames immediately preceding the cases being observed. This entailed collecting comments from question-and-answer engagements that involved these individuals in the House of Commons. I collected all such comments of over 1500 words that were made by the Prime Minister in the month preceding these events. For the other ministers I collected comments of over 1500 words in the preceding two months, since many members of the cabinet were involved in fewer speaking engagements of this sort than Prime Minister Thatcher. My source for this data was *Hansard*.

The dates I used for start dates for the events I examine (therefore, the first day following the data collection period) were as follows: March 31, 1982 for the Falklands case; June 21, 1986 for the South African case; September 20, 1988 for the Bruges speech; and June 25, 1989 for the Madrid ultimatum in the debate over EU policies. In the event that parliament was not in session for part of the data collection window, I adjusted this calendar by adding the preceding month to ensure that I obtained a large enough amount of timely data from which to measure these individuals' operational codes. I hand-coded the data according to the protocols laid down in chapter 2 (see also Walker, Schafer, and Young 1998). Another trained coder performed a reliability check on measurements I made pertaining to the Falklands and South Africa cases. He produced an intercoder reliability score of over 90 percent.

Given their central place in making strategic predictions in the manner put forward by Walker, Schafer, and Young (2003), and the fact that they are generally among the most fundamental cognitions influencing foreign-policy behavior, I concentrated my attention on three operational code variables. The first of these, Strategic Approach to Goals (I-1), addresses whether or not an individual is fundamentally oriented toward the use of cooperation or conflict. A leader's score on this variable is the percentage of positive or cooperative statements he or she makes about the self, or those with whom the self identifies, minus the percentage of negative or conflictual self references. Nature of the Political Universe (P-1), one's belief about whether the political world is fundamentally a place of cooperation or conflict, is coded much the same way, but in this instance the focus is on phrases in which the speaker does not identify with the subject of the phrase. Essentially, these two variables get at patterns that convey whether the self and, alternatively, others in their environment rely upon conflict or cooperation to achieve their aims, and the degree to which they hold on to those beliefs. The last variable I examine is Control Over Historical Development (P-4). This measure is the relative proportions of self and other attributions an individual makes. It illustrates the extent to which an individual decision maker believes the self or others have the ability to shape world events.

The Thatcher Cabinet

Through examining differences that exist across members of the Thatcher cabinet on key operational code variables, I seek to determine the degree to which its politics, especially splits within the cabinet over policy preferences on foreign policy matters, were the byproduct of its members approaching foreign policy from fundamentally different perspectives. In the case studies that follow, I examine the beliefs and behaviors of the following five decision makers. While I will discuss their beliefs and behavior in each case in which they took part, it is useful first to introduce these leaders as individuals, how they came to power, and the nature of their relationship with Prime Minister Thatcher.

Margaret Thatcher

Mrs. Thatcher served as Prime Minister from 1979 to 1990. Her election and her tenure marked several important turns in British politics. Under her leadership the Conservative Party was transformed. To some extent this was a matter of policy. Her government slashed state spending, cut many public services, and adopted a much more strongly free-market approach than had been the case previously. But her changes extended beyond that in altering the very nature of the membership of the party and its core beliefs. Her election led to the end of the dominance of the "wets," cautious, paternalistic politicians who feared extremism and sought "middle-minded" solutions to the country's problems (Young 1989, 198). In addition, the leadership of the party was no longer restricted to the traditional groups that had long dominated the party. To draw on Ian Buruma's description of Thatcher based on characters in E.M. Forster's *Howard's End*, "she was a Wilcox to the core," a sober, philistine conservative with a natural distrust, resentment, or dislike for social reformers, or those who valued the arts over industry (Buruma 1996, 23). She found many of the ideas of this set to be anathema. They were, therefore, either driven to the fringes of the party or were, at the least, much more fiercely questioned during her tenure in office.

Thatcher lacked expertise and knowledge, and even to some extent interest, in foreign policy topics in the early years of her government (Sharp 1991). While this would change greatly over time, early in her administration she would frequently turn to her top foreign policy advisors for guidance, or, in fact, largely turn policy decisions over to them. Nonetheless, being a woman of strong convictions, she held firmly to many opinions, even if she lacked a great deal of information on the issues at hand. And when she did take an active personal role in decision making, she played a powerful role.

John Nott

Nott was appointed defense secretary because he was judged to be a reliable hand who could be trusted to engage in what was in many ways the top priority of the leaders of Thatcher's first government, slashing spending. He had a strong background in economics and had proven to be a loyal administrator. Early on, he did not disappoint. For example, in 1980, fuel allocations were so tightly restricted that "many ships could not put to sea for months" (Hastings and Jenkins 1983, 11). His willingness to carry out these cuts, cuts that were deeply unpopular with many in the military establishment and many of the Prime Minister's Conservative allies, showed a considerable level of dedication and a deep commitment to many of the causes espoused by Mrs. Thatcher. But while he was in many ways a loyal team player, he was by nature at least slightly unpredictable.

A believer in many of the mantras of the rising side of the Conservative Party, Nott was also a bright, reflective man who was wary of walking in lock-step with his colleagues. This led him on more than one occasion to be a bit of a "maverick" (Howe 1994, 210). One example of this from his tenure as defense secretary shortly before the Falklands War was a shift in his views on defense spending. Basically, after slashing the budget to the bone (perhaps even through the bone), he contravened the wishes of No. 10 and balked at slicing them further. This move had endangered his position in the cabinet and cost him much of the influence he had with Prime Minister Thatcher. Shortly before the onset of the war the Prime Minister's office was letting it be known that he might soon be replaced (Young 1989, 270).

Francis Pym

Looking back, it may be hard to understand how Francis Pym came to serve as foreign secretary under Margaret Thatcher. After all, "Pym was . . . perhaps the most perfect epitome of the kind of Conservative politician Mrs. Thatcher detested" (267). He was "the man she least respected and least liked" (266). Thatcher had already removed him from high office once (he was John Nott's predecessor at the ministry of defense) for failing to support her initiatives. However, given the circumstances surrounding Lord Carrington's resignation as foreign secretary shortly after the Argentine invasion in 1982, Pym was (with the possible exception of Willie Whitelaw) the only man in government who could be reasonably expected to fill the job.

Why was this the case? For one thing, Pym's standing within the party as a whole was quite high. It is important to remember that in this time period the wets still played an influential role in Tory politics. Several were present in the cabinet, and Pym was one of the most prominent men on that side of the party. Additionally, he had experience that prepared him for the role. He had previously served in Thatcher's cabinet as defense secretary, and had shadowed the foreign secretary when the Tories were in opposition. Last, he was the only major figure in the government who could fill such a high-ranking role without necessitating a major cabinet reshuffle.

Such a reshuffle was out of the question given the impending crisis over the Falklands. So though she personally detested him, and thought extremely little of his politics, Margaret Thatcher named Pym to serve as her foreign secretary just as the country was facing momentous foreign policy choices. As she put it, "Francis's appointment undoubtedly united the Party. But it heralded serious difficulties for the conduct of the campaign itself" (Thatcher 1993, 187).

Geoffrey Howe

Geoffrey Howe was a central player in Margaret Thatcher's leadership of the Conservative Party throughout her entire tenure. She chose him to be her shadow chancellor immediately after her election as party leader, and during her reign as prime minister he held three of the highest posts in government: chancellor, foreign secretary, and deputy prime minister. In this study I am interested in Howe's behavior in the role of foreign secretary (1983–1989). He moved into the role from his position as chancellor shortly after the resounding Tory win in the 1983 election. At that time the prime minister viewed herself as having a new, strong mandate to proceed with the changes she sought in both the party and in the country as a whole. In that situation, Pym simply had to go. He had long been the focus of her "ineradicable displeasure" (Young 1989, 331), and she respected nothing "he had done during the war, or since" (332). Howe, on the other hand, had been a hardworking and trustworthy supporter of Prime Minister Thatcher for years. So she moved this valued ally to take over a ministry whose staff she distrusted. However, while Howe often performed in ways that met with Thatcher's approval, over time they grew apart, and he was dismissed from the Foreign and Commonwealth Office in 1989.

Nigel Lawson

Nigel Lawson was named chancellor in the 1983 reshuffle, filling the position made vacant by Geoffrey Howe's move to the Foreign Office. He became one of the people most closely associated with the economic reforms that occurred in the United Kingdom during Mrs. Thatcher's tenure as prime minister. Lawson lacked some of the natural political skills that some others in the government possessed. For example, Andrew Marr (1995) noted his "brutal candour" (267). But Lawson was brilliant, "probably the cleverest of the big names of the Thatcher administrations" (71). And he showed considerable skill in implementing the changes that the Tories sought in the 1980s. But over time rifts developed. And while he and the prime minister shared many economic beliefs, on certain topics they clashed, and by 1988 they were "almost publicly at each other's throats" (Howe 1994, 575). These clashes, perhaps most notably those related to Britain's role in the European economic system, eventually led him to resign.

Worldviews and Policy Debates

The Falklands War

The Falklands campaign was the grandest military adventure undertaken by the Thatcher government. Coming on the heels of an era in which British influence in global political and military affairs had been steadily shrinking for decades, it marked for many a return to Britain fulfilling the role of a great power. In launching a fleet to travel to the ends of the earth to protect the honor and integrity of the state, the government was performing in a manner matching a glorious, but distant, past.

Prior to the crisis in 1982, there was little reason to expect that the far South Atlantic would be the venue for such a consequential endeavor. While the status of the Falklands had been an intractable problem for both the British and Argentine governments, the Thatcher government had been proceeding apace to cut its commitments in the South Atlantic. There were plans to remove *HMS Endurance* from the area, and to close the station on South Georgia. Even the citizenship status of Falklands residents was at risk. The British government had begun to show a new willingness to engage in negotiations with Argentina over the status of the islands (Hastings and Jenkins 1983, 52).

Before the intensification of poor relations in March 1982, the British had made a string of de-escalatory moves. Prime Minister Thatcher was not active in setting policy at this juncture. Relations with Argentina were primarily managed by ministers in the Foreign Office. While Defense Minister Nott was apprised of the basic nature of relations with Argentina, his own role during this noncrisis period was to some extent the product of the resources he had at his disposal. The decisions he made that affected interactions with Argentina appear to have been made with the considerable economic constraints faced by his ministry very much in mind.

Relations between Argentina and the United Kingdom took a clear turn for the worse in March 1982. In the wake of a particularly threatening Argentine communiqué, both countries made policy choices that essentially created an escalatory spiral and eventually culminated in Argentina's invasion. By the end of this period, the principals (now including Pym as foreign secretary) had decided to send a large fleet to the South Atlantic and carry out a major war to retain control of the Falklands. I measured the operational codes of these three individuals during this crisis period to investigate whether or not the decisions of the political leadership in the United Kingdom were consistent with the foreign policy belief systems of the political leaders who played particularly prominent roles during the war: Margaret Thatcher (prime minister), John Nott (defense secretary), and Francis Pym (the leader of the House of Commons who was promoted to foreign secretary when Lord Carrington resigned immediately after the Argentine invasion).

The operational code scores of these cabinet members are compared in figure 4.1, which shows where these leaders would place Self and Other in the predicted strategies template. What do these scores in figure 4.1 predict about their strategies and tactics? Prime Minister Thatcher's scores place

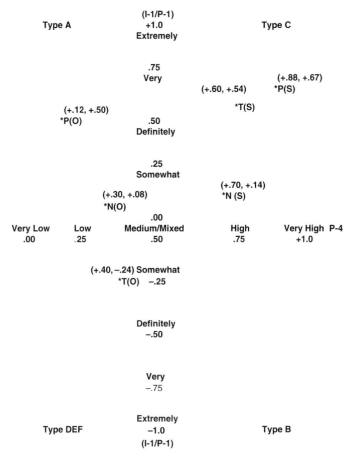

Figure 4.1 Consensus and Dissensus between British Leaders in Falklands Debate.

Note: T = Thatcher, N = Nott, P = Pym, (S) = Self, (O) = Other.

Self in Quadrant C and Other in Quadrant DEF. She prefers a conditional cooperation strategy of deterrence for Self and predicts a conditional conflict strategy of compellence from Other. Defense Secretary Nott's scores place Self closer to the border of Quadrants B and C and Other virtually on the border of Quadrants A and DEF. These sets of coordinates indicate that Nott prefers a cooperative strategy of exploitation or possibly a conflict strategy of bully for Self while predicting a mixed strategy of bluff and appeasement for Other. Foreign Secretary Francis Pym's scores show that he has a definite preference for a cooperative strategy of exploitation for

Self and clearly anticipates a cooperative strategy of appeasement by Other.[1]

From the variations that exist in their operational codes, we can predict that these three leaders are likely to disagree over what policies they believe the United Kingdom should pursue in this case. The construction of their respective subjective games in figure 4.2 allows us to compare their choice propensities following the escalation of tensions by Argentina in March, 1982. The "initial state" in each leader's Falklands War Game I is in quotation marks in the upper-right cell to which Argentina has moved from the upper-left cell that characterized the previous period of mutual de-escalation between Britain and Argentina. What does each leader think that the next move by Britain and the final (underlined) outcome should be and what are the likely strategic consequences? The answers are in the Theory of Moves (TOM) analyses of the subjective games constructed by TIP analyses of each leader's ranked preferences for the outcomes of settlement, domination, submission, and deadlock for Self and Other in figure 4.2.

Mrs. Thatcher's subjective game prescribes "move" ($\downarrow$) by the United Kingdom to deadlock (3,2) from submission (1,4) and predicts that Argentina will then move from (3,2) toward settlement (4,3) by shifting its strategy from conflict (CF) to cooperation (CO), followed by a similar shift by Britain. In Falklands War Game II, she is willing to "stay" ($|\leftarrow$) at deadlock as a new initial state until and unless Argentina shifts its strategy from conflict to cooperation, which implies that she will support the actual use of force in combat as well as its deployment to the South Atlantic. Mr. Nott concurs with the Prime Minister's prescription for Britain to move from submission (1,4) to deadlock (2,1) in Falklands Game I and anticipates that Argentina will then shift strategies from conflict to cooperation for a final outcome of British domination (3,2). Unlike the Prime Minister, the Defense Secretary believes that Britain will have to take the initiative in Falklands Game II, moving toward a "final state" of settlement (4,3) from a new initial state of domination (3,2). Both leaders believe that if Britain does not shift to a conflict strategy following Argentina's move to (1,4), the leaders in Buenos Aires will choose to stay at (1,4).

The Foreign Secretary Francis Pym disagrees with the strategic assessments of the other two leaders. His operational code scores for key beliefs locate Self in Quadrant C and Other in Quadrant A. He prescribes exploitation as a conditional strategy of cooperation backed by coercion for Self and predicts that Other's strategy is appeasement. While he recognizes that Britain should move eventually from submission (1,1) following Argentina's shift in strategies from cooperation to conflict in Falklands Game I, he believes that the two states are in a no conflict game with a

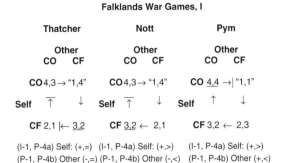

Falklands War Games, I

Thatcher	Nott	Pym
Other CO CF	Other CO CF	Other CO CF

CO 4,3 → "1,4"   CO 4,3 → "1,4"   CO <u>4,4</u> →| "1,1"

Self ↑ ↓   Self ↑ ↓   Self ↑ ↓

CF 2,1 |← <u>3,2</u>   CF <u>3,2</u> ← 2,1   CF 3,2 ← 2,3

(I-1, P-4a) Self: (+,=)   (I-1, P-4a) Self: (+,>)   (I-1, P-4a) Self: (+,>)
(P-1, P-4b) Other (-,=) (P-1, P-4b) Other (-,<) (P-1, P-4b) Other (+,<)

Falklands War Games, II

Thatcher	Thatcher	Nott
Other CO CF	Other CO CF	Other CO CF

CO <u>4,3</u> |← 1,4   CO <u>4,3</u> →|1,4   CO <u>4,3</u> →|1,4

Self ↓ ↑   Self ↑ ↓   Self ↑ ↓

CF 2,1 → "3,2"   CF 2,1← "3,2"   CF "3,2" ← 2,1

(I-1, P-4a) Self: (+, =)   (I-1, P-4a) Self: (+, =)   (I-1, P-4a) Self: (+, >)
(P-1, P-4b) Other (−, =) (P-1, P-4b) Other (−, =) (P-1, P-4b) Other (−, <)

Theory of Inferences about Preferences

(1) If (+, <), then Settle > Deadlock > Submit > Dominate: Appease Strategy
(2) If (+, =), then Settle > Deadlock > Dominate > Submit: Reward/Deter Strategy
(3) If (+, >), then Settle > Dominate > Deadlock > Submit: Exploit Strategy
(4) If (−, <), then Dominate > Settle > Submit > Deadlock: Bluff Strategy
(5) If (−, =), then Dominate > Settle > Deadlock > Submit: Compel/Punish Strategy
(6) If (−, >), then Dominate > Deadlock > Settle > Submit: Bully Strategy.

Figure 4.2 Subjective Games for British Leaders in Falklands War.

Note: Initial states are in quotations and final states are underlined.

shared preference for settlement (4,4) as the highest-ranked outcome. Therefore, he will be reluctant to move to deadlock (2,3) and will want to stay at (1,4) at least long enough to wait and see whether Argentina will reverse its strategy.

Pym will also be inclined to interpret Argentina's shift in strategy as due to exogenous shocks from the regime's domestic sector, which may be reversible with patience and further diplomatic communications, rather than a fundamental shift in the definition of the situation that would force him to alter his image of Other. While Pym shares the same strategic orientation of exploitation with Nott, their different diagnoses of Other's strategic orientation lead them to different choice propensities and assessments of final outcomes. The Foreign Secretary's disagreement with the Prime Minister is more fundamental, extending across choice and diagnostic propensities to strategic interaction outcomes in the conflict with Argentina.

Are these differences in the operational codes of the three leaders reflected in their behavior during the British decision-making process leading up to the Falklands War? Mrs. Thatcher's choices clearly match expectations based on her operational code. When faced with Argentina's escalatory moves, she responded in kind, pursuing a deterrence strategy. Nor did she waver from that approach. Indeed, she found the moves by some, particularly in the Foreign Office, to try to pursue negotiations "irksome," and she was not above publicly belittling those in her government who sought such tactics (Hastings and Jenkins 1983, 137). "Once military operations were underway she was firmly opposed to reverting to diplomatic measures which might interfere with their momentum" (Sharp 1997, 87).

Nott's behavior at the start of the war was not as vigorously aggressive as Thatcher's. He was not opposed to raising alert levels, but he was torn over whether or not to immediately launch a task force operation. Such an action could have been precipitous and imperiled Britain's best chance of maximizing its interests. He was not necessarily opposed to the move, but he felt it was best to proceed with caution given that events on this scale could spiral out of control, and the British fleet had many weaknesses (Hastings and Jenkins 1983, 68). It appears that he doubted the possibility of avoiding a larger conflict, but he was reluctant to immediately resign himself to that, and believed that such a turn of events might yet be avoided.

Nonetheless, it is clear he felt certain punitive and escalatory measures were required to respond to Argentina's behavior. Even though he had a basic preference for cooperation and caution, he was not, in the end, willing to rely on hope. He appears to have expected further escalatory moves by Argentina. In other words, he believed they were following a bluffing strategy that needed to be called. Therefore, he opted to support Thatcher and the navy and pursue a strategy of escalation. As was the case with Prime Minister Thatcher, Nott's actions appear generally consistent with his placement in the operational code strategic template.

Pym behaved in an exceptionally cooperative manner. He was not a supporter of the tit-for-tat escalatory spiral that both Prime Minister Thatcher and Defense Secretary Nott favored. He sought a diplomatic solution to the crisis, a course of action that infuriated Prime Minister

Thatcher. His de-escalatory signaling after Argentina's escalatory moves matches his definition of the situation as a cooperative game between Britain and Argentina. It is also consistent with the split between him and Mrs. Thatcher that the Prime Minister found so irritating. Even though he and the defense secretary agreed on Britain's strategic preference ordering of settlement > domination > deadlock > submission, their disagreement over Argentina's ranking of these outcomes led to a somewhat fragile strategic consensus between Nott and Thatcher while he became the "odd man out."

The Falklands War was won, though several ships and many men were lost in the endeavor. It became for Margaret Thatcher perhaps the signature foreign policy event of her tenure in office, and it did much to help her politically. Thatcher's force of personality and commitment to upholding her personal beliefs and convictions had a great deal to do with Britain's actions during the crisis. And those that she felt were either not loyal enough to her policies, or even simply not enthusiastic enough in moving ahead with them, found themselves displaced after she won reelection the following year. Both Pym and Nott were among those removed from office.

South Africa

In studying British behavior relating to South Africa in the mid-1980s, and the splits within the government on that issue, I chose to focus my examination on Margaret Thatcher (prime minister) and Geoffrey Howe (foreign secretary). Their operational code scores for this period are displayed in figure 4.3, and their respective subjective games are seen in figure 4.4. Their operational codes were somewhat similar during this period, sharing a preference for a strategy of cooperation. The foreign secretary had a somewhat negative view of others in the political universe while Thatcher's mixed view of others partly overlapped the foreign secretary's.

While both decision makers preferred to pursue a general strategy of cooperation leading to settlement as their highest-ranked preference, they may disagree over whether Britain should choose stay or move from an initial strategy of cooperation. We might expect Thatcher to be more conciliatory and reluctant to shift Britain's strategy from cooperation to conflict or perhaps argue that South Africa shared settlement as the highest-ranked outcome. Howe, on the other hand, should favor a shift to conflict from cooperation with the expectation that it would eventually cause a return to a strategy of cooperation by South Africa and a corresponding move by Britain and the international community toward a final outcome of settlement.

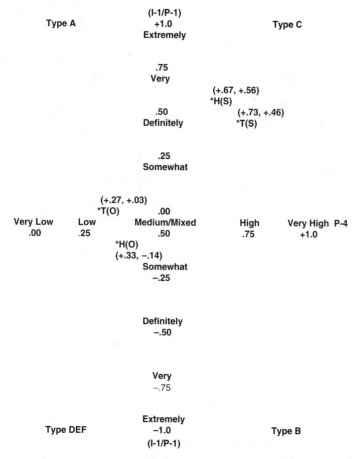

Figure 4.3 Consensus and Dissensus between British Leaders in South Africa Debate.

Note: T = Thatcher, H = Howe, (S) = Self, (O) = Other.

Does the historical record match these projections from their respective operational codes?

South Africa was a major international issue with important implications for British interests prior to Mrs. Thatcher coming to power, and that did not change once she took office. Even after the Lancaster House Agreement that led to the independence of Zimbabwe, the British retained substantial interests in the region. Beyond the matter of bilateral relations, South Africa was of vital importance to several Commonwealth countries, and the government had to deal with an array of interest groups that were actively pushing for change in the apartheid regime (Barber 1988). In addition, by the mid-1980s, the issue was getting a steady stream of media attention, which heightened the call for harsher action against the government in Pretoria.

This matter may have gained additional attention because the status of race relations in South Africa was a personal priority of some members of the administration. Most notably, the plight of the black African population had been a matter of considerable concern to Geoffrey Howe since his days at university. Howe and his wife had even taken a clandestine trip into Soweto in 1975 to investigate matters for themselves (Howe 1994, 476). Given this strong personal interest, in addition to national concerns, it is no surprise that Howe actively sought change in the South African regime.

Mrs. Thatcher, however, did not share Howe's perceptions of the situation or the priority he put on the issue. She lacked Howe's long-standing, deeply felt concerns. And the fact that as late as 1987 she was publicly branding the African National Congress as a "typical terrorist organization" shows that she was less than enthusiastic to associate herself or her government with key actors at the forefront of calling for change in South Africa (Barber 1988, 100). In the early 1980s Thatcher's government supported American policies of "constructive engagement" aimed at bringing change to the region (108). While there were calls for harsher measures and criticism of the government's reliance upon diplomatic maneuvering to try to affect change, the call for harsh sanctions did not gain much traction within the British government.

The British government's policy rested on the premise that their first, best chance to alter South African behavior was to work with them and maintain their trust. This policy also protected a number of British allies in Southern Africa whose economies would be seriously damaged if extensive sanctions were placed on the largest economy in the region. While this tactic won the support of the cabinet at first, the commitment that many in the government had to it began to change as time wore on without notable progress being made. In fact, in many ways the crisis began to intensify. The complexities of this issue increased as more and more of Britain's allies started to take stronger action against the Botha regime.

Particularly problematic was the behavior of international governmental organizations in which Britain was a member. These pressures reached a critical stage at the Commonwealth Heads of Government Meeting in Nassau in October of 1985. Of the 41 heads of state or prime ministers at the meeting, only Britain was willing to strongly defend the maintenance of its strategic approach that many thought had failed to alter the regime (Howe 1994). This meeting marked the beginning of the crisis period over British foreign policy toward South Africa from which I drew the sample of public statements by Mrs. Thatcher and Mr. Howe used to analyze these leaders' operational codes in figure 4.3 and subjective games in figure 4.4.

While both Thatcher and Howe remained opposed to especially severe action against the government in Pretoria, over time they began to move apart on the issue of what should constitute appropriate British action. In

South Africa Sanctions Games

Thatcher	Howe	Howe

	Other		Other		Other
	CO CF		CO CF		CO CF

CO "4,3" |← 1,4   CO 4,3 |←1,4   CO 4,3 →| 1,4

Self   ↓   ↑̄   Self   ↓   ↑̄   Self   ↑   ↓

CF 3,2 →| 2,1   CF 3,2 →| "2,1"   CF 3,2 ←"2,1"

(I-1, P-4a) Self: (+,>) (I-1, P-4a) Self: (+,>) (I-1, P-4a) Self: (+,>)
(P-1, P-4b) Other (−,<) (P-1, P-4b) Other (−,<) (P-1, P-4b) Other (−,<)

Thatcher's European Union Games

Bruges Period	Madrid Period	

	Other		Other		Other
	CO CF		CO CF		CO CF

CO "4,4"   1,2   CO 4,3 |←1,4   CO   4,3 →| 1,4

Self   Self   ↓   ↑̄   Self   ↑   ↓

CF 2,1   3,3   CF 2,1→"3,2"   CF   2,1←"3,2"

(I-1, P-4a) Self: (+,=) (I-1, P-4a) Self: (+,=)   (I-1, P-4a) Self: (+,=)
(P-1, P-4b) Other (+,=) (P-1, P-4b) Other (−,=)   (P-1, P-4b) Other (−,=)

Theory of Inferences about Preferences

(1) If (+, <), then Settle > Deadlock > Submit > Dominate: Appease Strategy
(2) If (+, =), then Settle > Deadlock > Dominate > Submit: Reward/Deter Strategy
(3) If (+, >), then Settle > Dominate > Deadlock > Submit: Exploit Strategy
(4) If (−, <), then Dominate > Settle > Submit > Deadlock: Bluff Strategy
(5) If (−, =), then Dominate > Settle > Deadlock > Submit: Compel/Punish Strategy
(6) If (−, >), then Dominate > Deadlock > Settle > Submit: Bully Strategy.

*Initial states are in quotations and final states are underlined.

Figure 4.4   Subjective Games for British Leaders in South Africa and EU Debates.

Note: Initial states are in quotations and final states are underlined.

Howe's view, the demands and concerns of the Commonwealth and the European Community altered the strategic equation, and he began to grow weary of increasingly bold South African intransigence, which to him represented their defection from a mutual cooperation strategy. While he would never advocate the sweeping punitive actions supported by some, as events unfolded in 1986 he began to feel that Britain should both follow and work with its allies, temper their excesses, and be willing to put more pressure on the South Africans. Essentially, he moved to supporting a conflict strategy of escalating pressure in response to South African intransigence to create a deadlock (2,1), and then following up South African inaction or escalation with a further punitive pattern of stay at (2,1) until South Africa moved from (2,1) toward settlement (4,3). This policy position is consistent with the predictions from the subjective game in his operational code.

In contrast, Prime Minister Thatcher was stridently opposed to sanctions even in the face of South Africa's unwillingness to change. Her view of the South Africans was from all sources vastly more positive than that of most other British leaders in 1986. In addition, her view of many of its opponents, both inside and outside South Africa, was unusually negative. She did not see South Africa's actions as unreasonably aggressive or uncalled for. For example, she may have seen South African military raids into neighboring states as understandable given unrest in the region and the nature of those regimes. Similarly, she may not have reacted as negatively as others to brutal action in Soweto, given her fears of the African National Congress. She also may not have believed that South Africa was escalating tensions, given that her prioritization of British interests in the region seems to have been quite different from that of many of South Africa's opponents. She apparently believed that they were still serving as a bulwark against radicals, and as such did not deserve to be the target of sanctions.

Beyond that, there are also reasons tied to matters of personality and governmental politics that could have contributed to her continual reluctance to put any sort of pressure on South Africa. As to personality, she was notoriously stubborn (Sharp 1991). In fact, she embraced a public self-image that was closely tied to that trait. She was extremely reluctant to jeopardize the image that she believed made her look tough and contributed to her popularity. Though of course even if such perceptions produced certain benefits, her stubbornness could also undermine her own policies, her relationships with allies, and, in turn, her ability to accomplish her aims (Howe 1994, 483).

Her decisions may have also been affected by governmental politics. There came a time when she believed that she had gained a firm grip on the country's policies toward South Africa. "I was firmly in charge of our approach to South Africa, making the main decisions directly from No. 10" (Thatcher 1993, 518–519). Given her hostility toward the Foreign and Commonwealth Office, which was even more intense than usual on South African policies, it is possible that she was extremely reluctant to acquiesce to any change that might be seen as vindicating the FCO, or allow them to reassert control over the agenda.

In 1986, the British government did eventually agree to support stricter measures against the South African government that had been approved by the European Community. But the personal roles played by both Howe and Thatcher in this dispute, and their growing disagreements, resulted in a difficult and distressing political process. Thatcher signed on to a "modest package of measures" (Howe 1994, 497), moving policy in the direction of the views of her foreign policy advisors and those of the majority of the British public. But trying hard to uphold her beliefs, she did so with the greatest reluctance, and only after a lengthy intra-government battle with her foreign secretary.

Thatcher and Howe shared a common definition of the situation as a subjective game, but they disagreed on the stability of the initial state for this game. Howe's view was that South Africa had shifted from (4,3) mutual cooperation to (1,4) while Thatcher argued that Pretoria's intransigence was not a shift in strategy. This disagreement led to the split between the two leaders over whether to shift British strategy from cooperation to conflict.

Relations with Europe

The final case I examine deals with British economic policies toward Europe in the late 1980s. I focus this study on Margaret Thatcher (prime minister), Geoffrey Howe (foreign secretary), and Nigel Lawson (chancellor of the exchequer). Their operational codes for this period, measured just before two prominent events relating to Britain's policies toward Europe, are displayed in figure 4.5. It is abundantly clear from the public record and the memoirs of the participants that during this period a schism developed between the policies advocated by Thatcher and those supported by Howe and Lawson. I will first discuss the areas of agreement and disagreement in these leaders' operational codes. Then I will discuss whether the patterns in their policy differences are matched by the differences found between the operational codes of these individuals.

I measured the operational codes of these leaders at two times, once in 1988 in the period preceding the famous Bruges speech, and again in 1989

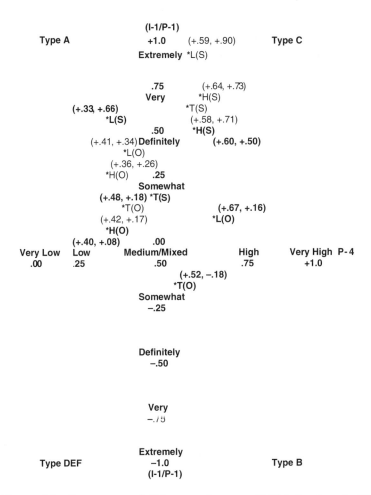

Figure 4.5   Consensus and Dissensus between British Leaders in EU Debate.

Notes: Madrid period is in bold and Bruges period is not. T = Thatcher, H = Howe, L = Lawson, (S) = Self, (O) 5 Other.

just before Howe and Lawson gave the prime minister an ultimatum demanding she alter her behavior and agree to implement economic integration policies that the United Kingdom had long promised to approve. Figure 4.5 shows us that in 1988 the three decision makers had generally similar operational codes. The subjective games of all three leaders were games of no conflict between Self and Other. The equilibrium (final outcome) for games in which both players rank settlement as their highest-ranked preference (4,4) have a non-myopic equilibrium of settlement no matter what initial state is postulated among the four cells in the game. There is also no incentive for either player to defect from this outcome unless it is to gain bargaining leverage on new issues or because one or the other player does not share the definition of the situation as a game of mutual cooperation (Stein 1990). All three leaders showed preferences for cooperative strategies (I-1) and also saw others as cooperative (P-1), but Thatcher was oriented toward less cooperative tactics than Howe and Lawson.

By 1989, we see that the worldviews of the Prime Minister and her two advisors in figure 4.5 were split over much more than tactical orientations. There were now serious fundamental differences in their operational codes on basic strategic points and their perceptions of other actors. Thatcher's general strategic orientation (I-1) plummeted, decreasing from +.71 to +.18, and her view of other political actors (P-1) shifted from friendly to hostile (+.17 to −.18). The latter shift redefined her subjective game to a mixed-motive game in which the two players do not agree on the highest-ranked outcome (see figure 4.4). Thatcher still ranks settlement as Self's highest-ranked outcome, but now she attributes domination as the highest-ranked outcome for Other. This shift in the image of Other, in turn, affects Thatcher's cooperative strategy in a mixed-motive game.

Thatcher prefers to stay at deadlock while predicting that Other will move from a strategy of conflict to cooperation. Her own strategy of cooperation is conditioned on this move by Other. This condition is the fundamental difference between a cooperation strategy in a mixed-motive game versus a no conflict game and, therefore, the fundamental difference in strategy between Thatcher and her two major foreign economic policy advisors. Both Howe and Lawson continued to be willing to make the first move to break a deadlock between Self (UK) and Other (EU), because their subjective games continued to define relations with Europe as mutual cooperation in 1989.[2]

At this key time in the history of Europe's economic integration, shortly before the creation of the European Union, the disputes within the cabinet on these issues became exceedingly acrimonious. Veritable chasms came to exist between the positions of the principals. Thatcher had long "held out resolutely" against joining the European Exchange Rate Mechanism (ERM) (Allen 1988, 44), though the government "had been committed to entry when the time was right since June 1979" (Seldon and Collings 2000, 51), and it was over this issue that the deepest splits in the cabinet existed.

Thatcher herself believed as early as 1987 that Lawson began "to follow a new policy, different from mine" (Thatcher 1993, 699) and started to work "in cahoots" with Howe to oppose her (704). The deep disagreements over the ERM had actually been easy for all to see since at least 1985 (Seldon and Collings 2000). What made 1987 different, and further enflamed an already major conflict, was that in that year Lawson began to manipulate the currency and interest rates in a manner that resulted in the United Kingdom effectively joining the ERM.

The Prime Minister was predictably infuriated. This is partially due to the fact that he was challenging her authority over the government. But it is also due to the fact that the man she had long relied on to direct economic policy, and a man whose economic policies had achieved a great deal of credibility in circles she admired, was now pushing an agenda that she thought imperiled the British economy (Seldon and Collings 2000). Obviously these moves were proving a strain on personal relationships, a strain that may have contributed to irreconcilable conflicts as Thatcher and her top advisers moved further apart on their basic beliefs and perceptions.

Howe was proving just as bothersome to the Prime Minister, if not more so. He was not only backing Lawson in the dispute over the ERM, he was also taking views on several issues tied to Europe with which she disagreed. For example, he had backed the reappointment of Lord Cockfield as EC commissioner, something Prime Minister Thatcher would not agree to given what she believed were Cockfield's pro-European sympathies (Howe 1994, 535). From Howe's perspective, Thatcher was rejecting decades of pro-European Conservative policies, playing upon nationalist and populist fears, trying to transform the party into something "Gaullist" (572).

These disputes reached a significant boiling point in the wake of Thatcher's famous speech in Bruges on September 20, 1988. In that address she mocked the concept of European integration, and in so doing held up for ridicule causes championed by many of her cabinet colleagues. It was this act that, according to Howe, "began to crystallize the conflict of loyalty" (538) represented in the shift from a cooperative game to a mixed-motive game in Thatcher's operational code following the Bruges speech. Relations worsened as the Prime Minister called for policy moves that were diametrically opposed to those favored by her foreign secretary and chancellor. In late June of 1989, just before the Madrid EC Summit, both men threatened to resign if she continued to block joining the ERM. Thatcher seemed to concede, but within a month Howe would be demoted to leader of the House of Commons, the first of the high-ranking personnel moves related to disputes on European and economic policy that would see all three of these individuals out of office before the end of the following year.

It is clear that the differences between the leaders on these matters, particularly the ERM, ran extremely deep and worsened as time went on. It is rare, particularly in a government as highly centralized as Thatcher's, to see the top members of the administration so strongly divided, and especially on a public matter of great national importance. Perhaps that is because these disputes were rooted in the emergence of divergent operational code beliefs. Thatcher's views of others and the nature of the political universe became more negative than the corresponding beliefs of her colleagues. Her strategic and tactical beliefs were also consistently less cooperative both before and after the Bruges speech (see figure 4.4). These differences may not have been the only influence that led her to act in such a less cooperative manner than her colleagues. But the differences in their operational codes are noteworthy, as is the fact that their core beliefs and strategies grew ever farther apart over time.

These disputes played a key role in Howe's removal from office and Lawson's resignation. And through those actions, which ignited further intra-administration disputes, these policy differences played a role in the ouster of the prime minister in 1990. With major figures in the administration holding so steadfastly to conflicting personal policy beliefs on a vital national issue the stage was set for their conflicting worldviews to result in major changes in the composition of the government. The choice that the prime minister and her advisors made, to hold fast to their convictions, undoubtedly exacerbated tensions in an already divided party.

Conclusion

In this analysis of intra-cabinet relations in the United Kingdom, we have seen evidence of the predictive power of the strategic template of subjective games in chapter 3. The results of this study should strengthen our appreciation for the important role that the beliefs and general foreign policy orientations of leaders have on the areas of consensus and dissensus regarding the choices that they make when acting in the international arena. While certainly not the only factor shaping the decisions of governments, they are a key influence. Here we have observed this link in multiple cases and demonstrated the usefulness of operational code analysis as a means of getting at these politically important connections. Through the use of the tools and classification procedures that are being developed as this research agenda is refined, we should be able to strengthen our ability to predict the future behavior of leaders and glean the key factors that have shaped the choices of presidents and government ministers in the past.

Even if every foreign policy action taken by world leaders does not fit the strategic template in every instance, it is apparent that the operational codes of the members of the Thatcher government shaped their general strategic orientations. The splits within the government on key foreign policy issues, and the tendencies for certain members of the cabinet to pursue conflicting strategies, were at least partly the result of fundamentally different views of Self and Other in the international system. Continuing to develop this line of research is important, both for what it reveals about the powerful role of beliefs in shaping the policy preferences of individuals, and for what it suggests about the possibilities for consensus around foreign policy decisions in the policy-making process of the state.

Notes

1. To link the Verbs In Context System (VICS) scores in figure 4.1 to the strategies in the Theory of Inferences about Preferences (TIP) in figure 4.2, I use the quartiles as cut points along the horizontal axis for P-4 scores and zero as a cut point on the vertical axis for I-1 and P-1 scores. P-4 scores are linked to low (<), equal (=), and high (>) beliefs about the balance of historical control between Self and Other in TIP's propositions by identifying the nearest quartile on the horizontal axis: low (.25), equal (.50), and high (.75). I-1 and P-1 scores are linked to cooperation (+) and conflict (−) strategies in TIP's propositions if they are at least half a quartile away from the zero point on the vertical axis. If they are less than a quartile away from the zero point, then they indicate a mixed strategy of cooperation and conflict.

2. Lawson's subjective games are not shown in figure 4.4 because the shared preference by Self and Other in these games, settlement (4,4) as the highest-ranked outcome, does not call for further analysis regarding his differences with the Prime Minister. Howe's subjective game is the same as Lawson's for the Bruges period and the same as Thatcher's for the Madrid period. Unlike the Prime Minister, however, he appears to have defined the initial state in the Madrid period as unchanged from the Bruges period while Thatcher perceived a shift in the EU from a cooperative to a conflict strategy and retaliated by also shifting to a conflict strategy with the expectation that the EU would move back toward settlement as a final outcome. This disagreement over the stability of (4,3) as the initial state led to their split over strategies with Howe preferring cooperation and Thatcher preferring conflict.

CHAPTER 5

GEORGE W. BUSH AND THE VULCANS: LEADER–ADVISOR RELATIONS AND AMERICA'S RESPONSE TO THE 9/11 ATTACKS

Sam Robison

Introduction

Since 9/11, the United States has engaged in two major military operations leading to a drastic reconfiguration of Afghanistan and Iraq, reduced and reinterpreted a significant number of domestic and international civil/human rights laws, and "presided over the most sweeping redesign of U.S. grand strategy since the presidency of Franklin D. Roosevelt" (Gaddis 2005, 2). These actions and changes have occurred for the ostensible purpose of reducing the threats of terrorism and the dangers of weapons of mass destruction following from the 9/11 attacks. The events of 9/11 have also had drastic effects upon the U.S. public, making foreign affairs more important than economics for the first time in years (A World Transformed 2005).

What is less clear is the effect that 9/11 has had on the fundamental political beliefs of key policy makers in Washington. Some argue that several members of the Bush administration already had a clear set of "hawkish" beliefs, and that the aftereffect of 9/11 was an increased level of political capital allowing for the realization of these principles in Iraq (Krauthammer 2001, 2002/2003; McGeary et al. 2001; Watson et al. 2001). Alternatively,

9/11 may have produced a significant shock to the beliefs of Bush and others within the administration, leading to a sharp break from preexisting foreign policy. Of course, it is possible that some major policy makers experienced a significant change in beliefs while others did not.

This project is an attempt to address this issue through an operational code analysis of George W. Bush and his major foreign policy advisors prior to and following 9/11. Previous work on the operational code suggests that an individual's beliefs are generally stable, though crisis events and high levels of persistent stress may affect one's core beliefs in important ways (Marfleet 2000; Schafer and Crichlow 2000; Walker and Schafer 2000; Walker, Schafer, and Young 1998). 9/11 is certainly one of the largest crises ever to occur within the United States. Did the terrorist attacks lead to major belief system changes in Bush administration officials?

Some argue that prior to 9/11, a clearly stated strategy of preemption and hegemony was lacking in the Bush administration. Robert Jervis (2003, 365) notes that during this time, Bush saw "American leadership . . . restricted to defending narrow and traditional vital interests," and this interpretation paints the picture of a pragmatic, consensus-minded presidency similar to that of Bush's father. Further, George W. Bush's heavy focus on economic versus security issues in the international domain also confirms this notion of pragmatism and continuity in U.S. foreign policy. Justin Brown (2001, 57) notes that early in the Bush administration, a continuation of Clinton's free-trade-oriented foreign policy was a priority, and quotes Bush as saying "I want the people of my country to understand that a foreign-policy priority of my administration will be this hemisphere," also indicating a provincially limited scope of U.S. action. This position clearly represents a divergence from the 2002 National Security Strategy Statement, which replaced such narrow, "realist" ideas with an aggressive, hegemonic, potentially preemptive foreign policy.

However, on closer inspection the changes following 9/11 may not have been as significant as they initially seem. After all, Bush's lobbying for a national missile defense system, the refusal to abide by the Kyoto Treaty, the Land Mine Treaty, and the International Criminal Court, and his support of Israeli policies of assassination against Palestinian terrorists were all actions and positions taken prior to 9/11 over international objections (Cheney 2001; Deats 2002; Krauthammer 2001; Prestowitz 2003). In February 2001, Charles Krauthammer (2001, 42) noted that "this decade starts with a return to the unabashed unilateralism of the '80s." Focusing on Bush's nuclear defense policies, an article in *Commonweal* (Stealth Foreign Policy 2001) noted trends foreshadowing the takeover of U.S. foreign affairs by the Pentagon in April of 2001.

A *Time Europe* article from July 2001 (McGeary et al. 2001, 19) called Bush's foreign policy "Reaganesque," presenting Bush as "a man who knows what he believes and charges fearlessly ahead." Further, Watson and colleagues (2001, 38) noted in February of 2001 that Bush was taking an interest in Iraq early that went beyond Clinton's focus, ordering Secretary of State Powell to "re-energize" U.S. policy here. Apparently in many instances the United States was already moving away from Bush's 2000 campaign advocacy of a humble, multilateralist approach to international affairs and toward an aggressive, unilateral perspective with Iraq as a target.

Thus, debates exist over U.S. foreign policy prior to 9/11, and the fact that discordant opinions exist demonstrates that the Bush administration had not found its footing during this early stage. Exploring the question of how chief administration officials viewed and approached the international arena might help to explain the influence these individuals had over policy outcomes. The issue of advisor influence is central here, and as such, Bush's major advisors will be analyzed in this study. These include Secretary of Defense Donald Rumsfeld, Secretary of State Colin Powell, Vice President Dick Cheney, Deputy Secretary of Defense Paul Wolfowitz, Deputy Secretary of State Richard Armitage, and Assistant to the President for National Security Affairs Condoleezza Rice.

As Bush had limited foreign policy experience prior to his taking office in 2001, he often relied on these experienced advisors to help establish policy and to teach him about international affairs (Mann 2004, 255). Thus, the beliefs of these advisors are compared here with Bush both before and after 9/11 to test their level of compatibility with the President. An analysis of the beliefs of different advisors may be helpful in producing a reference point from which Bush's decisions came to be influenced.

James Mann's analysis of Bush's advisors, *Rise of the Vulcans* (2004), identifies major cleavages between these individuals resulting in two distinguishable groups, and this distinction is used here in order to assess broader philosophical influences on Bush from subgroups of advisors. The first group consists of Rumsfeld, Wolfowitz, and Cheney, who are classified into the category of "hawks," and are often deemed "neoconservatives." Powell and Armitage, who make up the second group, are labeled "doves," because of their aversion to war and adherence to the "Powell Doctrine" of quick military operations and clear exit strategies supported by the public (Mann 120). Though the doves here are not *absolutely* dovish, they certainly are in relation to the hawks.

I hope to make several contributions to these debates about Bush's beliefs and relations with his advisors with an operational code analysis of Bush and the Vulcans. First, I seek to provide additional insight into the policy deliberations of the Bush administration, which has been very secretive about its internal affairs (Florini 2004; Keifer 2002). Second, I want to contribute to the general literature on group processes dealing with the dynamics of leaders and advisors in foreign policy decision making. Third, the data analysis will include an explicit examination of possible changes in belief systems as the result of a powerful external shock, thereby contributing to the belief system research focusing on individual learning and cognitive consistency processes.

Theories and Hypotheses

Several research questions are at the center of this study. The first is: what were Bush's beliefs prior to 9/11? During the 2000 presidential campaign, he was referred to as "friendly and approachable" (Carter 2000). As a Texas governor, Bush gave the impression on some issues of being a truly "compassionate conservative." This included the promotion of alternatives to more hard-line policies regarding capital punishment and birth control as well as a desire to improve the cohesiveness of civil society (Milbank 1999). On these issues, Bush would need to reach across ideological and cultural lines to build political support. On the other hand, Bush's support of the death penalty, heavy faith in private enterprise, and feelings on gun ownership seem to indicate a more hard-line perspective during his time as governor (Stephen 1999). The degree to which these competing perceptions of Bush are true and how they translate as ideological principles influencing foreign policy during the Bush presidency are examined here.

Ideological Theories

Two competing ideological explanations of Bush's beliefs prior to 9/11 emerge from these accounts. One is the compassionate conservative explanation, and the other is the "hard-line" explanation. These rival explanations anticipate that the president is either a dove or a hawk, depending on which of these ideological role identities he selects in the domain of foreign affairs. If Bush is a compassionate conservative, then he will likely have a dovish orientation toward foreign affairs. If he is a hard-line, then this orientation will likely be hawkish.

By extension, if the president takes a strong hand in guiding American foreign policy, then his ideological role identity will be reflected in American foreign policy decisions. On the other hand, a gap between the norms of his perceived role identity and U.S. foreign policy behavior may indicate that Bush delegates the conduct of American foreign policy to others, such as to Vice President Richard Cheney or to various cabinet officials such as the secretaries of state and defense, in conformity with his MBA executive training in the business world. The degree to which George Bush provides leadership in the domain of foreign policy may also vary by time period, pre- and post-9/11. These two explanations and theoretical amendments lead to the following rival hypotheses regarding the four major directional (cooperation vs. conflict) indicators in the presidential operational code:

Compassionate Conservative Hypotheses
Prior to 9/11, George W. Bush's operational code has:

H-1a. A friendly image of the political universe and the fundamental nature of one's political opponents (P-1).

H-1b. An optimistic view regarding the realization of fundamental political values (P-2).

H-1c. A cooperative approach toward the selection of goals for political action (I-1).

H-1d. A cooperative set of tactics for the pursuit of political goals (I-2).

Hard-Line Conservative Hypotheses
Prior to 9/11, George W. Bush has an operational code that has:

H-2a. A hostile image of the political universe and the fundamental nature of one's political opponents (P-1).

H-2b. A pessimistic view regarding the realization of fundamental political values (P-2).

H-2c. A conflictual approach toward the selection of goals for political action (I-1).

H-2d. A conflictual set of tactics for the pursuit of political goals (I-2).

Foreign Policy Linkage Hypothesis
The linkage between George W. Bush's operational code and American foreign policy decisions is likely to vary by time period following noncrisis and crisis environments (Brecher and Wilkenfeld 1997; Holsti and George 1975; Janis 1989). Buttressed further by the journalistic accounts of Bush as an "MBA President" early in his first term (Mann 2004; Woodward 2004),

I hypothesize that:

H-3. A gap between Bush's beliefs and U.S. behavior is more likely in a
    noncrisis (pre-9/11) period than in a crisis (post-9/11) period.

Of the two major groups of advisors examined here, hypotheses are
based upon perceptions of these groups following from their institutional
roles and personal backgrounds. Institutional role conflict is not expected
for Bush's more hawkish department of defense advisors as these individuals
carry with them role expectations and experiences that clearly dispose them
toward aggression and conflict, but this is less clear regarding Bush's department of state advisors. Long before taking the position of deputy secretary
of defense, Wolfowitz consistently argued for unilateral U.S. action abroad,
specifically in the Middle East (Mann 2004, 173, 236). His boss Donald
Rumsfeld previously held the post of secretary of defense, where he
consistently argued against Kissinger's détente policies. Further, in 1998,
Rumsfeld was appointed by Newt Gingrich as head of the "Rumsfeld
Commission," advocating heavy caution against potential WMD (weapons
of mass destruction) attacks (Mann 2004, 242). Both Wolfowitz and
Rumsfeld are commonly called "neocons," or advocates of an aggressive,
morality based foreign policy aimed at promoting democracy and freedom,
and this seems to succinctly represent the current Republican foreign policy
status quo.

State department doves Colin Powell and Richard Armitage also
embodied hawkish role identities in the past. Both doves started out in the
military, and Powell served as chair of the joint chiefs for both the elder
Bush and Clinton. Similarly, Armitage had extensive experience working
for the department of defense since the 1970s, and signed assorted letters from
the Project for the New American Century (or "PNAC"—a hawkish
foreign policy advocacy group) to Bill Clinton in the late 1990s, arguing
for the support of Taiwan against China and the removal of Saddam
Hussein from office (Letters and Statements 2005).

However, Powell's hawkish beliefs were likely leavened by the long-term
effects of his struggle (as a military advisor) against the perceived detached,
irresponsible civilian control over military affairs in Vietnam (Mann 2004, 41)
and his unique role as national security advisor immediately following the
Iran–Contra affair. Likewise, Armitage developed a special affinity for the
victims of war following his experience in South Vietnam (Mann 2004,
46–47), and since the mid-1980s has been viewed as a philosophical con-
federate of Powell, exemplified by his adherence to the "Weinberger/
Powell" Doctrine. The Vietnam experience seems to have set both Powell

and Armitage markedly apart from other hawks, in that they may advocate military action, but only after very careful deliberation. Therefore, prior to 9/11:

H-4. The hawks (Rumsfeld and Wolfowitz) will have an operational code that resembles the hard-line conservative belief system.
H-5. The doves (Powell and Armitage) will have an operational code that resembles the compassionate conservative belief system.

The vice president has an institutional role that is not clearly defined in the foreign policy domain. However, Dick Cheney's previous service as secretary of defense and his well-known background as a conservative hawk make him likely to exhibit a hard-line operational code.

H-6. Cheney will have a hawkish operational code that resembles the hard-line belief system.

Similar to President Bush, Condoleezza Rice's ideological preferences coming into the White House are more difficult to assess than those of the hawks and doves. Like the vice president, the national security advisor does not have a clearly defined role in terms of beliefs (Smith 2004). Further, Rice's role as an advisor to the elder Bush on Soviet relations and arms control policies does not necessarily entail hawkish or dovish role expectations either, as U.S. policies from Nixon to Reagan had shifted from détente to more aggressive policies aimed at running the Soviet economy into the ground and back again. The end of the cold war, removing Rice's primary academic focus from the international scene, may have then affected Rice's beliefs further, altering her opinions toward the international environment generally.

Despite the ambiguity in Rice's role and preexisting ideological allegiances, Rice has been a staunch advocate of the George W. Bush administration's hawkish policies since coming into office in 2001. And yet she seems to differ significantly from the philosophy of the hawks in important ways (Seymour 2005; Shock and Awe 2005). Rice's mentor in the elder Bush's White House was former National Security Advisor Brent Scowcroft, a temperate realist, and she is argued elsewhere to have been "pulled between her traditionalist mentor [Scowcroft] and her transformationalist president [George W. Bush]" (Rothkopf 2005, 33), placing her in the ideological center of the current Bush White House. Thus, Rice is not expected to precisely follow either the hawks or doves. Expectations do reflect the perception of Rice as the President's principal teacher on foreign policy issues (Heilbrunn 1999/2000; Mann 2004), and the notion that she gives Bush a great deal of emotional and cognitive support, being "passionately loyal" to the President for who she serves with "equal parts admiration and fondness" (Rothkopf 2005, 33). Thus, a reciprocal influence between Bush and Rice is expected.

H-7. Rice's operational code will be somewhat hawkish and relatively close to President Bush's operational code.

Learning and Cognitive Consistency Theories

How stable are the operational codes of the President and his advisors over time and across situations? It is possible that the beliefs of the hawks and doves after 9/11 remained fairly stable, following from the stability in beliefs toward international affairs demonstrated by these advisors over the years and the heavy constraints described by role theory (Holsti 1987; Smith 2004).

However, it is also possible that the traumatic effects of 9/11 may have affected Bush's advisors in important ways, regardless of their prior experiences. This event may have made these individuals more negative and conflict-oriented than they were prior to 9/11 despite role considerations and their previous beliefs. Learning effects would help to account for these outcomes. For example, new information in the form of the terrorist attacks may have led to a radical change in beliefs, which would then have consequently led to changes in policy preferences. More specifically, Levy (1994) argues that policy failures generally are an important cause of learning. Such a massive policy failure as the inability to ensure domestic security from terrorism would no doubt fall into this realm.

Cognitive Consistency Hypotheses

There is also the possibility that individuals will use historical experience to "learn" by strengthening preexisting beliefs. This type of learning may occur despite the kind of stimuli that would lead to belief change in a "rational actor" (Levy 1994, 306), particularly so for those with strong institutional role orientations and entrenched beliefs that reenforce these role expectations. Biases are ingrained within these individuals, and the forces of cognitive consistency are expected to be very strong, limiting the degree of learning that these individuals might undergo. This follows the notion that for an individual to function effectively, balance and congruence must take place within the individual's cognitive processing network (Simon and Holyoak 2002). Expectations are that a terrible shock to Bush's advisors would maintain or strengthen preexisting hawkish beliefs. Therefore, in response to 9/11:

H-8a. The hawks (Rumsfeld, Wolfowitz, and Cheney) will maintain or strengthen their beliefs in response to this stimulus.

H-8b. Rice's hawkish beliefs will be strengthened and any dovish beliefs that she had before 9/11 will weaken.

Role Conflict Hypothesis

In opposition to the potential strengthening of beliefs in the hawks, the doves in the state department (Powell and Armitage) may have experienced conflict between the expectations of their institutional roles calling for a diplomatic response to crises and the expectations of their president following the 9/11 attacks. Sarbin and Allen (1968) identify four role conflict resolution strategies: (i) the alternation of roles over time, (ii) the merger of roles so that the distinctive behavior associated with each is obscured, (iii) the interpenetration of roles so that both sets of behavior are performed at the same time, and (iv) altercasting the expectations of others so that one role trumps the other. Thus, the doves may have exhibited a flexible pattern of alternating, merging, or interpenetrating the roles of "diplomatic advisor" and "loyal soldier" (depending on the situation and stimulus) as a strategy of role conflict resolution between the expectations of their president and the expectations of their institutional positions. Therefore, I expect that:

H-9. The doves (Powell and Armitage) will shift their views in a hawkish direction after 9/11, but will not swing totally into the hawks' camp.

Either direction of change (weakening or strengthening of beliefs) may have occurred post-9/11 for the president, depending on his pre-9/11 beliefs. For Bush to achieve cognitive consistency following the terrorist attacks, 9/11 would have to coincide in some way with his preexisting cognitive framework, and if it did not, his beliefs would have to change. Specifically, a significant realignment of his preexisting belief system would have to occur if he was not already extremely pessimistic and conflictual toward the international environment.

The Leader-Advisor Hypothesis

The influence of advisors may play an integral role in explaining the president's own cognitive adaptation to role conflict in the context examined here, providing cognitive needs, emotional support, understanding, and political legitimacy in the eyes of others (George 1980). Thus, the president may need to hold beliefs similar to at least some of his advisors. Picking which advisors to heed over others may be dictated by cognitive consistency when conflicting viewpoints are expressed by hawks and doves, as cognitive dissonance would likely occur otherwise (Monroe, Hankin, and Vechten 2000). Thus, presidential role ambiguity and the need for cognitive reorientation post-9/11, in conjunction with the importance of advisors, seems to leave room open for crucial influences on a president by a given advisory group.

As president of the United States and titular head of the Republican Party, the expectations associated with these roles may have also caused George Bush to experience role conflict. Following 9/11, Bush becomes a self-styled "war president"; so whatever his previous beliefs, he seems to fully undertake the hawkish philosophy as his own, demonstrating some degree of belief "alternation." Therefore, I expect that:

H-10. The president's belief system will shift toward his hawkish advisors following the attacks on the Pentagon and the World Trade Center.

Methods and Results

Beliefs will be measured here through operational code indices, measures of belief systems inferred from the words of world leaders. Included in the operational code analysis are philosophical and instrumental beliefs about the international environment and the speaker's approaches to this environment. Speeches were chosen for the nine months prior to 9/11 and up to one year following. Speeches gathered after 9/11 start in October or later to reduce the extreme scores expected immediately after 9/11. These speeches were taken from respective departmental websites for given advisors (Armitage 2004; Bush 2004; Cheney 2004; Powell 2004; Rice 2004; Rumsfeld 2004; Wolfowitz 2004) as well as Lexis-Nexis for Cheney. The coded information reflects foreign affairs contents almost exclusively. Prepared comments from press conferences and congressional hearings were also used, but responses to questions were not included in this analysis. The number of speeches for each individual in a given time period ranged from four to sixteen. When a large pool of speeches were available (e.g. Bush after 9/11), a random sample of available foreign policy speeches was selected.

Two types of analyses are performed following data collection. The first is a basic means test for all leaders measured through the Verbs In Context

System (VICS). This step leads to the creation of z-scores, a measure of deviation from a sample mean. To determine z-scores, raw data for each leader are aggregated prior to calculation of index scores. Once preliminary scores are obtained for each index, means and standard deviations from a comparison sample of post–World War II U.S. leaders are used to compute z-scores. A single z-score is calculated on each index for every individual at both time periods. A z-score of 2 (two standard deviations from the mean) or more is interpreted as extremely high, a score of 1.5 is high, and a score of 1 or approaching 1 is moderately high. The second type of assessment used is analysis of variance (ANOVA), in which we are mainly interested in comparing the means of the two main subgroups of advisors with one another and with Bush over time.

Comparative Individual Analyses

George W. Bush

Based on z-score comparisons, Bush's pre-9/11 scores on critical measures of P-1 (z = .35) and P-2 (z = .74), though positive, are less than one standard deviation from the sample of U.S. leaders (the means and standard deviations for which are located in table 5.1). These scores indicate that Bush held beliefs typical to other U.S. leaders regarding the image of the international system (P-1) and the ability to realize his political values (P-2). His P-4 (z = .01) score is also insignificant, showing that Bush sees control over international affairs similarly to other U.S. leaders as well. However, Bush's scores on I-1 (z = 1.08) and I-2 (z = .91) indicate a moderately strong, positive belief in the use of cooperation toward achieving his policy objectives. Regarding role conceptions, Bush sees the image of the "self" (I-1) as more cooperative than that of the "other" (P-1), and the locus of control (P-4) does not seem to be a factor. Bush sees himself as a benign leader in a moderately friendly world. Based on these findings, Bush's beliefs are typical of a U.S. leader prior to 9/11, though somewhat more cooperative than average.

Following 9/11, Bush's belief system changes significantly. His P-1 (−1.36) and P-2 (−1.16) z-scores are now significantly below the average and have shifted nearly two standard deviations below his pre-9/11 scores. This means that Bush's view of the political universe became much more negative after 9/11. Bush's P-4 (.40) measure increases, indicating that his belief about control over historical outcomes also changes somewhat following 9/11. On the I-1 (−1.71) and I-2 (−1.21) measures, Bush's scores change over two standard deviations in the negative direction versus his pre-9/11 score. This shows that Bush strongly prefers conflict over cooperation in tactics and strategies after 9/11.

Condoleezza Rice

The pre- and post-9/11 dynamics for the White House Assistant for National Security Affairs Rice show that she is similar to other U.S. leaders on P-1, P-2, I-1, and I-2 indices prior to 9/11 (indicating that her perceptions of the environment, outlook on value-realization, and strategic/tactical orientations are average), while her P-4 score is strongly negative (indicating a low belief in control over historical events). Following 9/11, Rice scores negatively on every measure of interest, approaching or surpassing a one standard deviation change on P-1, P-2, and I-1 while her P-4 score becomes more average. Thus, compared to other U.S. leaders, Rice sees the international environment as hostile, becomes pessimistic about realizing political values, and is increasingly conflict-oriented in her strategic and tactical orientations following 9/11.

Hawks and Doves

Table 5.1 indicates that on the philosophical measures of P-1 and P-2, Rumsfeld's scores are strongly negative prior to 9/11, whereas Wolfowitz's scores are moderately strong and negative on P-1 and P-2. These profiles indicate a generally hostile, pessimistic view of the political universe for both hawks. Cheney, however, is fairly average on P-1 and P-2, scoring similar to Bush in the moderate, positive direction. All hawks examined score negatively on I-1 and I-2 prior to 9/11 (though Rumsfeld's score on I-2 is only moderately low, $z = -.64$), indicating a preference for conflict-oriented strategies and tactics by each of the hawks. These scores are very different from Bush's cooperative, positive perspective prior to 9/11. Regarding perceived control over the political universe (P-4), only Cheney's score is significant, though all hawks score in the negative direction, indicating a weaker belief in control than others over historical developments. Overall, the hawks are hostile, conflict-oriented, cautious regarding others' intentions, and pessimistic prior to 9/11.

Changes after 9/11 on P-1 and P-2 are negligible for Rumsfeld, Wolfowitz, and Cheney. This degree of stability carries over for Rumsfeld and Wolfowitz to their insignificant, though negative, P-4 score. However, Cheney becomes much more confident post-9/11 in his ability to control outcomes (P-4) than he did previously. Although he becomes only slightly more confident than the average U.S. leader, this is a drastic change from Cheney's pre-9/11 score. Following 9/11, both Rumsfeld and Wolfowitz become significantly more conflict-oriented on I-1. On I-2,

Table 5.1 Z-Scores of Bush and His Advisors Compared to the Average Post–World War II Leader

	Bush	Hawks			Doves			Comparison sample	
		Cheney	Rumsfeld	Wolfowitz	Powell	Armitage	Rice	Mean	Std. Dev.
Pre-9/11 z-scores									
P-1:Nature of politics	0.35	0.13	−1.72	−1.15	0.61	1.06	0.47	0.27	0.19
P-2:Value realization	0.74	0.48	−1.37	−0.88	0.77	1.32	0.70	0.13	0.14
P-4:Historical control	0.01	−1.26	−0.39	−0.26	0.82	−0.72	−1.95	0.21	0.06
I-1: Strategic orientation	1.08	−4.09	−1.10	−1.50	0.12	0.95	−0.68	0.38	0.22
I-2:Tactical orientation	0.91	−3.23	−0.64	−1.38	−0.01	0.05	0.06	0.14	0.15
Post-9/11 z-scores									
P-1: Nature of politics	−1.36	−0.50	−.47	−1.12	−0.81	−0.51	−0.95	0.27	0.19
P-2: Value realization	−1.16	0.05	−.27	−0.92	0.54	−0.31	−0.98	0.13	0.14
P-4: Historical control	0.40	0.12	−0.64	−0.54	0.17	−0.49	−0.51	0.21	0.06
I-1: Strategic orientation	−1.71	−1.96	−2.23	−2.55	0.28	0.00	−1.49	0.38	0.22
I-2: Tactical orientation	−1.21	−1.26	−1.75	−1.46	0.24	0.31	−0.06	0.14	0.15

★Z-scores were calculated by subtracting the "Comparison Sample" (post–World War II U.S. leaders) mean score from the leader's mean VICS score (not listed) separately for each period and dividing this number by the "Comparison Sample's" standard deviation. Z-scores represent the number of standard deviations the subject's mean is located above or below the sample mean.

Rumsfeld changes notably, and though Wolfowitz does not, they both remain on the conflictual side of the continuum. Dick Cheney's strategic and tactical scores (I-1 and I-2), though remaining conflictual, become somewhat less extreme following 9/11. Overall, the hawks' scores are consistently negative over time, making them directionally stable.

Colin Powell is fairly typical of other U.S. leaders on both instrumental and philosophical scores before 9/11, not scoring one standard deviation away from the average U.S. leader on any major score. Powell scores moderately in the positive direction on the philosophical indices, displaying a degree of optimism and a perception of friendliness abroad slightly above that of the average U.S. leader. Richard Armitage's philosophical scores of P-1 and P-2 approach or exceed one z-score in the positive direction, indicating an even friendlier, more optimistic perception of the international environment than Powell. Armitage also scores significantly and positively on I-1, indicating a preference for strategic cooperation over conflict, though his I-2 score is average. Regarding control over historical development (P-4), though Powell scores moderately positive, Armitage scores moderately negative, indicating a divergence in dovish perceptions of control. Apart from feelings of control, however, the doves score in the optimistic and cooperative direction, though this must be qualified by Powell's somewhat average scores and Armitage's insignificant I-2 ($z = 0.05$) score.

Figure 5.1 shows in graphical form how strongly Bush differs from the hawks prior to 9/11. Though Cheney and Bush hold similar, moderately friendly images of others (P-1), among all those plotted on figure 5.1 (including Cheney), Bush alone prefers cooperation over conflict (I-1), and sees himself as having more influence over outcomes than others (P-4). Conversely, following 9/11, the *similarities* between Bush and the hawks become evident. All individuals plotted on figure 5.1 following 9/11 fall into the lower two quadrants, indicating pervasive preferences for conflict and perceptions of the external environment as hostile. However, Bush is again set apart from Rumsfeld and Wolfowitz based upon his positive belief in control over historical development (P-4). Similarly to Bush, Cheney also scores positively on the P-4 index following 9/11, and as the close concentration of scores in figure 5.1 shows, the hawks seem divided into two subgroups based upon perceptions of the self's degree of control, one group consisting of Bush and Cheney (in the lower right quadrant) and the other of Rumsfeld and Wolfowitz (in the lower left quadrant), which may reflect a subtle disparity in the post-9/11 role perceptions of those hawks occupying the White House and the Pentagon.

Figure 5.2 compares Bush to the doves, and, contrary to the examination of Bush with the hawks, all three individuals plotted on figure 5.2 score in

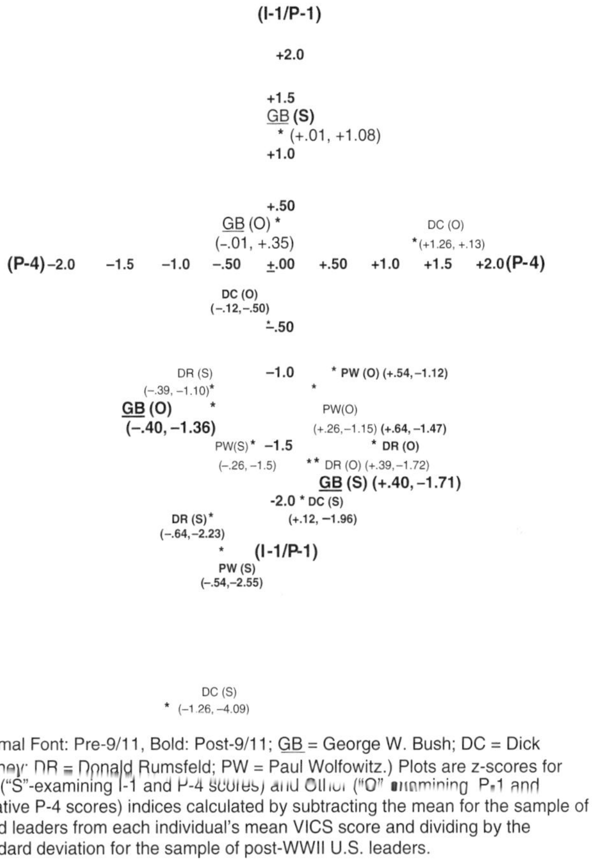

(I-1/P-1)

+2.0

+1.5
GB (S)
* (+.01, +1.08)
+1.0

+.50
GB (O) *   DC (O)
(−.01, +.35)   *(+1.26, +.13)
(P-4)−2.0   −1.5   −1.0   −.50   ±.00   +.50   +1.0   +1.5   +2.0(P-4)

DC (O)
(−.12,−.50)
±.50

DR (S)   −1.0   * PW (O) (+.54,−1.12)
(−.39, −1.10)*   *
GB (O)   *   PW(O)
(−.40, −1.36)   (+.26,−1.15) (+.64,−1.47)
PW(S)* −1.5   * DR (O)
(−.26, −1.5)   ** DR (O) (+.39,−1.72)
GB (S) (+.40, −1.71)
-2.0 * DC (S)
DR (S)*   (+.12, −1.96)
(−.64,−2.23)
*   (I-1/P-1)
PW (S)
(−.54,−2.55)

DC (S)
* (−1.26, −4.09)

(Normal Font: Pre-9/11, Bold: Post-9/11; GB = George W. Bush; DC = Dick
Cheney; DR = Donald Rumsfeld; PW = Paul Wolfowitz.) Plots are z-scores for
Self ("S"-examining I-1 and P-4 scores) and Other ("O" examining P-1 and
negative P-4 scores) indices calculated by subtracting the mean for the sample of
world leaders from each individual's mean VICS score and dividing by the
standard deviation for the sample of post-WWII U.S. leaders.

Figure 5.1   Self and Other Images of Bush and Hawks Pre– and Post-9/11.

Note: Normal font: pre-9/11; bold: post-9/11; GB = George W. Bush; DC = Dick Cheney; DR = Donald Rumsfeld; PW = Paul Wolfowitz. Plots are z-scores for Self ("S"—examining I-1 and P-4 scores) and Other ("O"—examining P-1 and negative P-4 scores) indices calculated by subtracting the mean for the sample of world leaders from each individual's mean VICS score and dividing by the standard deviation for the sample of post–World War II U.S. leaders. The asterisks here refer to the specific points on the plot referred to by the coordinates in parentheses.

the upper two quadrants prior to 9/11. This indicates that Bush and the doves all share friendly perceptions of the other and prefer cooperation more highly than conflict prior to 9/11. Interestingly, on the P-4 measure of control over historical outcomes, Bush's score lays directly in between Powell's strong feelings of personal control and Armitage's feelings of relative weakness. Armitage's weak belief in control over historical development

(I-1/P-1)

+2.0

+1.5 <u>**GB**</u> (S)
       (+.01, +1.08)

RA (S)
(−.72, +.95)
    *

+1.0   * RA (O)

CP (O)   * CP (O)   (+.72, +1.06)
(−.82, +.61)*   (−.17, +.81)

CP (S)

<u>GB</u> (O) *   *CP (S)   (+.82, +.12)
(−.01, +.35)(+.17, +.28)   *

(P-4)–2.0   **–1.5**   **–1.0**   –.50*   +.00   +.50   +1.0   **+1.5**   **+2.0(P-4)**
RA (S)
(−.49, 0.00)

     –.50   * RA (O)
          (+.49, −.51)

<u>GB</u> (O)   –1.0
(−.40, –1.36)
     *

     –1.5   * <u>**GB**</u> (S)
          (+.40, –1.71)
     –2.0

(I-1/P-1)

(Normal Font: Pre-9/11, Bold: Post-9/11; <u>GB</u> = George W. Bush; CP = Colin Powell;
RA = Richard Armitage.) Plots are z-scores for Self ("S"-examining I-1 and P-4
scores) and Other ("O"-examining P-1 and negative P-4 scores) indices calculated
by subtracting the mean for the sample of world leaders from each individual's
mean VICS score and dividing by the standard deviation for the sample of
post-WWII U.S. leaders.

Figure 5.2   Self and Other Images of Bush and Doves Pre– and Post-9/11.

Note: Normal font: pre-9/11; Bold: post-9/11; <u>GB</u> = George W. Bush; CP = Colin Powell;
RA = Richard Armitage. Plots are z-scores for Self ("S"—examining I-1 and P-4 scores) and
Other ("O"—examining P-1 and negative P-4 scores) indices calculated by subtracting the
mean for the sample of world leaders from each individual's mean VICS score and dividing by
the standard deviation for the sample of post–World War II U.S. leaders. The asterisks here
refer to the specific points on the plot referred to by the Coordinates in parentheses.

foreshadows his movement in a hawkish direction following 9/11, which
is apparent in figure 5.2. Despite a clear shift toward the hawks, however,
Armitage remains relatively positive and sees the world as friendly in comparison to Bush and the hawks post-9/11. Figure 5.2 also makes clear that
Powell is the only dove (and the only individual measured in this study) to
score positively on the P-1 and I-1 indices following 9/11.

    Prior to 9/11, figures 5.1 and 5.2 clearly show that based on z-score
comparisons, Armitage and Powell are both markedly dovish, while
Rumsfeld, Wolfowitz, and Cheney (excluding Cheney's perceptions of
others) are undeniably hawks. During this initial time period, the hawks
and doves seem to balance each other out in terms of their beliefs. Whereas
all the hawks score negatively on I-1 and I-2, the doves score positively.
Excluding Dick Cheney, this finding holds for P-1 and P-2 as well. Thus,

face validity is found for denoting the hawks as favoring conflict and the doves as preferring cooperation within the administration prior to 9/11.

There is also stability within Bush's major advisory groups, as changes following 9/11 are negligible for all advisors except Armitage and Cheney. Powell, Rumsfeld, and Wolfowitz are fairly consistent on every major measure, whereas Cheney becomes more moderate and Armitage approaches or surpasses a one z-score change on P-1, P-2, and I-1 in the negative direction. Armitage seems to have regressed toward the mean, as his post-9/11 scores are fairly average compared to that of other U.S. leaders. However, this movement in Armitage indicates a clear shift away from dovish beliefs, and is consistent with the role conflict hypothesis (H-9) that doves would be expected to merge, "interpenetrate," or alternate between hawk and dove orientations following 9/11. Colin Powell does not exhibit this degree of role conflict following 9/11.

Comparative Group Analyses

Selected ANOVAS below compare and contrast hawks, doves, and the Bush/Rice pair with one another overall as well as from period one (pre-9/11) to period two (post-9/11). The first step determines the plausibility of treating hawks, doves, and the Bush/Rice pair as separate groups through general within-group comparisons over time and across-group comparisons generally. Then the differences between groups are compared across time periods, followed by an assessment of the relative influence of cognitive consistency and learning effects from the 9/11 attacks on their belief systems.

Hawks and Doves Comparisons

Separate ANOVA comparisons of both the hawk and dove groupings over time show no significant differences at the .05, two-tailed level on any operational code index for either group, indicating a high degree of consistency for these groups. Thus, ANOVA findings generally give support to the z-score comparisons mentioned earlier. In contrast, ANOVA results looking at all speech acts (at both time periods) show that the hawks and doves differ significantly from each other on every major index: P-1 [$F_{(1, 62)} = 17.562$, $p < .001$], P-2 [$F_{(1, 62)} = 9.415$, $p < .05$], P-4 [$F_{(1, 62)} = 6.123$, $p < .05$], I-1 [$F_{(1, 62)} = 7.952$, $p < .05$], and I-2 [$F_{(1, 62)} = 7.781$, $p < .05$]. Thus, the hawks in table 5.2 see the world as a more hostile place where their political values are less likely to be realized, hold less faith in control over historical outcomes, and are more conflict-oriented than their dovish counterparts.

Group comparisons were then examined for doves versus hawks both before and after 9/11 to see if these differences in beliefs held across time.

Table 5.2 ANOVA Comparison Data for Bush and His Advisors

General comparisons	Hawks Mean*	Std.Dev.	Norming Group Mean	Std. Dev.	Doves Mean	Std. Dev.
P-1: Nature of politics	.24	.20	.27	.19	.47	.19
P-2: Value realization	.13	.14	.13	.14	.25	.14
P-4: Historical control	.23	.08	.21	.06	.28	.09
I-1:Strategic orientation	.38	.35	.38	.22	.63	.28
I-2: Tactical orientation	.16	.20	.14	.15	.31	.21
N**	44				22	

Time-specific comparisons	Bush Pre-9/11 Mean	St. Dev.	Post-9/11 Mean	St. Dev.	Rice Pre-9/11 Mean	St. Dev.	Post-9/11 Mean	St. Dev.
P-1: Nature of politics	.47	.23	.15	.35	.50	.20	.27	.11
P-2: Value realization	.30	.18	.06	.24	.29	.14	.10	.69
P-4: Historical control	.26	.10	.30	.08	.09	.04	.22	.02
I-1: Strategic orientation	.78	.23	.41	.22	.67	.47	.42	.33
I-2: Tactical orientation	.43	.16	.18	.13	.53	.65	.29	.21
N	9		13		2		4	

Time-specific comparisons	Hawks Pre-9/11 Mean	St. Dev.	Post-9/11 Mean	St. Dev.	Doves Pre-9/11 Mean	St. Dev.	Post-9/11 Mean	St. Dev.
P-1: Nature of politics	.29	.24	.22	.18	.49	.19	.47	.19
P-2: Value realization	.15	.15	.11	.15	.28	.15	.24	.13
P-4: Historical control	.22	.09	.23	.07	.30	.09	.25	.09
I-1: Strategic orientation	.51	.34	.31	.34	.65	.19	.63	.33
I-2: Tactical orientation	.20	.19	.13	.21	.31	.17	.30	.23
N	16		28		10		12	

* "Mean" scores reflect post-speech aggregation means used in ANOVA, as opposed to the means of individual speeches.
** Sample size represents the number of post-aggregated speeches analyzed through ANOVA. A minimum of 20 "sumverbs" (total number of verbs coded by VICS) per speech were required to run ANOVA, and this required the aggregation of smaller speeches. Thus, the "N" here generally under-represents the number of speeches examined.

Prior to 9/11, the doves and hawks approach or exceed a significant difference from each other in their philosophical beliefs: P-1 [$F(1, 24)=5.41$, $p<.05$], P-2 [$F(1, 24)=3.87$, $p=.06$], and P-4 [$F(1, 24)=5.56$, $p<.05$]. Interestingly, their I-1 and I-2 scores for strategic and tactical instrumental beliefs are not significantly different at the .05 level. Post-9/11, however, the hawks and doves differ significantly on both philosophical and instrumental beliefs: P-1 [$F(1, 38)=15.196$, $p<.001$], P-2 [$F(1, 38)=6.969$, $p<.05$], I-1 [$F(1, 38)=7.599$, $p<.05$], and I-2 [$F(1, 38)=5.513$, $p<.05$]. No significant difference is found for P-4 post-9/11.

Finally, a MANOVA with period (pre- and post-9/11) and group (doves and hawks) as factors was run to test the degree to which either cognitive consistency or learning best explains the dynamics affecting these groups. The results showed no significant interaction effects at the $p = .10$, two-tailed level of significance. Further, echoing the one-way ANOVAs earlier, no significant differences were found for time, while statistically significant differences were found for group on every index examined at the .05 level. The dynamics of each group over time support the cognitive consistency hypothesis rather than the learning hypothesis regarding the impact of external shocks on belief systems.

Bush/Rice Group Comparisons

Results from the comparison of means in table 5.2 indicate significant changes for Bush between period one and period two at the .05, two-tailed level that occurred on P-1 [$F(1, 20)=5.81$, $p<.05$], P-2 [$F(1, 20)=6.30$, $p<.05$], I-1 [$F(1, 20)=14.5$, $p<.001$], and I-2 [$F(1, 20)=17.597$, $p<.001$]. Bush becomes more conflictual, sees the world as more hostile, and holds less faith in the realization of his political values following 9/11. However, no significant change is found on Bush's P-4 score. An ANOVA for Rice over time indicates a change approaching significance on P-2 [$F(1, 4)=6.131$, $p<.10$] and a strong, significant change on P-4 [$F(1, 4)=28.944$, $p<.05$]. Rice appears less confident in the realization of her political values following 9/11, and she perceives an increased degree of control over historical development. Rice's P-1, I-1, and I-2 scores do not differ significantly over time.

An ANOVA between Rice and Bush overall shows a significant difference only on the P-4 index [$F(1, 26)=7.915$, $p<.05$], indicating that Bush's feelings of control are stronger than those of Rice generally. Based on separate ANOVAs comparing Bush and Rice at each time period, again, significant differences are found only on the P-4 index both prior to [$F(1, 9)=5.47$, $p<.05$] and following [$F(1, 15)=4.203$, $p<.10$] 9/11, as Bush sees himself as having more control over historical development than

Rice at both time periods. No other significant differences were found between Bush and Rice either before or after 9/11, indicating a high degree of harmony between these individuals in terms of their operational beliefs over time and identifying them as a "group" apart from hawks and doves.

A MANOVA was then run between Bush and Rice with group (Bush vs. Rice) and "time" (pre-9/11 and post-9/11) as factors. No significant interaction effects were found at the p = .10, two-tailed significance level. Not surprisingly, the group had a strong, significant effect on the P-4 index [F(1, 24)=10.79, p<.05], but no other variables were significant. However, the time factor did yield significant effects on every major index: P-1 [F(1, 24)=3.97, p=.058], P-2 [F(1, 24)=4.85, p<.05], P4 [F(1, 24)=4.80, p<.05], I-1 [F(1, 24)=6.26, p<.05], and I-2 [F(1, 24)=6.73, p<.05], indicating that the operational codes of both Bush and Rice were significantly altered following 9/11.

Bush/Advisor Relations

Analysis of Bush versus the doves on all speeches shows a significant difference only on the P-1 score [F(1, 40)=4.59, p<.05], demonstrating that Bush perceives the political universe as more hostile than the doves. Conversely, Bush differs significantly from the hawks overall on I-1 [F(1, 64)=4.554, p<.05], I-2 [F(1, 64)=5.882, p<.05], and P-4 [F(1, 64)=6.779, p<.05]. This indicates that Bush places much more faith in cooperation abroad and has a stronger feeling of control over events than the hawks. This general analysis shows that Bush falls somewhere in between his advisory groups in terms of beliefs. If anything, Bush seems generally more similar to the doves than the hawks, as he significantly differs from the latter on three of the five indices examined here.

However, disaggregating these comparisons by time (crisis/noncrisis situation) reveals that this apparent middle ground in Bush is an artifact of his different positions pre- and post-9/11. Based on ANOVA results, there are no significantly different beliefs at the p=.05, two-tailed significance level between Bush and the doves as a group prior to 9/11. During this same period, the ANOVA results show Bush and the hawks reaching or approaching a statistically significant difference on philosophical indices P-1 [F(1, 23)=3.67, p=.068, two-tailed] and P-2 [F(1, 23)=4.30, p<.05], indicating that Bush sees the world as more friendly and is much more optimistic toward realizing his political values. Further, on the instrumental indices I-1 [F(1, 23)=4.75, p<.05] and I-2 [F(1, 23)=9.62, p<.05], Bush is much more cooperation-oriented than the hawks. There is no significant difference between Bush and the hawks regarding control over historical events (P-4) prior to 9/11. Overall, Bush scores more similarly to the doves than hawks prior to 9/11.

Following 9/11, however, Bush differs from the doves significantly on philosophical scores P-1 [$F(1, 23) = 7.50$, $p < .05$] and P-2 [$F(1, 23) = 5.205$, $p < 0.05$], indicating that he now sees the world as much more hostile and is more pessimistic about realizing his political values than the doves. However, there is no significant difference between Bush and the doves on the control measure (P-4). Bush also differs significantly from the doves on I-1 [$F(1, 23) = 3.812$, $p < .10$] and I-2 [$F(1, 23) = 3.022$, $p < .10$], though only at the $p = .10$, two-tailed level. Following 9/11, Bush becomes more conflict-oriented in foreign policy than the relatively peaceful doves.

Bush's only significant difference from the hawks after 9/11 is that he believes more strongly in his ability (P-4) to control historical development [$F(1, 39) = 6.683$, $p < .05$]. On all other measures of importance, Bush is not significantly different from the hawks, indicating concurring conflictual, hostile, and pessimistic views. Thus, Bush's belief system exhibits learning effects as he switches from a dovish to a hawkish orientation following 9/11, accompanied by Rice in a similar shift of views.

Discussion

The major finding from the ANOVA group and z-score individual analyses regarding Bush is that he changed dramatically following 9/11. Measured against the average post–World War II U.S. leader, Bush scores unexceptionally prior to 9/11, though he is somewhat more cooperative than average regarding strategic and tactical beliefs. These results support hypotheses (H-1c and H-1d) consistent with the interpretation of Bush as a friendly, "compassionate" conservative leader early in his first administration. Following 9/11, however, Bush becomes more conflict-oriented and hostile toward the rest of the world, and is more pessimistic regarding the realization of his goals. This supports the hypothesis that major crises are able to significantly alter an individual's belief system, as Bush's beliefs roughly parallel a dove prior to 9/11 and a hawk afterward (H-10).

Regarding the beliefs of his advisors, hypothesized expectations were generally found regarding direction and intensity of beliefs. Prior to 9/11, the hawks (including Cheney, H-6) held hard-line beliefs (H-4); the doves held compassionate conservative beliefs (H-5); and Rice generally believed as Bush did, following his lead (H-7). Further, a fair to high level of stability was found for these individuals over time. As figures 5.1 and 5.2 show, even when significant changes occurred, the *directionality* of beliefs generally remained constant (H-8a) for both the hawks and doves even after 9/11.

Conversely, Bush's shift in beliefs following 9/11 was stronger than that of any other advisor examined, changing directionality (H-10) from positive to negative on every major index except P-4. The type of negative, conflictual change demonstrated by Bush is also generally found in Rice (H-8b), though to a lesser degree.

Bush's advisors in the department of defense adhered to their hypothesized conflict-oriented roles (H-8a) following the terrorist attacks. The only advisor who strayed from his pre-9/11 beliefs substantially is Armitage who, as figure 5.2 shows, becomes somewhat more hostile and conflict-oriented following 9/11. Armitage seems to have been the most affected by role conflict (H-9) as described by Sarbin and Allen (1968). The fact that Armitage's beliefs regress to the mean after 9/11, falling between those of the hawks and Powell, indicate that his roles either merged (an obfuscation of role expectations) or became "interpenetrated" (an adherence to hawkish and dovish roles simultaneously), though a more in-depth analysis of post-9/11 trends would be necessary to precisely tease out the types of role conflict resolution strategies pursued by Armitage.

Although hypothesis H-9 (that the doves would become somewhat more hawkish following 9/11) is supported in Richard Armitage's case, this is not so for Powell, whose beliefs remained cooperative, friendly, and optimistic. Powell seems to have experienced little, if any, role conflict throughout the time period examined here. It would be interesting to see if Powell's consistency in dovish beliefs held up leading to the war in Iraq, when he began more explicitly toeing the administration's line. It might be expected that role conflict would increase for Powell leading up to his United Nations speech.

Bush himself, and perhaps Cheney and Rice, had no fixed set of institutional guidelines as role expectations to follow either before or after 9/11. A high degree of role ambiguity, stemming from the vagueness of the presidential role, in conjunction with issues of learning and the need for cognitive consistency, made it relatively easy for Bush to undergo an extreme shift in beliefs following 9/11. Additionally, the hostile nature of U.S. foreign policy after 9/11 follows from Bush's post-9/11 beliefs, indicating that this president's belief system strongly correlates with foreign policy actions and supports the linkage hypothesis (H-3) associating a leader's beliefs with a state's behavior during crisis periods.

If Bush's beliefs mesh with U.S. action following 9/11, how can the realist and unilateralist actions taken by the administration during the early Bush White House be explained in conjunction with Bush's friendly, positive beliefs during that time period? As mentioned earlier, Bush initially claimed that he would rely heavily on the knowledge and advice of his more experienced advisors regarding issues of U.S. foreign policy. The findings here suggest this seems to have largely been the case prior to 9/11. As mentioned earlier, U.S. foreign policy became *more* aggressive and unilateral following 9/11, but in many respects it was already heading in this direction. Perhaps the hawks received the lion's share of foreign policy influence delegated by the President prior to 9/11. Though it seems intuitively as if Bush would look to those who thought similarly to himself for advice (the doves prior to 9/11), qualitative accounts indicate that the doves' level of influence was minimized versus the hawks from the beginning.

For example, Mann (2004, 278), using a skiing analogy, argues that Colin Powell first experienced the feeling of being "pushed . . . back on his heels" by the Bush White House in March of 2001, when Dick Cheney and company are shown to have run the show. Bob Woodward (2004, 15, 22–23) also notes that Powell had become "increasingly skeptical" regarding Donald Rumsfeld's justifications for going after Iraq prior to 9/11, and though these feelings were relayed to the President, Powell's pleas were largely ignored. Perhaps Dick Cheney, whose pre-9/11 tactical and strategic preferences are more conflictual than anyone at any time period, was indeed playing a significant policy-making role before 9/11. Thus, analysis of these individuals' operational codes supports the suggestion by Mann (2004) and Woodward (2004) that Cheney and his ideological colleagues were the most important influences on George W. Bush's foreign policy, at least prior to 9/11.

Following 9/11, Bush's beliefs converge with those of the hawks, which generally remained stable, and hawkish influence in the White House grew even more. Rumsfeld, Wolfowitz, and Cheney started out seeing conflict and pessimism as the appropriate perspective toward the world, and this not surprisingly held after 9/11. Perhaps following 9/11, the hawks' philosophy started making more sense in Bush's eyes, and the doves looked more like naïve idealists than truly constructive counselors. This interpretation supports the hypothesis that the hawks also strongly drove Bush's foreign policy after 9/11.

Colin Powell and Richard Armitage stepped down from their respective posts in the state department following the Bush administration's first term, and a look at their operational codes may help to understand why this happened. Powell and Armitage are called doves in this analysis, and this label seems appropriate based on their operational code beliefs. The doves' beliefs remained cooperative and friendly when Bush's changed so much after the terrorist attacks, and these differences seem to have fostered heated conflict over time (Mann 2004; Woodward 2004). The fact that the doves are now gone, replaced by a presumably less antagonistic state department headed by Bush's like-minded confidante Condoleezza Rice, may speak volumes about where the administration is headed in the second term.

If international conflict escalation was truly viewed as the last option in the minds of influential policy makers after 9/11, then a war in Iraq would not have happened in the fashion that it did. Bush seemed to believe after 9/11 that taking the offensive in the "war on terror" was a critical objective that needed to be achieved. Those advocating the necessity of international support and UN resolutions would only get in the way of this agenda. With Cheney, Rice, and Rumsfeld securely at his side, Wolfowitz heading the World Bank, Republican politician Porter Goss running the CIA, and like-minded hawks such as John Bolton and Karen Hughes representing Bush's conception of "diplomats," the President's shift toward a more hawkish foreign policy orientation is a trend that seems likely to continue.

PART IV

APPLICATIONS: THE DOMAIN OF INTERNATIONAL SECURITY

CHAPTER 6

REAGAN AND GORBACHEV: ALTERCASTING AT THE END OF THE COLD WAR

Akan Malici

Introduction

Observing the evolution of international relations theory, one scholar wrote "Students coming of age in the post–cold war era seem to grasp intuitively that the study of international relations . . . is ultimately about human beings, and that the way in which human beings engage in such relations . . ." is difficult to comprehend through the lenses of theories that dominated throughout the cold war era (Gaddis 1992/1993, 55). Conventional international relations theories, such as neorealism and institutionalism, traditionally reject the impact of ideational variables on politics (Keohane and Martin 2003; Waltz 1979). By the end of the cold war it was evident that these theories were in trouble as they had to face an increasing number of empirical anomalies. The reason they were in trouble appeared to be a denial of ideational variables and the importance of leaders in the conduct of world politics.

To consider actors as amorphous entities and to rob them of any consciousness is equivalent to denying the sociopsychological character of politics (Ashley 1986; Cox 1986; Kratochwil 1986, 2001). Such an understanding of international interactions is impoverished and can only be enriched by an effort to develop a better understanding of the agents of political action (Carlsnaes 1992; Dessler 1989; Wendt 1987). This position was carried into the discipline of political science by the "constructivist turn" in the early 1990s (Checkel 1998). Consistent with this effort, I argue that the end of the cold war cannot be adequately understood without systematically examining and tracing the beliefs of Ronald Reagan and Mikhail Gorbachev.

No two leaders exemplify Alexander Wendt's (1992) claim that "anarchy is what states make of it" better than superpower leaders Ronald Reagan and Mikhail Gorbachev. For the sake of theory advancement it is necessary to reexamine "what really happened" at the end of the cold war. Was it just brute power politics? Or was there more going on? I shall argue the latter, that Gorbachev engaged in *altercasting*. This strategy entails continuous gestures (moves and tactics) that an opponent would not expect and the goal of transforming the very beliefs of an opponent. Then I will ask: did Reagan merely adapt to Gorbachev's initiatives and play along, or did he go further? Did he go so far as to alter his definition of the situation and the Soviet Union as an effect of experiential learning? And finally, did his beliefs and possible learning patterns impact the foreign policy behavior of the United States at the end of the cold war?

My argument is consistent with constructivists who consider politics to be a social–psychological affair, arguing that this is "a world of our making" (Onuf 1989). Constructivists criticize mainstream theories of international relations for "ontological reductionism" (Wendt 1987, 342). Intending to deliver a *social* theory of international politics, they argue that relevant actors must be problematized because they exist within a psychological reality of interactions and a socially constructed world (Berger 1966, 111). Despite the suggestion of a dialogue between sociological constructivism and the cognitivist research program in political psychology, systematic efforts to synthesize both approaches remain largely absent (Walker 2004b; Wendt 1999, 134, 394).

The agent in the "agent-structure debate" is still not comprehended sufficiently and remains undertheorized (Buzan, Jones, and Little 1993; Carlsnaes 1992; Dessler 1989; Gould 1998; Hollis and Smith 1991, 1992, 1994). One reason is a lack of rigorous methods that would enable the scientific study of ideational variables (Ruggie 1999). Historically, constructivists rely on interpretations as a methodological tool. Interpretations are by definition subjective, however, which makes an effort to derive firm knowledge elusive. As one scholar acknowledged, "Not all interpretations are equally valid," leading to the problem of "how to justify a claim about unobservables" (Wendt 1999, 85).

My methodological goal is to make the unobservables observable by engaging in analysis at the interface of constructivism and cognitivism. The constuctivist turn in the 1990s heralded the return of ideational variables into the study of international relations. Constructivists have argued that actors are not to be considered passive agents who merely respond to environmental stimuli as much of international relations theory would have it. Instead, they are selective agents actively shaping their environment—problem solvers who aim to make sense of a complex environment and derive alternatives for decisions. While such claims speak to our immediate intuitions of "what politics is about," there is still missing a tool kit for systematically demonstrating the existence and the impact of ideation on politics. Operational code analysis provides such a tool kit to contribute to the scientific study of ideational variables—a necessity that is increasingly acknowledged by representatives of most paradigms within the discourse of international relations (Brooks 1997; Christensen and Snyder 1990; Keohane and Martin 2003; Walt 1987; Wohlforth 1994/1995).

In the following pages, I first review in more depth the constructivist challenge to structural theories of international relations. Then I discuss the response offered by the application of operational code analysis and game theory to meet this challenge. Finally, I illustrate the application of these tools to the challenge of explaining the end of the cold war posed by constructivist theorists.

The Constructivist Challenge

The events surrounding the end of the cold war cast serious doubt on the universal applicability of structural theories. These theories were "caught flat-footed" by events that they could not explain (Koslowski and Kratochwil 1994; Lebow 1994; Lebow and Risse-Kappen 1995; Wohlforth 1998, 653–655). The reason is that structural theories ignore that international relations are conducted by "conscious entities capable of reacting to, and often modifying, the variables and conditions they encounter" (Gaddis 1992/1993, 55). More specifically, the reason for the failure of structural approaches is their ontological reductionism. Most problematic is the assumption of exogenously defined preferences:

> By taking preferences as given we beg what may be the most important question on how they were formed . . . Economic theory treats tastes and preferences as exogenous. Analysis is therefore facilitated, but at the cost of drawing attention away from areas that may contain much of the explanatory "action" in which we are interested. (Jervis 1988, 319, 324–325)

As actor's preferences and causal beliefs are unproblematic "givens," and insofar as these are left unexplained, structural theories cannot account for "how individuals under given conditions produce new conditions" (Przeworski 1985, 401; see also Carlsnaes 1992, 251; Elster 1986). Such shortcomings led to the agent-structure debate, first in sociology and then in international relations theory, marked by the birth of the so-called constructivist challenge (Bhaskar 1979; Carlsnaes 1992; Dessler 1989; Giddens 1979, 1984; Hollis and Smith 1991; Wendt 1987).

Constructivists argue that structural approaches deal only with one dimension of a multidimensional reality. Since they ignore changes taking place in consciousness, they are incomplete and hence do not enable an understanding of how interests change as a result of changes in the belief systems of agents. Their approaches obscure rather than illuminate the sources of states' foreign policy preferences (Keohane 1988, 391). The result has been a fundamentally ahistorical approach to world politics which denies the "significance of practice" (Ashley 1986, 290).

Constructivists contend that not only are identities, interests, and subsequent preferences of agents socially constructed in the course of practice, but that they must also share the stage with other ideational factors that emanate from human capacity and will (Ruggie 1999, 216). Constructivists deny the structuralist assumption that the "world exists independent of human beings" (Wendt 1999, 216). While structural approaches emphasize existing circumstances, constructivists emphasize the *making* of these circumstances by agents. Constructivists consider *making* to have at least two meanings: "What do people make of their circumstances in the sense of understanding them? And what do they make of them in the sense of acting on whatever understanding they hold?" (Ruggie 1999, 237).

The key toward an answer is to understand that the most fundamental fact about international politics is the nature of the socio-psychological consciousness of actors about themselves and others. These constitute identities and interests by helping actors define the situation of ensuing interactions. For analytic purposes two aspects of the ensuing interactive process are distinguished—"role-taking" and "altercasting" (Schwalbe 1988; Turner 1956). Role-taking "involves choosing from among the available representations of the Self who one will be, and thus what interests one intends to pursue" (Wendt 1999, 329). Subsequent interactions are then literally constructed through the role-taker's (ego) gesture toward another actor (alter). This gesture may consist, for example, of a threat, a retreat, a concession, or an attack. For ego, "this gesture represents the basis on which it is prepared to respond to alter." This basis, however, is not known to alter, and so it must make an inference about ego's motivations and intentions, respond, and hence subject the latter to an interpretative process of inferences (404). This communicative process between ego and alter constitutes a "social act" and leads in turn to a reinforcement or a novel creation of intersubjective meanings between the actors.

New intersubjective meanings are created, for example, if ego takes a different role than alter expects and if ego subsequently succeeds in alter-casting alter. Altercasting is "a technique of interactor control in which ego uses tactics of self-presentation and stage management in an attempt to frame alter's definition of the situation in ways that create the role which ego desires alter to play." Thus, "ego tries to induce alter to take on a new identity (and thereby enlist alter in ego's effort to change itself by treating alter as if it already had that identity" (Earle 1986; Goffman 1959; Weinstein and Deutschberger 1963; Wendt 1992, 421). The underlying logic here is the self-fulfilling prophecy: by treating the other as if he is to respond in a certain way, ego is literally trying to "teach" its definition of the situation to Alter. If alter is "willing to learn," then both actors will emerge with a newly created intersubjective understanding of each other (Blumer 1969, 2; Merton 1996; Wendt 1999, 330–331).

While constructivists' challenges to our traditional understanding of interaction are quite forceful, these scholars have demonstrated little success in applying a scientific method to the study of ideational variables. Relying often on interpretation as a methodological tool, constructivists have justi-fiably been charged with subjectivism. Both constructivists and cognitivists reject the assumption of given preferences and the implicit relegation of beliefs to a residual role. According to their reflectivist understanding of politics, beliefs are a central element of all research because "knowledgeable practices constitute subjects." Being reflectivists, they also "share a cognitive, intersubjective conception of process in which identities and interests are endogenous to interaction, rather than a rationalist-behavioral one in which they are exogenous" (Biersteker 1989; Lapid 1989; Wendt 1992, 392). "Social and political life," in short, "comprises a set of practices in which things are *constituted* in the process of dealing with them" (Campbell 1998, 5).

Both cognitivists and constructivists have been criticized for advancing underspecified models lacking rigorous conceptualization and operational-ization (Achen and Snidal 1989; Morrow 1997). I address these criticisms by using methods capable of systematically and quantitatively identifying ideational variables. I also use a model that conceptualizes ideational variables (beliefs) and preferences specified within a rigorous framework provided by sequential game theory (Brams 1994).[1]

This symbolic-interactionist (ideational) usage of game theory is in stark contrast to a traditional, materialistic, game-theoretic analysis of interaction (Axelrod 1984; Fearon and Wendt 2002; Taylor 1976). In the latter, the structure of the game—of the actor's beliefs about each other and their preferences—is exogenous to interaction and, as such, does not change. Consequently, only structural learning—an adjustment of means without a change in the intersubjective understanding of the involved actors—is possible. Interaction is merely *regulative*. Constructivists, in contrast, argue that interaction can have *constitutive* effects—a cognitive process of experiential learning in which actors do not only alter actions employed toward each other but change the ideas or, in other words, the very beliefs they hold about each other (Rawls 1955; Ruggie 1999; Searle 1995).

Thus, traditional game-theoretic analyses of international interactions emphasize "behavioral effects, treating interests and identities as constant and focusing on how the acquisition of new information about the environment enables actors to realize their interests more effectively . . ." (Wendt 1999, 326–327). In contrast, the constructivist assumption is that interaction entails learning and perspective-taking processes, which may also change identities and interests. As Wendt (334) explains: "Over time, as Alter and Ego mutually adjust to the representations of Self and Other conveyed in each other's actions, their ideas about who they are and what they want will come to reflect the appraisals of the Other, at first perhaps for instrumental reasons, but increasingly internalized." Whether this claim is indeed so, has not been demonstrated conclusively by constructivists.

Constructivists caution against endogenizing preferences within a game-theoretic framework arguing that "game theory was not designed for this task and so its relevant conceptual repertoire is relatively underdeveloped" (327). Yet, exactly this task ought to be the goal—to *develop* the conceptual repertoire of game theory and thereby contribute to the scientific study of ideational variables. Indeed, I argue that endogenizing preferences within a game-theoretic model is especially promising because the latter carries *positive* statements about what *ought* to be expected if decisions are indeed influenced by beliefs.

Therefore, it is important to recognize at the outset the fundamental difference between what I assume and the assumption of traditional game-theoretic approaches. In the latter, interaction is regulative. If actors fail to achieve their goals, they engage in *structural learning* and adjust their actions. I argue that "more is going on." Actors are not only trying to "get what they want," they are also trying to sustain or change "who they are," that is to say, the conceptions of self and other that generate those wants in the first place (316). In other words, interactions can also have constitutive effects via a cognitive process of *experiential learning*. Here actors alter the beliefs they hold about each other, which redefines the menu of rational foreign policy actions. Which form of learning occurs—structural or experiential—"is an empirical question that needs to be investigated, not assumed away a priori" (334).

Since constitutive rules operate on the basis of agents' interpretations and perceptions, issues of cooperation and conflict are of a psychological nature (405). Wendt acknowledges further that a constructivist approach is "at base cognitive rather than behavioral" and also suggests "constructivism has to be enriched with . . . insights about learning and cognition which it has neglected" (394). The irony is that almost no one has followed this recommendation so far (Walker 2004b).

Learning and International Interactions

Intersubjective understandings that exist among actors may change over time as a result of experiential learning, which is formally defined as "a change in beliefs (or degree of confidence in one's beliefs) or the development of new beliefs, skills, or procedures as a result of the observation and interpretation of experience" (Levy 1994, 283; Wendt 1999). Such an understanding of international interactions suggests that operational code analysis provides a satisfying method for examining the research questions mentioned earlier. The operational code research program conceptualizes actors (self and other) in an intersubjectively constituted context with self having diagnostic propensities about and prescriptive propensities toward other.

A leader's philosophical and instrumental beliefs, respectively, determine his subjective definition of the context in which he finds himself and the tactical and strategic orientations he considers to be appropriate for self within this situation (George 1969). What distinguishes this study from a conventional constructivist analysis of international interactions is that it uses systematic research procedures to quantitatively demonstrate the impact of ideational variables and learning patterns. In order to determine Reagan's operational code, this study employs the Verbs in Context System (VICS) of content analysis to identify his philosophical and instrumental beliefs (Walker, Schafer, and Young 1998, 2003).

With the progress of time a leader's operational code, that is to say, his intersubjective understanding of self and other, might change as a result of *experiential learning*. Conceptualized within an operational code framework, learning occurs if and when an actor's beliefs about the nature of the political universe and the most effective means to achieve political goals are strengthened, weakened, or altered altogether. Operational code analysis also allows us to distinguish among three levels of experiential learning: simple, diagnostic, and complex (Deutsch 1963; Levy 1994; Malici and

Malici 2005a, 2005b; Malici and Malici 2005; Nye 1987; Tetlock 1991; Walker, Schafer, and Marfleet 2001). *Simple* learning is defined as changes in instrumental beliefs about the best means for the self to achieve goals, and *diagnostic* learning is defined as changes in philosophical beliefs about others in the political universe. *Complex* learning occurs when an actor's key philosophical beliefs about political goals and key instrumental beliefs about the most effective means to achieve them are modified so as to alter a leader's strategic preferences.

If Gorbachev pursued a successful altercasting strategy to end the cold war, then we should expect that an operational code analysis of Reagan's beliefs over time will display learning patterns.[2] I measure Reagan's operational code beliefs in three different intervals between the years 1985 and 1988.[3] The first interval starts in March 1985 and terminates in January 1986. Reagan's operational code in this period will serve as a baseline from which subsequent levels of learning can be assessed. The second interval starts in February 1986 (after the Twenty-Seventh Congress of the Communist Party) and ends in December 1986. In this interval Gorbachev clearly intensified his strategy of altercasting. Did this have any effect on Reagan's beliefs? The third and final interval starts in January 1987 (shortly after the famous Reykjavik summit) and ends in December 1988. In this period, Reagan clearly shows more behavioral reciprocation to Gorbachev's initiatives (Garthoff 1994; Malici 2004). What are Reagan's beliefs about the Soviet Union in the last two years of his presidency?

While these comparisons inform us about the beliefs of Ronald Reagan and whether he learned, they do not inform us about any behavioral impacts. For this purpose I utilize the Theory of Inferences about Preferences (TIP) from operational code analysis and the Theory of Moves (TOM) from sequential game theory (Brams 1994; Malici 2004). By using TIP to determine the distribution of payoffs and TOM to specify strategies and outcomes, I move beyond traditional game-theoretic analyses of interaction. Traditional game-theoretic analyses *passively* represent the situation between two actors. My analysis *actively* constructs their situation. An application of game theory is especially promising because it carries positive statements about what *ought* to happen if U.S. foreign policy behavior at the end of the cold war was indeed influenced by Reagan's beliefs and perceptions of the Soviet Union.

If the characteristics of decisions and outcomes are congruent with the actor's beliefs, there is at least a presumption that the beliefs may play a causal role (George 1979, 105–114; George and Bennett 2005). The congruence procedure is no panacea for the difficulties of establishing causality, yet as long as it is not carried out in an "atheoretical" manner, it "can make an important contribution to the establishment of general propositions and thus to theory building in political science" (Lijphart 1971, 691). The value of such an endeavor is that it can refine concepts, generate novel theoretical ideas, and assess the credibility of certain types of propositions (Goldmann 1988, 224).

Reagan Faces the Gorbachev Challenge

The Gorbachev Challenge

Beginning in March 1985, Gorbachev posed a challenge to the practice of cold war international politics. During his tenure the Soviet Union stopped playing power politics, despite "the insistence of international relations theory that this could never happen" (Gaddis 1992). Indeed, given Reagan's hostility, Gorbachev's actions were difficult to comprehend at first. On the day that Gorbachev assumed the Soviet leadership, Reagan stated, "There's a great mutual suspicion between [our] two countries. I think ours is more justified than theirs" (quoted in Mandelbaum and Talbott 1987, 44). And just one week after Gorbachev's accession, Reagan reaffirmed an assertive U.S. position, stressed the need for an intensified defense effort, and renewed charges of Soviet violations of political and arms control agreements (Garthoff 1994, 208). He also declared that the United States would "actively, and if necessarily unilaterally, sponsor insurgencies seeking the overthrow of pro-Moscow leftist regimes in the Third World" (Mandelbaum and Talbott 1987, 61).

Instead of responding in kind, Gorbachev chose a strategy of altercasting. He recognized that the forces that constituted the superpower security dilemma "are themselves ongoing effects of, not exogenous to the interaction" (Wendt 1992, 407). Gorbachev aimed to change them. He set out to demonstrate to Reagan that his past perception of the Soviet threat was a social construction no longer warranted. Gorbachev's goal was to deconstruct this construction. His foreign policy process toward the United States took the form of a social process, "one of constructing and reconstructing self and social relationships" (Stryker 1987, 93). This required tireless endurance. Reagan was one of the most anti-Soviet presidents ever (Mandelbaum and Talbott 1987, 182).

Reagan's beliefs would not allow for mutual rapprochement. His aggregated VICS scores specify a Compel/Punish strategy for both Self (I-1 = .30, P-4a = .26) and Other (P-1 = .20, P-4b = .16) in the period between March 1985 and January 1986. His strategic preferences for this period rank domination over settlement over deadlock over submission and he attributes the same preference order to Gorbachev (see figure 6.1).[4] The initial state of (2,2) deadlock in this subjective game of prisoner's dilemma represents Reagan's belief that both superpowers had deadlocked with each other in the past. Based on calculations of strategic rationality the prediction is that neither Reagan nor Gorbachev would "move" and concede for fear of being dominated by the other. Empirically, the prediction

Reagan's Prisoner's Dilemma Game

		Gorbachev					Gorbachev	
		CO	CF				CO	CF
	CO	3,3 $\mid\leftarrow$ 1,4				CO	3,3 $\rightarrow\mid$	1,4
Reagan		$\downarrow$ $\uparrow$			Reagan		$\uparrow$ $\downarrow$	
	CF	4,1 $\rightarrow$ "2,2"				CF	4,1 $\mid\leftarrow$ "2,2"	

Reagan's Predicted Strategy   Gorbachev's Predicted Strategy
(I-1, P-4a) Self (-, =)   (P-1, P-4b) Other (-, =)

Period 1: March 1985–January 1986 and Period 2: February–December 1986

Reagan's Mutual Assurance Game

		Gorbachev					Gorbachev	
		CO	CF				CO	CF
	CO	4,4 $\leftarrow$ 1,2				CO	4,4 $\rightarrow\mid$ 1,2	
Reagan		$\downarrow$ $\uparrow$			Reagan		$\uparrow$ $\downarrow$	
	CF	2,1 $\rightarrow$ "3,3"				CF	2,1 $\leftarrow$ "3,3"	

Reagan's Predicted Strategy   Gorbachev's Predicted Strategy
(I-1, P-4a) Self (+, =)   (P-1, P-4b) Other (+, =)

Period 3: January 1987 – December 1988

Theory of Inferences about Preferences

(1) If (+, <), then Settle > Deadlock > Submit > Dominate: Appease Strategy
(2) If (+, =), then Settle > Deadlock > Dominate > Submit: Reward/Deter Strategy
(3) If (+, >), then Settle > Dominate > Deadlock > Submit: Exploit Strategy
(4) If (-, <), then Dominate > Settle > Submit > Deadlock: Bluff Strategy
(5) If (-, =), then Dominate > Settle > Deadlock > Submit: Compel/Punish Strategy
(6) If (-, >), then Dominate > Deadlock > Settle >Submit: Bully Strategy

Figure 6.1   Reagan's Subjective Games in Three Cold War Periods.

Note: The initial state is in quotation marks, and the final state is underlined for each game. The symbols " $\rightarrow$ " and " $\rightarrow\mid$ " indicate the respective strategic choices of "move" or "stay" by the player with the next move given the initial state.

would hold true for Reagan, but not for Gorbachev. Instead, he set out to initiate his altercasting strategy.[5] Shortly after he assumed power, Gorbachev announced on April 7 a six-month, unilateral moratorium on deployment of intermediate-range missiles (SS-20) in Europe. On April 17, he went further and proposed a moratorium on all nuclear weapon testing (Stein 1994, 179).

As we would expect from Reagan's beliefs, he did not perceive Gorbachev's conciliatory gestures as such. Instead, he chose to push ahead with the development of the United States' Strategic Defense Initiative (SDI), declaring that the United States would "demonstrate that communism is not the wave of the future," and that it would "prevent the further expansion of totalitarianism throughout the world" (quoted in Goshko 1985, 220). He also considered abandoning the unratified but so far observed Strategic Arms Limitation Talks II (SALT) Treaty (Garthoff 1994, 219). Gorbachev, for his part, continued his altercasting strategy and responded on July 30, 1985, with the following statement:

> Wishing to set a good example, the Soviet Union has adopted a decision to unilaterally end any nuclear explosions . . . The Soviet Union expects that the United States will react positively to this initiative and end its nuclear explosions. (Quoted in Goldstein and Freeman 1990, 112)

Although Gorbachev invited Reagan's reciprocation, he did not make his decision contingent upon it. However, Reagan's response was "to counter the burgeoning Gorbachev peace offensive by a rebuttal" (Garthoff 1994, 222). On August 17, the United States conducted nuclear tests. The following week experienced further escalations of hostile U.S. activities. Reagan announced that the United States would soon carry out the first live tests of an antisatellite missile and stressed U.S. determination to continue the development of SDI. On August 25, the United States test-launched its MX missile for the first time from an underground silo. Despite vehement Soviet protests, missile and laser tests continued in September, and the escalation culminated in a U.S. announcement regarding the creation of a space command to coordinate all military systems in space (Goldstein and Freeman 1990, 118).

Gorbachev continued his "peace initiative" nevertheless (Sternthal 1997, 43). He acknowledged the deterioration of U.S.–Soviet relations and nevertheless argued in favor of the Soviet moratorium. Gorbachev went even further in September when he proposed reductions of 50 percent in strategic offensive arms to a number of 6000 nuclear warheads, accompanied by an agreement not to develop, test, or deploy "space-strike weapons" (Goshko 1985, 220). Any concession on SDI, however, was out of question for Reagan. He rejected reciprocation not only in this matter, but to almost any of Gorbachev's cooperative moves. On September 27, the United States conducted another nuclear test and soon afterward, in an unprecedented move, sent the battleship USS Iowa (armed with long-range cruise missiles) into the Baltic Sea.

Further U.S. moves of escalation followed in November through a unilateral American reinterpretation of a key provision of the Anti-Ballistic Missile (ABM) treaty. Reagan argued that the ABM treaty permits the development and testing of space-based ABM systems and components— "theretofore believed banned by the treaty" (Garthoff 1994, 230; Oberdorfer 1998, 123–127). This reinterpretation was controversial to the degree that even close U.S. allies such as West German Chancellor Kohl and British Prime Minister Thatcher would contest it (Garthoff 1987). The protest motivated Reagan to defer but not diffuse the issue.

In November, Reagan and Gorbachev met for their first summit in Geneva. The agreements they reached at the summit were not very substantial. The main agreement concerned a reduction of strategic arms by 50 percent ("in principle") and on negotiations that were to follow regarding a prospective intermediate-range nuclear forces (INF) agreement. Nevertheless, after the meeting, Reagan spoke of a "fresh start" in U.S.–Soviet relations and of "heading in the right direction." On December 23, he stated that the United States would continue to adhere to the SALT II provisions after the expiration of the unratified treaty at the end of the year (Goldblatt and Fern 1986, 593; Mandelbaum and Talbott 1987, 4–6). At the same time, however, he ordered a continuation of nuclear tests and SDI research, and accused the Soviet Union of various violations of arms control agreements. Reagan's beliefs about the Soviet Union kept him from engaging in any substantial reciprocation to Gorbachev's initiatives. Gorbachev, however, remained committed to moving the superpower relationship from a Hobbesian world of enemies toward a Kantian world of friends (Wendt 1999).

Reagan Resists the Winds of Change

At the 27th Party Congress of the Communist Party on February 25, 1986, Gorbachev "identified himself with a new concept of security alien to traditional Soviet thinking" (Risse-Kappen 1994, 201). He argued that "[o]ne cannot resolve . . . global problems . . . by the efforts of any one state . . . For this cooperation on a global scale is required . . ." He emphasized that security between the superpowers can only be mutual, and "if one takes international relations as a whole, can only be universal." He continued to say that the two superpowers "have not a few common interests, and there is the objective imperative to live in the world at peace with one another, and to compete on an equal and mutually advantageous basis" (quoted in Garthoff 1994, 257). Gorbachev was convinced that anarchy would not necessarily lead to conflictual international relations as much of conventional IR theory would have it (Mearsheimer 2001; Waltz 1979). He was to prove this in subsequent years through continuous, unilateral gestures. These would, however, be met in the short run by Reagan's continuously rigid beliefs about the Soviet Union.

Table 6.1 shows the mean scores for Reagan's operational code beliefs and identifies statistically significant differences. These mean scores differ from the aggregated scores used earlier to construct Reagan's subjective game. The former are the average scores for Reagan in each period while the latter are cumulative scores for each period. While the mean scores for a number of Reagan's instrumental beliefs shifted slightly toward cooperation between Period 1 and Period 2, overall he continues to display a conflictual posture. The only statistically significant difference in table 6.1 between Period 1 and Period 2 also supports this conclusion. In the period between February and December 1986, Reagan believed even more in the utility of oppose tactics than he did previously. This represents simple learning in which the President's confidence in oppose tactics strengthened rather than weakened or remained the same.

Reagan's aggregated VICS scores for Period 2 continue to specify a Compel/Punish strategy for both Self (I 1 − .32, P-4a = .22) and Other (P-1 = .21, P-4b = .20). As in the previous year, his strategic preferences rank domination over settlement over deadlock over submission. He attributes the same preference order to Gorbachev during the February–December 1986 period (see figure 6.1). The initial state of deadlock (2,2) represents Reagan's belief that superpower relations had not improved substantially in the previous year. Reagan's beliefs displayed a high need for cognitive consistency and he discarded any of Gorbachev's conciliatory gestures from the previous period.[6] Although Gorbachev had de facto moved toward a cooperative stance during the previous year, in Reagan's mind the superpowers remained deadlocked in a prisoner's dilemma game. The prediction is that the apparent deadlock would continue. Reagan would choose to "stay" with a conflict strategy in response to his diagnosis of Gorbachev's strategic preferences.

In March, Reagan declared that he would not regret his 1983 labeling of the Soviet Union as the "evil empire" (Mandelbaum and Talbott 1987, 45). At the same time, the U.S. battleship USS Yorktown and the USS Caron,

Table 6.1 Reagan's Beliefs in Three Cold War Periods

Philosophical & instrumental beliefs	Period 1*	Period 2**	Period 3***
P-1. Nature of political universe (Conflict/Cooperation)	0.225	0.204	0.360[a]
P-2. Realization of political values (Pessimism/Optimism)	0.071	0.028	0.150[a]
P-3. Political future (Unpredictable/Predictable)	0.098	0.121	0.128
P-4. Historical development (Low control/High control)	0.255	0.224	0.237
P-5. Role of chance (Small role/Large role)	0.975	0.974	0.970
I-1. Strategic approach to goals (Conflict/Cooperation)	0.262	0.303	0.539[a]
I-2. Intensity of tactics (Conflict/Cooperation)	0.024	0.089	0.223[a]
I-3. Risk orientation (Averse/Acceptant)	0.179	0.189	0.279[b]
I-4. Timing of action			
a. Conflict/Cooperation	0.714	0.697	0.461[a]
b. Words/Deeds	0.567	0.532	0.424
I-5. Utility of means			
a. Reward	0.106	0.126	0.128
b. Promise	0.066	0.051	0.079
c. Appeal/Support	0.460	0.474	0.562[b]
d. Oppose/Resist	0.104	0.156[a]	0.110[b]
e. Threaten	0.063	0.046	0.037
f. Punish	0.202	0.147	0.084[a]

* Period 1: March 1985–January 1986 (n = 14); ** Period 2: February–December 1986 (n = 13); *** Period 3: January 1987–December 1988 (n = 18). Significant differences between mean indices at the following levels: [a] $p \leq 0.05$, [b] $p \leq 0.10$ (two-tailed test). Significant differences noted on indices in the Period 2 column indicate that there is a significant difference between Periods 2 and 1. Significant differences noted on indices in the Periods 3 column indicate that there is a significant difference between Periods 3 and 2.

a specially equipped intelligence-collection destroyer, entered Soviet territorial waters in the Crimean Sea. Reagan also ignored ongoing U.S.–Soviet talks on regional matters. On March 22, 1986, he accused Moscow of a "continuing horror of the Soviet attempt to subjugate Afghanistan," and authorized "another $300-plus million in 'covert' military assistance" (Garthoff 1994, 272). Ten days later it was disclosed that the United States was to supply Stinger antiaircraft missiles to insurgents in Afghanistan and other third world countries led by pro-Moscow regimes (272).

However, Gorbachev persisted with his altercasting strategy. At the end of March, he renewed the nuclear testing moratorium under the provision that the United States would follow suit. Reagan did not reciprocate, and instead ordered a new nuclear weapons test on April 4. In May, he finally declared that SALT II is "dead" (Oberdorfer 1986, A1). Although "the picture looked bleak, . . . the Soviet leadership was not giving up on prospects for developing relations" (Garthoff 1994, 275). In June, Gorbachev engaged in "a serious offer of negotiations" regarding a "substantial reduction" of conventional forces in Europe. He anchored the Warsaw Pact in this proposal, and suggested the establishment of the Conference on Disarmament in Europe. Furthermore, he initiated a development in Soviet military doctrine toward "defensive principles" and a "balance of military forces at the lowest possible levels," combined with the "reduction of military potentials to the limits necessary for defense."[7]

In addition, Gorbachev proposed a reduction of "operational-tactical nuclear arms with a range of up to 1000 km," which had posed a major concern to West European North Atlantic Treaty Organization (NATO) allies (Sternthal 1997, 73). Gorbachev kept pushing even further. On June 16, he conceded a toleration for U.S. "laboratory research" regarding SDI—an unprecedented move on this issue. Another gesture of this kind followed when he suggested setting INF systems, apart from Intercontinental Ballistic Missiles (ICBMs) and Submarine Launched Ballistic Missiles (SLBMs), at a zero level in Europe pertaining to the Soviet Union and the United States and not to other NATO states such as Britain and France.

Reagan's reaction was somewhat positive, attributing "a serious effort to the Soviets" (Oberdorfer 1991, 169–174). He nevertheless advocated the realization of SDI without any signs of compromise. U.S. hostilities escalated further when in September a "naval battle group, for the first time featuring the nuclear-missile-armed battleship USS New Jersey, passed through the Kuril Islands into the Sea of Okhotsk for an exercise simulating an attack on Soviet bases (Garthoff 1994, 296). The signs before the Reykjavik summit were not much different from the signs before the Geneva summit and, as the latter approached, it became increasingly clear that "although Reagan was prepared to negotiate on his own terms, he was not disposed to seek a real compromise" (286).

Gorbachev's agenda at the summit carried unprecedented concessions. He accepted, for example, an equal 50 percent cut in ICBMs, SLBMs, and heavy bombers (Zemtsov and Farrar 1989, 168). He also agreed to include a cut in the Soviet heavy (SS-18) missiles. Furthermore, he agreed "to exclude all American forward-based shorter-range systems capable of striking the Soviet Union from the 'strategic forces' to be counted and limited" (Garthoff 1994, 287). With regard to space weapons and defensive systems, Gorbachev moderated his initial demand from a fifteen-year nonwithdrawal commitment from the ABM treaty to ten years. He also reiterated his concession about SDI research. On the issue of INF, Gorbachev reiterated his zero-level suggestion, but also went further as he dropped his earlier demand that French and British weapons should be frozen at existing levels.

As we can expect from Reagan's beliefs, his position was much less conciliatory. He was able to accept the removal of Soviet and U.S. INF missiles in Europe, which was not a real concession because NATO allies of the United States were in a position to maintain their missiles. On SDI and space weapon testing, he remained uncompromising. Reagan was prepared to consider a ten-year period regarding a nonwithdrawal from the ABM Treaty, as suggested by Gorbachev. He conditioned it, however, by the call for an agreement with the provision that at the end of the period each side would legitimately be able to deploy ABM defenses.

In Reykjavik, Reagan and Gorbachev reached "near-agreements" on the elimination of nuclear weapons, an elimination of Soviet and U.S. INF missiles in Europe, and the prospect of removing all ballistic missiles. Given that these agreements did not include British and French cuts, given that an elimination of ballistic missiles would be significantly more disadvantageous to the Soviet Union than to the United States, and given that Reagan would make no concession regarding SDI, the Soviet hope for a *quid pro quo* was disappointed. Worse, upon the conclusion of the summit, the United States declared that it would "actively oppose any application by the Soviet Union for membership in the World Bank or the International Monetary Fund" (296).

Although by the end of the year superpower relations were still in a slump, there was nevertheless value to Gorbachev's persistence. His New Thinking had "made inroads in American public opinion and among the domestic opponents of Reagan's hard-line foreign policy" (Goldstein and Freeman 1990, 122). It was the mounting pressure from this arena that would soon serve as a stimulus for Reagan to reevaluate his stance toward the Soviet Union. Other stimuli would emanate from further interaction with the Soviet Union, in which the latter would push increasingly toward cooperation.

Reagan Reverses Course

In the last two years of the Reagan administration, Gorbachev remained "committed to change" although he was frustrated by the "slow U.S. response" (Zemtsov and Farrar 1989, 122–123). Through his preceding efforts, Gorbachev had experienced failures and now he set out for new trials. These would soon bear fruit.

Although Reagan's actions toward the Soviet Union had not changed much in the first two years, his beliefs underwent changes in the next two years, revealing that he engaged in complex learning. Overall, the significant differences in mean scores in table 6.1 indicate that Reagan's enemy image of Gorbachev in Periods 1 and 2 gave way to a new image in Period 3 of friendlier attributes and a corresponding shift in Reagan's own strategic image of how to manage Soviet–American relations. Reagan now views the political universe (P-1) in significantly more cooperative terms and is significantly more optimistic (P-2) about the realization of his political values. In the realm of instrumental beliefs, the results indicate that Reagan's strategic approach to goals (I-1) and intensity of tactics (I-2) become significantly more cooperative. He is more likely to take risks (I-3) in order to achieve cooperation, and he has a significantly lower propensity to shift between cooperative and conflictual tactics (I-4a). Here he values appeal tactics (I-5c) significantly more than previously, and his belief in the utility of oppose (I-5d) and punish tactics (I-5f) decreased significantly.

Similarly, Reagan's aggregated VICS scores for Period 3 indicate a mutually cooperative stance in the period between 1987 and 1988. They specify a Reward/Deter strategy for Self (I-1 = .53, P-4a = .23) and Other (P-1 = .38, P-4b = .19). Reagan's redefined strategy ranks settlement over deadlock over domination over submission. At the same time he perceives Gorbachev to have the same preference ordering. The initial state of deadlock (3,3) reflects Reagan's belief that there continued to be points of mutual contention between the superpowers after Reykjavik. However, he appears to believe now that rapprochement would be possible. The conflict game of prisoner's dilemma during the previous two years, in Reagan's mind, had been transformed into a no conflict game of mutual assurance. This game predicts that the player with the next move will move toward a final state of (4,4) with the anticipation that the other player will reciprocate.

The most significant gesture came first from Gorbachev. In an unprecedented move, he decoupled SDI from any INF missiles agreements on February 28 (Crockatt 1995, 361). This concession put the INF element of the nuclear arms talks, which had been deadlocked after the Reykjavik summit, back on track. At the same time Gorbachev also kept stressing his agenda of "reasonable sufficiency" in military affairs. A subsequent willingness by the United States to cooperate was shown in bilateral diplomatic consultations throughout 1987. In March 1987, the United States initiated various diplomatic exchanges continuing through September. Discussions were held regarding communication exchanges, the UN, human rights, and regional conflicts. Of particular importance was that both sides together attempted to bring a resolution to conflicts in the Middle East, the Far East, and Southeast Asia.

Reagan clearly welcomed these steps and displayed a cooperative attitude as well. However, now he challenged the Soviet Union to include shorter-range INF (SRINF) missiles in any agreement to protect allied security interests. Gorbachev conceded and proposed to first freeze and then cut these systems. On July 23, he proposed a global double zero, eliminating all INF and SRINF in Asia and in Europe. This offer was very generous as the Soviet Union had approximately 160 SRINF missile launchers operationally deployed while the United States had none (Garthoff 1994, 312; Gormley 1988). At this point Reagan started to signal further cooperation. Negotiations on INF continued throughout the summer and culminated in a summit in Washington in December.

Relations between the superpowers clearly improved. In July, Reagan argued that his objective was to "break out of the stalemate of the Cold War . . . to dispel rather than to live with the two great darkening clouds of the postwar era . . ." (Reagan 1987a). He then asked the Soviets to reduce military secrecy. Already prior to Reagan's statement, Gorbachev "expressed readiness for joint calibration tests for nuclear tests that could verify a ban on virtually all tests" (Garthoff 1994, 317). Gorbachev engaged in still more unilateral efforts. In the fall, for example, "Soviet ballistic missile submarine patrols off the U.S. coast were discontinued. And for the first time in a decade, there was no Soviet naval visit to the Caribbean" (318).

In September, Reagan met with Soviet foreign minister Shevardnadze in Washington. They agreed to negotiate the elimination of INF and SRINF, and reached an agreement on the implementation of "full-scale, stage-by-stage negotiations" on nuclear testing (Reagan 1987b). In contrast to earlier negotiations where Reagan did not include European missiles, he now agreed to withdraw the nuclear warheads from 72 German missiles. Furthermore, Shevardnadze and his American counterpart Schultz signed an agreement committing both sides to establishing "Nuclear Risk Reduction Centers in Washington and Moscow to exchange information and notifications required by various arms agreements in order to reduce the risk of miscalculation or misunderstanding . . ." (Garthoff 1994, 320).

On December 8, Reagan and Gorbachev convened in Washington and signed the INF Treaty.[8] It entailed the "complete elimination of an entire class of U.S. and Soviet nuclear arms" (Reagan 1987c). Both sides agreed to destroy all of their intermediate and shorter-range land-based missiles and their launchers. The treaty also set in place the mutual monitoring arrangements of nuclear facilities and deemed it legitimate for both sides to engage in extensive and intrusive verification inspections (Garthoff 1994, 327). Regarding the Strategic Arms Reduction Treaty (START), both sides agreed that they would "find a mutually acceptable solution to the question of limiting the deployment of long range nuclear armed SLCM's (Ship Launched Cruise Missiles)." Summarizing further, Garthoff writes that "[s]everal procedures for verification were agreed on, building on the INF breakthrough. Another agreement was reached on an overall ceiling of 4900 ballistic missiles within the agreed-on ceiling of 6000 delivery vehicles" (328). Where the two sides found no agreements was on SDI and the ABM Treaty. Nevertheless, until their next meeting in Moscow relations continued to improve.

On February 21, Schultz went to Moscow to meet with Shevardnadze and Gorbachev in preparation for the planned summit. On this occasion progress was made for the first time in the economic realm. Schultz conveyed Reagan's commitment to work toward a reduction of the Western Coordinating Committee (COCOM) restrictions on trade with the Soviet Union and also to ease its own restraints. On March 23, Schultz and Shevardnadze implemented their agreement from September of the previous year: Nuclear Risk Reduction centers were opened in Moscow and Washington. One month later both signed bilateral agreements on Afghanistan (Schultz and Reagan 1988). In a final presummit meeting, Schultz and Shevardnadze signed "an agreement specifying that the INF Treaty covered similar categories of intermediate-range weapons based on other physical principles, plugging a gap in INF Treaty Coverage" (Garthoff 1994, 347).

Diplomatic consultations between the superpowers also continued in the meantime. Assistant Secretary Murphy met Shevardnadze in March to discuss Middle East issues, and the following month Deputy Minister Rogachev and Assistant Secretary Schiffer discussed politics in East Asia and the Pacific. Again one month later, Assistant Secretary Crocker met with Deputy Minister Adamishin to discuss the African region. Probably the most important meeting (and the first of its kind since 1979) was between Secretary of Defense Carlucci and Minister of Defense Yazov. The subjects of discussion were military doctrine and conventional force reductions. Both sides "expressed satisfaction with the meeting and

committed themselves to continue contacts at various levels."
Congressional visits increased and so did "unofficial cooperation, including
trials of nuclear testing detection equipment in January at both the Nevada
and Semipalatsink nuclear test ranges" (342–343).

At the Moscow summit, Gorbachev and Reagan made progress with
regard to the long-stalemated START negotiations, in particular with
respect to mobile intercontinental missiles and air-launched missiles. The two
foreign ministers signed agreements regarding advance notifications of ICBM
test launchings and on joint efforts regarding the monitoring of underground
nuclear test limitations. Reagan and Gorbachev also extended a 1973 agreement on peaceful uses of nuclear energy. Further cooperative arrangements
were concluded on fishing rights, sea search and rescue, long range radio
navigation in the northern Pacific region, transportation technology,
expanded civil space cooperation, and cultural exchanges.

The traditional dynamic at previous meetings was that Gorbachev
conceded more than Reagan. So it happened this time. Gorbachev
concluded that "more could have been achieved" (quoted in Garthoff
1994, 359). However, he also concluded some substantial new Soviet initiatives were necessary to move Soviet–U.S. relations further forward.
Between the Moscow summit and the next major event in Soviet–U.S.
relations, which would follow with Gorbachev's appearance at the UN,
negotiations on strategic arms reductions continued. So did negotiations
toward a ban on chemical weapons as well as diplomatic consultations on
bilateral and regional issues.

At his UN speech on December 7, Gorbachev laid out new Soviet
initiatives. He expressed "keen interest in an invigorated role of the United
Nations with active Soviet cooperation, publicly signaling an end to the
traditional Soviet position of regarding the United Nations as a forum for
continuing Cold War competition" (Sternthal 1997, 127–128). For
Gorbachev, the practice of international politics had departed from realist
zero-sum assumptions. He announced a unilateral reduction of the Soviet
armed forces by 500,000 troops, with a particular emphasis on withdrawals
and reductions from Eastern Europe. He included a withdrawal and dis-
banding of offensive weaponry—six tank divisions from central Europe,
including 5000 tanks and 50,000 men. Additionally, "Gorbachev noted
that in all the Soviet forces in Europe would be cut by 10,000 tanks, 8500
artillery pieces, and 800 combat aircraft." He concluded by emphasizing a
"deideologization of foreign policy" and an endorsement of "freedom for
choice" for all peoples (Blacker 1991, 437; Crockatt 1995, 363; Sakwa
1990, 334; White 1990, 151–161).

Reagan welcomed these steps and signaled further U.S. reciprocation, which would later be implemented by his successor. By the time Reagan reached the end of his presidency in 1988, international politics had been transformed and the most prominent theory within the realm of security studies, namely realism, was in trouble. One of the two superpowers had stopped playing power politics, although states in a realist account are described as being "engaged in a never-ending struggle to improve or preserve their relative power positions" (Gilpin 1975, 35). The unexpected would continue in 1989 and beyond.

Conclusion

Forecasting the future of U.S.–Soviet relations in 1987, two observers write: "Whoever they are, and whatever changes have occurred in the meantime, the American and Soviet leaders of the next century will be wrestling with the same great issue—how to manage their rivalry so as to avoid a nuclear catastrophe—that has engaged the energies, in the latter half of the 1980s, of Ronald Reagan and Mikhail Gorbachev" (Mandelbaum and Talbott 1987). Yet, this scenario never came to be *because* of these two leaders. "It takes two to tango," was Reagan's reply to a query about the prospects for improving relations with the Soviet Union (quoted in Mandelbaum and Talbott 1987, 33). I agree, as I have demonstrated in this study that it takes a teacher *and* a learner. Through his strategy of altercasting, Gorbachev managed to change the constitutive rules of the game and to overcome the enduring rivalry between the Soviet Union and the United States. By the end of 1988, international politics had undergone tremendous change. Reagan and Gorbachev together demonstrated that this is "a world of our making," that anarchy has no predetermined logic, indeed that "anarchy is what states make of it" (Onuf 1989; Wendt 1992).

Through the use of operational code analysis in combination with sequential game theory, I have shown that a systematic, quantifiable, and thereby reproducible study of ideational variables is possible. It is crucial to employ objective and replicable methods to escape the recurring (and valid) criticism of subjectivism. If carried out properly, ideational scholarship can contribute to our understanding of political behavior by encouraging the problematization of actors' preferences and investigating the ways in which they shape actors' behavior. Ultimately, it is leaders who make and implement decisions. Therefore, we cannot dispense with a systematic study of these agents of foreign policy change and the transformation of international relations.

Notes

1. For previous interesting attempts to endogenize preferences within a general rationalist or game-theoretic framework, see Becker (1996), Clark (1998), Cohen and Axelrod (1984), Elster (1982), and Raub (1990).

2. For evidence that Gorbachev did, in fact, pursue an altercasting strategy, see Malici (2004).

3. For each interval I constructed a pool of public statements that were subjected to the following coding procedures. In sampling Reagan's public statements, I followed Walker, Schafer, and Young (1998, 182) who set the following criteria for foreign policy speeches: "(1) the subject and object are international in scope; (2) the focus of interaction is a political issue; (3) the words and deeds are cooperative or conflictual." The sample of speech acts was drawn from the *Lexis Nexis Academic Universe* and the Public Papers of President Ronald W. Reagan database at the University of Texas (http://www.reagan.utexas.edu/resource/speeches/rrpubpap.asp). Each speech act had to be at least 1500 words long in order to be subjected to the coding procedures. Due to the relatively short time periods and small number of statements in the sampling frame, a random sample from a large pool was not necessary. The final pool contained a total of 14, 13, and 18 public statements, respectively, for the three intervals.

4. The Compel/Punish strategies attributed to Reagan and Gorbachev are determined through TIP and by reference to speech acts by a norming group of different world leaders from various regions and historical eras. Important questions for applying TIP are whether Reagan's I-1 and P-1 beliefs are above or below the mean for the norming group and whether his P-4 beliefs are greater, less than, or within one standard deviation of the mean for the norming group. Since these questions investigate variation rather than central tendency, aggregated scores rather than mean scores for Reagan are calculated to determine distance from the mean scores ($n = 255$) for the norming group (P-1 = .25, SD = .32; I-1 = +.33, SD = .47; P-4 = .21, SD = .12).

5. Brams (1994, 77–78) classifies the prisoner's dilemma game as a magnanimity game in which his sequential game theory prescribes a mutual cooperation (3,3) solution rather than a (2,2) deadlock solution when the initial state is either (4,1) or (1,4). His rationale for magnanimity is that the player with the highest rank preference in one of these initial states will move to (3,3) in order to prevent the player with the lowest ranked preference from moving to (2,2). When the initial state is (2,2), however, TOM's nonmyopic solution is a final state of (2,2) in a single play of the game. Brams does not consider the possibility that, under the assumption of repeated plays of the game, altercasting by one player is an extension of the logic of magnanimity and may be considered a rational strategic choice. By shifting to a cooperative strategy in moving toward the cell with his lowest-ranking preference, this player may induce the other player to reciprocate and

move toward (3,3) rather than risk a subsequent return to (2,2) in the absence of reciprocation. In effect, an altercasting strategy by Gorbachev is an attempt to create a new initial state in which Reagan will then recognize that it is now magnanimous to move to (3,3).

6. On cognitive consistency, which discusses an individual's relative openness or resistance to new information, see Abelson et al. (1968), Abelson and Rosenberg (1958), Glass (1968), Heider (1958), Osgood (1960), and Zajonc (1960). For some applications to foreign policy analysis, see Adelman (1973), Hermann (1984), Holsti (1967), and Jervis (1976).

7. *Pravda*, June 12, 1986. The proposal called for mutual force reductions of 100,000–150,000 troops within a period of two years, to be then followed by additional reductions of 350,000–400,000 troops.

8. The text of the INF Treaty is reproduced in *Survival* 30 (March/April 1988), 162–180.

CHAPTER 7

CRISIS DEFERRED: AN OPERATIONAL CODE ANALYSIS OF CHINESE LEADERS ACROSS THE STRAIT

Huiyun Feng

With increasing tensions over the Taiwan Strait after the reelection victory of the independence-oriented, Democratic Progressive Party (DPP) of Chen Shuibian, speculations and concerns over the future of Taiwan and Sino-American relations have intensified. Will China use force against Taiwan? A crucial related question is what should the United States do? The implications of a Taiwan Strait conflict for the United States are complicated and far-reaching. Discussions have focused on what strategies the Chinese People's Liberation Army will adopt to overcome the defense of Taiwan and avoid direct counterforce by the United States. The Taiwanese are debating whether Taiwan should get more offensive weapons systems.

The Taiwan issue is one of high political sensitivity to three major parties—Mainland People's Republic of China (PRC), Taiwan, and the United States. The repercussions of a potential military conflict between the Mainland and Taiwan may draw the United States in under the Taiwan Relations Act (TRA) signed in 1979. As a close U.S. ally with self-interested considerations Japan may also get involved in the conflict, which would draw in the three major powers in the Asia-Pacific region. The crisis over Taiwan's recent election has already drawn the major parties toward an arms race that is darkening the whole East Asian security future.

Is war across the Strait unavoidable? If yes, who will provoke it, the Mainland or Taiwan? If not, how can the crisis be deferred? This chapter focuses on these questions by examining Mainland and Taiwan leaders' beliefs and belief changes during the recent election crisis. I argue in this chapter that in assessing the future conflict over the Taiwan Strait, it is necessary to consider leaders' beliefs in addition to situational factors. The chapter proceeds in four parts: (i) a review of the general situation regarding the Taiwan Strait; (ii) theoretical assumptions about crisis analysis and leaders' beliefs; (iii) operational code analyses of the two current leaders from Mainland and Taiwan and the subjective games in their belief systems; (iv) conclusions and policy implications.

Dire Strait?

Taiwan's two elected presidents, Lee Tenghui and Chen Shuibian, seem to have consistently and gradually pursued "the Taiwan identity" from the middle of the 1990s (Shlapak, Odetsky, and Wilson 2000). Lee's speech on a "state-to-state" relationship with the Mainland initiated a period of crisis[1] with China's launching of missile tests in late 1995–1996. Although Chen Shuibian initiated the "five nos" in his first term inauguration speech in 2000,[2] which ended that crisis with the Mainland, his defensive referendum[3] and proposed constitutional revisions precipitated a new crisis in 2004. Perceptual differences over the issue of Taiwan's political status have hindered further Cross-Strait talks. Making the situation worse, one of the most crucial negotiators initiating the talks, Gu Zhenfu from Taiwan, died recently. Taiwan's past two presidents, Lee Tenghui and Chen Shuibian, seem to be pushing further on the drive for independence and causing more tension.

With the reelection to a second term of Taiwan's Chen Shuibian in March 2004, tensions between the Mainland and Taiwan increased again. On the one hand, Chen initiated a defensive referendum held together with the election in March 2004, advocated possible changes of titles for Taiwan's diplomatic offices abroad, and planned constitutional change for Taiwan in the form of a referendum in 2006 and final revisions in 2008. On the other hand, mainland officials and the State Council's Taiwan Information Office issued a strong message to Taiwan over the defensive referendum and constitutional change. The constitutional revision in Beijing's eyes is tantamount to a declaration of independence. Beijing distrusts Chen deeply, believing that Chen is playing a strategy of moving gradually toward independence under disguise.

China watchers are concerned that before the 2008 Olympics, there might be a confrontation.[4] Former Taiwan President Lee Tenghui even mentioned that, due to the Chinese concern over the Olympic games, it might be a good opportunity for Taiwan to declare independence in 2008. Pessimists believe that it is an urgent situation because the Taiwan leader Chen is a risk taker. They argue that as Taiwan's independence is his and his party's lifelong pursuit, he will definitely give it a try before his second term is over. The PRC military posture is also pushing many Taiwanese further away rather than drawing them closer as expected from closer economic and cultural exchanges. It is generally believed that Chinese aggressive polices, such as the military exercises across the Strait, have turned out to be counterproductive, as seen from the victory of the pro-independent DPP's Chen in Taiwan in 2000.

Views differ over the level of danger posed by the reelection of Chen Shuibian. Some think that despite "all the rhetoric, there is little immediate risk of conflict" (Taiwan's Elections, Seen from the Mainland 2004) due to the lack of a concerted policy position from the PRC side over the referendum in particular. Many do agree that the danger for military conflict is real, possible, and foreseeable; however, some also believe it is avoidable (Carpenter 2005). David Lampton (2004) stresses, "[C]ross-Strait relations are entering a new and more dangerous phase." David Shambaugh points out that, "The issue is shifting, therefore, from one of deterrence and balance to one of confidence-building and tension reduction . . . The question is whether the Taiwan government, after the elections, will be inclined to move in this direction" (Luard 2004). China scholars have detected a trend in the Chinese media following the reelection of Chen Shuibian toward a harder line on Chen, indicating an increasing sense of impatience (Mulvenon 2004). Despite the victory of the Pan-Blue camp led by Kuomingtang (KMT) with the First People's Party and the New Party in the December Legislative Yuan (LY) election, Beijing has stressed that tensions across the strait may continue (Cross-Strait Tensions May Continue despite Elections 2005).

Beijing's Concerns

Taiwan was part of the Chinese territory back in the Qing Dynasty. The Qing was defeated in a war with Japan in 1894–1895, and Taiwan was taken by Japan for 50 years. After the anti-Japanese War (World War II), the Nationalist government then took back the Island, which became their refuge in 1949 after being defeated in the Civil War with the Chinese Communist Party (CCP). The CCP ever since has stressed the course of reunification with Taiwan. The military effort at reunification was interrupted by the Korean War in the early 1950s and the extension of U.S. military assistance to Taiwan.

The Taiwan issue was constantly in the minds of the Chinese leaders during the cold war. For Mao, it was the unfinished business of the Civil War. He advocated unification of the motherland by the use of force. Deng proclaimed that China can wait one hundred years but it will never give up Taiwan. "It is true that under Deng, China's policy altered dramatically from liberation by force to peaceful unification" (Scobell 2002, 31).[5] According to Scobell, this policy change was more tactical than strategic. The strategic significance of Taiwan was not forgotten by the Chinese leaders. Deng proposed Hong Kong's "one country, two systems" framework to Taiwan, which was followed by Jiang during his administration. In addition, Jiang put forward his "Eight-Point Proposal" in 1995 as the guiding principle concerning Cross-Strait political relations.

The basic line for Beijing over reunification has stressed the policy of "peaceful reunification and one country, two systems."[6] The "One China Principle"[7] was the most fundamental. There is only one China and Taiwan is an inalienable part of China. The PRC government is the sole representative of China who opposes any separatist moves. Although the Mainland proposes "peaceful" reunification, it has never given up the use of force should Taiwan declare independence.

Since Hu Jintao came to power in 2003, the Mainland's Taiwan policy has became even tougher and more aggressive because of Taiwan leaders' provocative pro-independence policies. Beijing has emphasized through official media and academic sources that reunification, sovereignty, and territorial integrity are more important than economic achievements and the Olympics. In other words, China is ready to sacrifice all of these for reunification. At the Fourth Plenum of the sixteenth Central Committee of the Communist party held in September 2004, Hu took over the military's high command from Jiang. As the chairman of the Central Military Committee, Hu's first speech stressed the determination and will to use force should Taiwan declare independence. An anti-secession Law was also forwarded to the National People's Congress for consideration at their next session in March 2005.

In the recent 2004 Defense White Paper (see note 6), the Chinese government points out that "Taiwan independence forces have increasingly become the biggest immediate threat to China's sovereignty and territorial integrity as well as peace and stability on both sides of the Taiwan Strait and the Asia-Pacific region as a whole." Hu's leadership stressed "[S]hould the Taiwan authorities go so far as to make a reckless attempt that constitutes a major incident of 'Taiwan independence,' the Chinese people and armed forces will resolutely and thoroughly crush it at any cost." Some scholars point out that although this year's Defense White Paper was not as tough as the 2000 one, it shows the extent of Chinese leaders' resolve over Taiwan. Mainland officials had been tough regarding the Taiwan elections, trying to sway voters to vote for their preferred candidates. However, their two efforts in 1996 and 2000 only met with increased opposition from Taiwan. This year the Chinese government has conducted less saber rattling, yet the Taiwanese leader Chen's defensive referendum stirred up another round of criticism of his and the DPP's independence orientation.

The Taiwan issue has turned into one of political legitimacy for the current Chinese leadership. Therefore, even though there might be changes and reforms in foreign policies in general, there will not be any change in the Taiwan policy (Suettinger 2004). The urgency over the Taiwan issue has only increased. Despite dissensions within and between the leadership, neither Jiang and Hu nor their successors can afford to lose Taiwan. In addition, the Taiwan issue is directly linked to other regions with separatist activities, Tibet and Xinjiang. The Chinese government defines the Taiwan issue as one of internal affairs; therefore, international interference goes directly to encroaching on the sovereignty and territorial integrity of China. This calls to mind the historical Chinese humiliation over foreign exploitation. While the Taiwan authorities stress that there is a unique Taiwan identity, the Chinese government stresses that people on both sides of the Strait share a great Chinese identity. A common culture, shared history, and the Confucian tradition are the determining factors for this identity. The strategic importance of Taiwan to the Mainland is also undeniable as a further extension of its coastlines.

Both parties have let rhetoric be the main weapon up to now. Both displayed restraint while the United States was moderating and mediating.[8] The United States tries to deter Beijing from exerting its military posture to threaten the Island and keeps on providing highly advanced defensive weapon systems to Taiwan under the TRA. At the same time it seems more and more difficult to rein in Taiwan president Chen Shuibian. George Bush is trying to warn Taiwan to refrain from actions that might change the status quo, thus provoking Beijing and dragging the United States into a confrontation with Beijing.

On the one hand, time is running out for the Mainland as the new generations in Taiwan and the Mainland are less concerned with the reunification of the motherland. On the other hand, the military balance is leaning toward the mainland with its increasing number of short-range missiles and kilo-submarines. The arms sales from the United States to Taiwan are constantly drawing criticisms from the Mainland while domestic pressure is also increasing on the Taiwan leadership for the procurement of arms systems from the United States even for defensive purposes. To show somehow their resolve to attack and to defend, respectively, both Mainland and Taiwan have followed their threats with military exercises in which the other party is the potential target.

Crises and Leaders' Beliefs

Scholars analyze the Taiwan situation from different perspectives, focusing either on the international system or domestic politics, which affect leaders' decisions. Both of the previous two elections Taiwan held in 1996 and 2000 resulted in crisis situations short of a military confrontation between the two sides, although U.S. warships ended up in the Taiwan Strait in 1996. The 2004 election witnessed fewer military moves by both parties; however, tension again intensified when Chen initiated the defensive referendum. During the two previous crises, how political leaders made decisions affected the final outcomes of the events. If Jiang had not conducted military exercises across the Strait, the pro-independence leaders, such as Lee in 1996 and Chen in 2000, might not have been elected. By the same token, if Chen were not reelected in 2004 and had not pushed for the referendum, the tension across the Taiwan Strait might not have heated up again. Therefore, to explain and predict the Taiwan situation, we cannot neglect the role of key political leaders from both sides.

Decision makers' beliefs are a critical factor in understanding, diagnosing, and prescribing the decision-making process of states particularly under situations featuring high uncertainty and incomplete information. "The belief system sets bounds within which interpretations are accepted or rejected" (Vertzberger 1990, 123). Besides the international structural constraints on rational actors and domestic political influences on actors' choices, beliefs also limit and influence the choices by directing and causing state decision-making elites (the key decision-making individuals, small groups, or key bureaucracies) to orient toward particular preferences in policies.

As anarchy is what the state makes of it (Wendt 1992), so individual leaders' beliefs "serve as guides to information processing and become a baseline for interpretations, expectations, and predictions of others' behavior" (113). To study beliefs in situations like crises is essential, as the individual's belief system takes on a central role in the processing of information by representing all the hypotheses and theories that a leader is convinced are valid at a given moment in time. They help to make sense of the cues and signals picked up from the environment. "Thus beliefs provide him with a relatively coherent way of organizing them" (114). Beliefs can have three major causal effects on foreign policy decisions: mirroring effects, steering effects, and learning effects (Goldstein and Keohane 1993;

Walker 2002; Walker and Schafer n.d.).[9] The joint impact of beliefs and the environment condition a leader's capability to make decisions and may lead to policy choices that are suboptimal. In Chinese decision making, despite the high consensus for key decisions, the influence of key decision makers, for example, Mao, Deng, Jiang, and Hu, as the core decision figures is prominent and exceptional. Therefore, studying the beliefs of these key decision makers is essential and valid in understanding and explaining Chinese foreign policy behavior.

To better understand Chinese foreign policy behavior, cultural factors are important but not easy to understand. Scholars disagree about how many strategic cultures China has, specifically, if there is one or two strategic cultures. Some state that China has only one strategic culture, which is realpolitik because Confucianism does not function in actual policy making (Kane 2001).[10] Johnston (1995a, b) argues that China's security behavior actually originates from its strategic culture and Chinese decision makers have internalized a strategic culture of *realpolitik*. He claims that a Parabellum strategic culture of realpolitik, and not a Confucian strategic culture of accommodation, guides Chinese foreign policy behavior as seen from its grand strategy (Johnston 1995a; Scobell 2002; Wang 2002). Others stress that China has one strategic culture, but it is the Confucian strategic culture that influences the beliefs and behavior of Chinese leaders (Zhang 2002). A more complex view is that there are two strategic cultures, and the Chinese apply the Confucian strategic culture when building upon their self image while resorting to the realist Parabellum norms when encountering other countries (Scobell 2002). Scobell (2001) calls this a "Chinese Cult of Defense."

Whether it is a Confucian or Parabellum strategic culture that is functioning in Chinese decision making is actually a very complex question. It is not either/or, but rather when/which. Chinese leaders may be Confucian or Parabellum in general, but they may change to the opposite type under different situations and before different audiences. In particular, any leader might turn more aggressive under a high security threat as in the case of crisis and war. A leader may be stable, or he or she may change due to external factors. These questions deserve further exploration when studying leaders' beliefs. I employ operational code analysis here to study the individual's beliefs under different situations in order to assess what kind of strategic culture is influencing Chinese decision making particularly under crisis situations.

Operational Code Analysis

Although both Mainland and Taipei try to show their strength, determination, and will in what they say, whether their beliefs show the same intended effects is worth studying. In order to study the intentions and motivations behind leaders' speeches regarding the Taiwan Strait, this study employs an automated content analysis of Beijing and Taiwanese leaders' public speeches. In particular, in this chapter I focus on the two current Mainland and Taiwan leaders and the 2004 election crisis. I analyze and compare Hu's and Chen's operational codes in an effort to speculate on the future of Cross-Strait relations.

To compare and contrast the general operational code beliefs of Hu Jintao and Chen Shuibian, a series of Analysis of Variance (ANOVA) tests are conducted to compare the mean scores of these leaders with each other and with a norming group of world leaders. These comparisons are to test their general beliefs toward the world and their general strategic orientations. A Multivariate Analysis of Variance (MANOVA) test of the influence of leader versus situation is also conducted to assess the impact of audiences and crises on these leaders' beliefs.

Table 7.1 presents the general operational code beliefs of Hu Jintao and Chen Shuibian. Comparing their general beliefs to a norming group of world leaders, we can see that the two leaders differ significantly from the average world leader in all their major beliefs. They are more cooperative in their view of the nature of the political universe (P-1), and in their strategic (I-1) and tactical (I-2) orientations. They are also more optimistic toward the realization of political values (P-2) compared with the average world leader. Hu shows lower control over historical development compared with the Taiwan leader whose view of control over historical development is close to the average world leader (P-4).

A one-way ANOVA of Hu and Chen was also conducted to see if there are any significant differences between them. The results show ($p < .05$ 2-tailed) that Hu and Chen's general operational code beliefs differ significantly for most of their philosophical beliefs (P-1, P-2, P-3, P-4). In general, Hu sees the nature of the political universe as friendlier than Chen (P-1), thus he is more optimistic about the realization of political values (P-2). Hu sees the political future as more predictable than Chen (P-3) but Hu shows lower historical control than Chen (P-4). There are also a few differences in their instrumental beliefs. Chen's shift propensity between words and deeds (I-4b) is much lower than Hu and the norming group. Hu is less likely to use threaten and promise strategies (I-5TH, I-5PR) than Chen and more likely to use reward means (I-5RE). These results remain stable in 2004.[11] The MANOVA analysis later assesses the stability of these results in crisis and noncrisis situations and before domestic and international audiences.

Table 7.1   A Comparison of the General Operational Codes of Hu Jintao and Chen Shuibian with the Norming Group

		Hu (N = 50)	Norming Group (N = 255)	Chen (N = 32)
Philosophical beliefs				
P-1	Nature of political universe (Conflict/Cooperation)	0.55★★★	0.250	0.46★★★
P-2	Realization of political values (Optimism/Pessimism)	0.38★★★	0.118	0.28★★★
P-3	Political future (Unpredictable/Predictable)	0.19★★	0.148	0.13
P-4	Historical development (Low control/High control)	0.15★★	0.212	0.21
P-5	Role of chance (Small role/Large role)	0.97	0.968	0.97
Instrumental beliefs				
I-1	Strategic approach to goals (Conflict/Cooperation)	0.62★★★	0.334	0.57★★
I-2	Intensity of tactics (Conflict/Cooperation)	0.32★★★	0.139	0.27★★
I-3	Risk orientation (Averse/Acceptant)	0.37★	0.304	0.33
I-4	Timing of action			
	a. Conflict/Cooperation	0.37★★	0.509	0.41★
	b. Words/Deeds	0.17	0.525	0.29★★★
I 5	Utility of means			
	Reward	0.20	0.167	0.11★
	Promise	0.07	0.073	0.15★★
	Appeal	0.55★★	0.427	0.53★★
	Oppose	0.12	0.147	0.13
	Threaten	0.02★	0.047	0.05
	Punish	0.05★★	0.138	0.04★★

★   Significant at p ≤ .10 level (two-tailed) from the norming group.

★★   Significant at p ≤ .05 level (two-tailed) from the norming group.

★★★   Significant at p ≤ .001 level (two-tailed) from the norming group.

Crisis and Audience Effects

To test the impact of crisis on the two current leaders' beliefs during crisis periods in front of domestic and international audiences, a three-way MANOVA test of leader, situation and audience is conducted for Hu and Chen. The public statements of both leaders are divided into crisis and noncrisis periods for domestic and international audiences.[12] This three-way MANOVA design is to determine whether the differences between the two leaders are stable across crisis and noncrisis periods and before domestic and international audiences. In addition, does the additional burden of facing reelection in the case of Chen have an impact on his operational code during crisis periods? Specifically, the following directional hypotheses are tested. During a crisis situation, both Hu and Chen will:

H-1: View the political universe as less friendly (P-1).
H-2: Be less optimistic about the realization of political goals (P-2).
H-3: See the political future as less predictable (P-3).
H-4: Believe that control over historical development is lower (P-4).

These hypotheses test the stability of the previous differences in the philosophical beliefs between Hu and Chen, controlling for situation (crisis/noncrisis) and audience (domestic/international). These two variables may interact with one another to qualify further the stability of these differences. The MANOVA will also be run with the remaining VICS indices as dependent variables to see if they are affected by the addition of these control variables. The difference between the two leaders for one philosophical belief (P-4) control over historical development remains significant before both audiences during both crisis and noncrisis situations with Hu (.160) showing lower control than Chen (.215). The MANOVA results in table 7.2 also show that there are some three-way interaction effects on the philosophical beliefs (P-1, P-2, P-3, P-5).

In front of a domestic audience, Hu views the nature of the political universe (P-1) as slightly less cooperative during crisis situations while Chen's view is much less cooperative. Facing an international audience, Hu sees a less friendly world during crisis situations while Chen sees a friendlier world in a similar situation. Addressing a domestic audience, Hu is slightly more optimistic (P-2) during crisis than during noncrisis situations but Chen is much less optimistic. When facing an international audience, Hu turns less optimistic during crisis while Chen turns more optimistic. With a domestic audience, Hu views the political future (P-3) as more predictable during crisis, but Chen sees the political future as less predictable.

Table 7.2 (a) Hu and Chen's Beliefs in a Three-Factor Multivariate Analysis of Variance Design (Leader x Audience x Situation)

		Main effects (N = 69)	
Independent factors		F (1, 64)	P Value★ (two-tailed)
Leader	P-4	4.633	.035
	I-4b	2.886	.095
	I-5 RE	3.225	.078
Audience	N.S.		
Situation	N.S.		
Leader x situation	I-5PR	3.076	.084
Audience x situation	I-3	3.584	.063
	I-5PU	2.780	.101
	I-5PR	4.412	.039
Leader x audience	N.S.		
Leader x situation x audience	P-1	9.688	.003
	P-2	5.826	.019
	P-3	4.549	.037
	P-5	3.188	.079

(b) Hu and Chen's Mean Scores for the Interaction Effects of Leader x Audience x Situation

P-1	Hu		Chen	
	Noncrisis	Crisis	Noncrisis	Crisis
Domestic	.461	.456	.770	.443
International	.643	.595	.320	.503
P-2	Hu		Chen	
	Noncrisis	Crisis	Noncrisis	Crisis
Domestic	.310	.336	.475	.264
International	.426	.415	.198	.312
P-3	Hu		Chen	
	Noncrisis	Crisis	Noncrisis	Crisis
Domestic	.152	.161	.205	.119
International	.206	.181	.105	.145
P-5	Hu		Chen	
	Noncrisis	Crisis	Noncrisis	Crisis
Domestic	.979	.975	.950	.970
International	.952	.975	.975	.974

★ P ≤.10 level (two-tailed)

Facing an international audience, Hu sees the political future as less predictable in crisis while Chen shows more confidence. Finally, Hu attributes a lesser role to chance (P-5) during a crisis facing a domestic audience while Chen attributes a greater role. With an international audience, Hu attributes more to the role of chance while Chen attributes slightly less.

The leader still matters for some instrumental beliefs. Hu (.193) is in general more likely to use rewards (I-5RE) than Chen (.107). Hu (.482) is also more likely to shift in his words/deeds (I-4b) than Chen (.285). Situation and audience do not have independent effects. One instrumental belief (I-5PR) has interaction effects between leader and situation when controlling for the audience factor. Chen tends to use more promises during crisis situations (from .082 to .168) while Hu uses fewer promises during crisis situations (from .080 to .068).

There are also some interaction effects for instrumental beliefs (I-3, I-5PU, and I-5PR) between audience and situation controlling for leader effects. When there is a crisis, the two leaders turn more risk averse facing a domestic audience (from .385 to .272) but more risk acceptant facing an international one (from .227 to .435). During crisis, they tend to use more promises domestically (from .028 to .149) and less so facing an international audience (from .121 to .106). Although they use less punishment rhetoric during crisis situations facing either a domestic audience (from .107 to .037) or an international audience (from .047 to .039), the change in front of a domestic audience is much sharper.

In general, the leaders' philosophical belief changes under different situations and audiences display some consistent diagnostic propensities. Hu displays the features of the head of a rising authoritarian state. Hu is more responsive to an international constituency. To maintain the credible claim of territorial integrity over Taiwan, Hu is less cooperative before the international audience to show his strong will during Taiwan's elections against Chen's inclination toward independence. Chen, as a democratically elected and reelected president, is more responsive to the domestic constituency. To draw voters and support, Chen is a strong advocate of Taiwan's independent identity before a domestic audience. If both leaders are more likely to take chances during crisis situations, the future of Cross-Strait relations still remains in the hands of the strategic interaction between the two sides.

Strategic Interaction Analysis

To further compare and contrast the strategic orientations of Hu and Chen during crisis and noncrisis periods, I use the scores from figure 7.1 to map

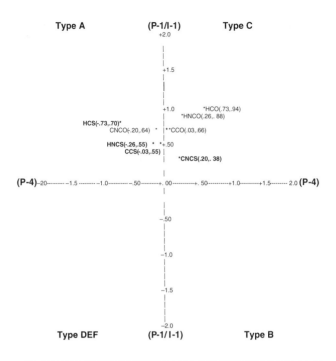

Self scores are in bold. The following abbreviations are used above: HCS = Hu Crisis Self; HCO = Hu Crisis Other; HNCS = Hu Non-Crisis Self; HNCO = Hu Non-Crisis Other; CCS = Chen Crisis Self; CCO = Chen Crisis Other; CNCS = Chen Non-Crisis Self; CNCO = Chen Non-Crisis Other. Scores are aggregated indices from statements in crisis and non-crisis situations for each leader expressed as standard deviations from means for the sample of world leaders in Table 7.1.

Figure 7.1   Operational Codes of Hu and Chen for Crisis and Noncrisis Situations.

Note: Self scores are in bold. The following abbreviations are used in the figure: HCS = Hu Crisis Self; HCO = Hu Crisis Other; HNCS = Hu Noncrisis Self; HNCO = Hu Noncrisis Other; CCS = Chen Crisis Self; CCO = Chen Crisis Other; CNCS = Chen Noncrisis Self; CNCO = Chen NonCrisis Other. Scores are aggregated indices from statements in crisis and noncrisis situations for each leader expressed as standard deviations from means for the sample of world leaders in table 7.1. The asterisks are rough approximations of the coordinates being referred to in parentheses.

their beliefs into sequential games using the Theory of Inferences about Preferences (TIP) in figure 7.2.[13] The two leaders have the same subjective game in both crisis and noncrisis situations. Their Self (I-1) and Other (P-1) scores fall in the upper (cooperative) half of the quadrants in figure 7.1 and cluster within one standard deviation of the mean for the P-4 index of historical control. The subjective game in figure 7.2 is the same for each

Hu and Chen Subjective Game for Crisis and Non-Crisis Situations

	Other				Other	
	CO	CF			CO	CF
CO	4,4 ← 1,2			CO	4,4 →| 1,2	

Self   ↓   ↑   Self   ↑   ↓

| CF | 2,1 | "3,3" | | CF | 2,1 ← | "3,3" |

Self's Strategy   **Other's Strategy**
(I-1, P-4a) Self (+, =)   (I-1, P-4b) Other (+, =)

Chen Subjective Game from New Year 2005 Speech

	China				China	
	CO	CF			CO	CF
CO	3,4 ← 1,2			CO	3,4 →|1,2	

Taiwan ↓   ↑   Taiwan   ↑   ↓

| CF | 4,1 → | "2,3" | | CF | 4,1 \| ← "2,3" | |

Taiwan's Strategy   **China's Strategy**
(I-1, P-4a) Self (−, =)   (I-1, P-4b) Other (+, =)

THEORY OF INFERENCES ABOUT PREFERENCES

(1) If (+, <), then Settle > Deadlock > Submit > Dominate: Appease Strategy
(2) If (+, =), then Settle > Deadlock > Dominate > Submit: Reward/Deter Strategy
(3) If (+, >), then Settle > Dominate > Deadlock > Submit: Exploit Strategy
(4) If (−, <), then Dominate > Settle > Submit > Deadlock: Bluff Strategy
(5) If (−, =), then Dominate > Settle > Deadlock > Submit: Compel/Punish Strategy
(6) If (−, >), then Dominate > Deadlock > Settle > Submit: Bully Strategy.

Figure 7.2   Subjective Games of Hu and Chen.

Note: Initial states are in quotations and final states are underlined. The symbols "→" and "→\|" indicate the respective strategic choices of "move" or "stay" by the player with the next move given the initial state.

leader during both noncrisis and crisis periods. During noncrisis periods, both Hu and Chen prefer to stay at settlement and believe that the other side will also stay. When there is no election or crisis pressure, therefore, the status quo is likely to be maintained. During crisis periods, both leaders will have the opportunity to move to settlement (4,4) as a non–myopic equilibrium, no matter what the initial state is, while predicting the other side will also move to settlement. However, deadlock (3,3) is also a Nash equilibrium for this game.

Although a crisis developed during an election year (2004), neither the elected nor the nonelected leader wanted to escalate into real military conflict. These results may reflect the influence of the United States on the two protagonists. The United States protection of Taiwan under the TRA and potential involvement in a Taiwan Strait conflict causes the Mainland to be cautious. The United States is also a restraining factor on Taiwan's moves toward independence, as is the fear of fighting another war with the PRC.

In order to examine the trend of future strategic interactions between the Mainland and Taiwan, I have also chosen the New Year speeches by Hu and Chen in 2005 for a subjective game analysis.[14] Will the future bode well for Taiwan, as seen from the two leaders' beliefs expressed in these speeches? Talks between Mainland and Taiwan had not yet resumed in January 2005. In his New Year's speech, Hu's subjective game remains unchanged. He continues to think that Mainland China and Taiwan will move toward settlement, which signals an opportunity to resolve the issue peacefully. In the following paragraph from Hu's New Year speech, he offers accommodative words as well as warnings.

> In the coming year, we will continue to implement the basic principle of "peaceful reunification and one country, two systems" and the eight-point proposal on developing Cross-Strait relations and advancing the process of the motherland's reunification in the current stage; promote cross-strait personnel, economic and cultural spheres; and maintain stability in the Taiwan Strait region. Here, I would like to reiterate once again that we are ready to display the greatest sincerity and make the greatest effort in striving for the prospect of peaceful reunification; and we are ready to resume Cross-Strait dialogue and negotiations on the basis of the one China principle. However, we will absolutely not permit anyone to separate Taiwan from China in any form. The Chinese government and the Chinese people will unswervingly defend national sovereignty and territorial integrity. (China's National Defense in 2004, 2004)

The subjective game in Chen's 2005 New Year speech predicts that he will choose to move to settlement while he believes that Mainland China will stay at the initial state of deadlock. Chen's New Year's game in figure 7.2 has a Nash equilibrium of deadlock (2,3) and a non-myopic equilibrium of settlement (3,4) when the initial state is deadlock. However, this non-myopic equilibrium is unstable unless Hu exercises deterrent threat power to keep Chen from moving from (3,4) to (4,1) by shifting from a cooperation (CO) to a conflict (CF) strategy (Brams 1994, 217, Game 27). The effective exercise of threat power by Hu would require either a credible deterrent threat in pre-play communication from an initial state of (3,4) or else a willingness to tolerate repeated plays of the game at higher levels of mutual tension in which China moves to deadlock (2,3) by mobilizing its forces after Chen moves to (4,1). Taiwan has moving power from (3,4), in other words, the ability to cycle in repeated plays of the game (Brams 1994).[15]

Chen may hope to deter Hu from exercising threat power by exploiting Taiwan's relationship with the United States. He wants the United States to continue arms sales under the TAC and protect Taiwan. Thus, a future crisis may only be deferred between the Mainland and Taiwan even if Chen moves to (3,4), and tensions may also escalate if he proves to be in no hurry to move from the (2,3) Nash equilibrium. Although Hu's subjective game predicts that both sides will move to a (4,4) settlement outcome from an initial state of deadlock (3,3), it is not the case that this NME settlement outcome is equally stable as a final outcome in both subjective games.

From this analysis, we can see that although the future of Cross-Strait relations remains ambiguous and difficult to manipulate for all parties concerned, settlement is not unachievable. However, the trend of development up to now is not an optimistic one, as both leaders are becoming more confident in their positions. With Chen in his second term and with Hu consolidating his power over the state, the party, and the military, both need to show resolve for domestic purposes and for international credibility. Chen's loss for taking any risk is less, because he will not need a third term of office. For Hu, a loss will be much more serious for himself and the Party in both the domestic and international arenas.

Conclusion

To sum up, the general operational codes of Hu and Chen show cooperative orientations rather than aggressive ones. Although they do not matter independently, situation and audience do interact with leaders to have different effects on the two leaders' beliefs during a crisis. Retaining the current status quo is a better outcome for both sides, because Beijing will neither have any excuse to take action while Taiwan will neither have to face the fate of conflict with the Mainland nor problems with Washington. However, Chen still wants to move toward a Taiwan identity, and the Mainland does not want this to happen. Therefore, the most preferred outcome by each side is not acceptable as well to the other side, specifically, if Taiwan gets "widely recognized de jure independence" or Beijing realizes "reunification of China on the same 'one country, two systems' basis as Hong Kong" (Taiwan Strait IV 2004).

Even though both sides undertake precautions, there is still the danger of potential conflict if either party's intentions are misperceived or misunderstood. Given the current situation across the Strait, the danger level is indeed high and communications are essential when talks are stalled. Misperception is highly possible with the current level of communications across the Strait, so it is even more essential to analyze what decision makers have on their minds, whether they are stable, and what may affect them to take action. As Hu has just assumed the highest command of the PRC and Chen faces another four years as president, how they think about the Cross-Strait relationship is of long-term interest for all relevant parties.

Finally, an important and crucial factor in the Cross-Strait relationship is the U.S. role. Beijing sees the United States as having heavy leverage in its relationship with Taiwan and, therefore, is upset over continuous U.S. arms sales to Taiwan. In the case of a military conflict over Taiwan, some draw the conclusion that the PLA (People's liberation army) cannot prevail over Taiwan should they choose to attack given U.S. military superiority (Brown, Prueher, and Segel 2003; Shambaugh 2002; Whiting 2005). U.S. policy toward the Taiwan issue had followed strategic ambiguity until George W. Bush stated that the United States would use all means to defend Taiwan in an interview in 2001. The U.S.–China relationship has fluctuated with the Taiwan situation. Now with the focus of the United States on antiterrorism and nuclear proliferation in Northeast Asia, the United States and China are cooperating broadly over these issues.

As China retains the right to use force over Taiwan and the United States continues to be bound under the TRA to provide defense for Taiwan, the situation demands that the United States maintain an ambiguous position and hope the status quo continues. So far, U.S. allies in Asia (Australia, Japan, South Korea, and Singapore) have refrained from promising support in case of sudden Taiwan contingencies. Japan remains a strong ally of the United States, and the China–Japan relationship is deteriorating. Even U.S. arms sales to Taiwan met with strong opposition from the Taiwan public. The Chen administration officials have tried to sell the idea of buying offensive weapons given the perceived Chinese missile threat. The Chinese government strongly opposed U.S. arms sales to Taiwan and the upgrading of Taiwan defense systems or including Taiwan in the Theater Missile Defense system.

Although the U.S. army may be overstretched worldwide now with fighting going on in Afghanistan and Iraq, some analysts stress that it is a wrong perception that Washington will not intervene should Beijing invade Taiwan (Lampton 2004). But will the United States fight for Taiwan? The U.S. resolve to protect or not to protect Taiwan affects policies and policy changes in both the Mainland and Taiwan. As a major third party with military forces deployed in the area and strategic interests in the region, the U.S. role is vital. None of the parties involved want war. However, the deep and even further deepening distrust in the triangular relationship—between Beijing and Taipei, the United States and China in particular—might lead to consequences unwanted and unintended by all parties. Lampton (2004) points out, "[T]he recent elections and broader development in Taiwan, when combined with counterproductive policy in Beijing and some missteps in the Bush Administration, have made conflict more likely." Both Beijing and the United States will need to continue to adjust their Taiwan policies in light of the ongoing developments on the Island.

Notes

1. Michael Brecher defines a foreign policy crisis as a situation in which three conditions, deriving from a change in a state's external or internal environment, are perceived by the highest-level decision makers of the state: (i) a threat to basic values; (ii) an awareness of a finite time for response to the external threat to basic values; and (iii) a high probability of involvement in military hostilities (Brecher 1977).

2. The five nos are no declaration of independence; no change in the "national title"; no "state- to-state description in the Constitution"; no referendum to change the status quo; no abolition of the National Unification Council nor the Guidelines for National Unification.

3. On March 20, the day of the election, Chen's administration held a "defensive referendum" under the legislature's referendum law to decide if the island's sovereignty is under imminent threat from Mainland's military threat, specifically its increasing defense budget and increasing numbers of missiles deployed opposite Taiwan. Therefore, the referendum is "antimissile" and "antiwar." Chen claims that its effect is also to raise the awareness of Taiwanese to the magnitude of the threat for a consensus on self-defense.

4. Some think 2005 is crucial and some believe 2006 is the year that the Mainland will consider using force (Minnick 2004).

5. A message released by the Standing Committee of the National People's Congress in 1979 named " A Message to Taiwan Compatriots," first states the basic lines for Cross-Strait relations that Deng Xiaoping said indicates "the sincere, fair and reasonable" attitude of the Mainland. www.chinataiwan.org/web/webportal/W5023254/, accessed December 12, 2004.

6. In the 2004 Defense White Paper released in December 2004, it is emphasized that "The Chinese Government continues to adhere to the basic principles of 'peaceful reunification' and 'one country, two systems' along with the eight-point proposal on developing Cross-Strait relations and

advancing the process of peaceful reunification of the motherland at the current stage." The 2004 Defense White Paper can be downloaded from Lexus Nexus Internet Index.

7. Divergent views exist over what is the one-China policy/principle: Beijing stressed that there is only one China and Taiwan is a province of China. In Vice President Richard Cheney's speech during his 2003 visit to Beijing, he put it in a way that a one-China policy is based on the three joint communiqués and the Taiwan Relations Act.

8. To what extent the U.S. role is a mediator is under discussion between the Chinese and American governments.

9. Mirroring effects refer to when beliefs serve as a necessary condition and reflect the situational environment. Beliefs can be both necessary and sufficient for decisions when they act as a steering force in situations when beliefs differ from situations. Leaders still refer to their beliefs for policy references by looking for cognitive shortcuts, or by blocking different information or cues from the environment (cognitive bias), or referring back to familiar strategic choices made in the past (through analogies or comparisons with significant historical events). In this case, beliefs may also activate deep motivations, because of the interactive relationship between basic needs for affiliation and for achievement and power on the one hand and beliefs on the other as people tend to adopt beliefs that are compatible with their core needs. Learning effects refer to beliefs' changes resulting from adjustments made as "new information (perceptions) reinforces or reverses old information (beliefs)" (Walker and Schafer n.d.). Learning may affect strategies, tactics, or simply moves by states in strategic interactions depending on the transparency of the situation and the complexity of an individual's belief system. See also Walker (1983).

10. Thomas Kane argues for the influence of Legalism, which is the realpolitik counterpart of Confucianism. He argues that even if China benefits from world markets and the existing balance of power, the Chinese regime will not be satisfied with that balance because China depends on other powers to protect its wealth through means of arms. The Chinese will want to retain the potential to challenge the existing order by force. See also Johnston (1995a); Wang (2002).

11. A follow-up one-way ANOVA of Hu's and Chen's beliefs in 2004 shows that some of their beliefs still differ *significantly* $p < .10$ (two-tailed). In 2004, Hu is more optimistic about the realization of political values (P-2 for Hu = .38; Chen = .28), and sees the political future as more predictable than Chen (P-3 for Hu = .17; Chen = .12). Hu still shows lower historical control than Chen (P-4 for Hu = .13; Chen = .19). Chen is more likely to use promises than Hu (I-5PR for Hu = .07; Chen = .19).

12. For this MANOVA test, noncrisis situation is coded as 1 and crisis situation is coded as 2. Public statements are selected after Hu and Chen

assumed head office of Mainland and Taiwan, specifically, for Hu after November 2002 and for Chen from his 2000 party and presidential elections. Crisis over the Taiwan Strait for Hu is mainly during the 2004 election but for Chen both 2000 and 2004 elections ended up with intensified Cross-Strait tensions. The 2004 crisis starts with the defensive referendum that Chen held with the presidential election and was temporarily calmed with the Legislative Yuan election in December 2004 when the Guomindang (nationalist) pan-blue camp won over Chen's DPP party. Statements given for domestic purposes only and without particular attention to the international effect are coded as domestic audience = 1, e.g., Chen's inauguration speeches; those statements given abroad by the leaders or in front of international press or with particular attention to the international community are coded as international audience = 2, e.g., Hu's APEC speech.

13. The scores in figure 7.1 are expressed as standard deviations from the means for the norming group in table 7.1. The means and standard deviations for I-1, P-1, and P-4 for this norming group were provided by Professor Mark Schafer, department of political science, Louisiana State University. Mean scores for the norming group are I-1 = .33, SD = .47; P-1 = .25, SD = .32, P-4 = .21, SD = .12.

14. The VICS scores for Self (I-1, P-4a) and Other (P-1, P-4b), expressed as standard deviations from means for these key beliefs in the norming group, are as follows. In Hu's speech I-1 = .48, P-4a = -.10, P-1 = .72, P-4 = .10, and in Chen's speech I-1 = -.01, P-4a = -.02, P-1 = .53, P-4b = .02.

15. Deadlock (2,2) is a Nash equilibrium in Chen's game because neither player can improve the immediate outcome for itself by shifting its strategy. Brams (1994, 222) defines deterrent threat power as "a threat to move to another strategy to induce the threatened player to choose a state, associated with the threatener's initial strategy, that is better for both players than the state threatened." Moving power "is the ability to continue moving when the other player must eventually stop; the player who possesses it uses [it] to induce a preferred outcome" (Brams 1994, 224).

CHAPTER 8

LINKS AMONG BELIEFS AND PERSONALITY TRAITS: THE DISTINCTIVE LANGUAGE OF TERRORISTS

Elena Lazarevska, Jayne M. Sholl, and Michael D. Young

Introduction

Much of the activity in identifying terrorists focuses on doing so among non-terrorists in public places such as airports and train stations (see, e.g., Atick 2001 and Willing 2003). Although this is an understandable concern, it would be at least equally valuable if we were able to identify likely terrorists or supporters of terrorism before they engaged in overt acts of terrorism, either to increase surveillance or to engage in policies to reduce the opportunities for such individuals to gain influence. For example, although he is not classified as a terrorist by the state department, Muqtada al-Sadr has verbal behavior patterns that closely resemble those of terrorists and these patterns were evident in 2004 when he ordered or encouraged his militia to take up arms against U.S. forces in Iraq. Early warning of this potential would have been useful for U.S. policy makers. Differences in the use of language between terrorists and non-terrorist political leaders may be useful for understanding the beliefs and motivations of potential leaders in volatile societies.

This study does not attempt to resolve the debate as to whether there is a *terrorist personality* that may account for an individual predisposition to support or engage in terrorism. Our more modest objective is to explore the differences between the verbal behavior of terrorists and non-terrorist political leaders. The goal is to see if "at-a-distance" assessment techniques can identify common characteristics of terrorists' verbal communication that may not be present in the verbal communication of non-terrorist political leaders. We look at the verbal behavior of political leaders using the tools of leadership assessment. Seven indicators from the Leadership Trait Analysis (LTA) and two from the Operational Code Analysis (OCA) approaches to the psychological assessment of political leaders are used to look for common verbal behaviors among identified terrorists (Hermann 2003; Walker, Schafer, and Young 2003).

LTA focuses on a leader's individual personality traits in order to draw inferences about his leadership style (Hermann 2003). The goal is to identify relatively stable traits that differentiate political leaders from one another in kind or degree. These traits include conceptual complexity, self-confidence, control over events, need for power, in-group bias, distrust of others, and task orientation. OCA focuses on a leader's beliefs about the "self-in-situation," in order to draw inferences about his or her leadership style. Both interviews and prepared speeches may be used for this task, which is to reconstruct the leader's cognitive propensities for diagnosing the political universe as cooperative, mixed, or conflictual and prescribing cooperation or conflict as the most effective means for realizing fundamental political values (Walker, Schafer, and Young 1998, 2003).

Methods

For this study we collected speeches, interviews, press conferences, and parts of published books for 23 terrorists, 65 non-terrorist political leaders, 4 former terrorists, and 7 leaders from states that sponsor terrorism. The latter two groups are not part of the central analysis in the study, but are included as interesting additional comparison groups. Individuals are identified as terrorists based on: (i) the U.S. department of state designation of terrorist organizations and their leaders in the 2002 and 2003 editions of *The Patterns of Global Terrorism* (2003) (http://www.state.gov/s/ct/rls/pgtrpt), and (ii) FBI sources for classification of U.S. terrorists. The sample of non-terrorist political leaders includes both current heads of state and government, as well as either former political figures or other prominent individuals who have influence on the state's political processes.

Former terrorists are individuals who have had ties with a terrorist organization, but for whom we have documents after their affiliations with terrorist organizations have ended, or who have assumed a public political role. Leaders from states that sponsor terrorism are leaders of countries that the U.S. Department of State in *Patterns of Global Terrorism* has classified as state sponsors of terrorism. This list includes leaders from Iran, Iraq, Syria, Libya, and Cuba.

We have included individuals from various geographic regions in order to reduce any effects that cultural and linguistic patterns may have on an individual's verbal behavior. Our sample of terrorist leaders includes members of terrorist organizations and non-terrorist political leaders from North America, Europe, the Middle East, Latin America, and Asia. Similarly, groups with various ideological backgrounds were included to account for the possible effects that their ideological distinctions may have on their speech patterns. Hence, our sample includes organizations with different missions: religious (Armed Islamic Group, Kach, Branch Davidians), separatist (Liberation Tigers of Tamil Eelam, Basqe Fatherland and Liberty, Popular Front for the Liberation of Palestine), radical socialist (Communist Party of the Philippines, or Shining Path), or radical environmental (Earth Liberation Front).

Although the data in this study do not allow us to assess whether differences exist in speech patterns across these subgroups, we did find statistically significant differences among terrorists from the Americas and the Middle East on one indicator (View of the Political Universe). This suggests, in a very preliminary way, that future research might look for differences in subgroups based upon such things as geography, culture, or mission.

Whenever possible, we collected at least 50 documents for each individual, with each document containing at least 50 codable words. Although the documents for most individuals exceed the minimum required, in some cases, 50 documents could not be found for some terrorists leaders. Because of the diversity of document lengths, we used counts of words and punctuation (tokens) to determine whether an appropriate amount of material was available for a particular individual. A minimum of 10,000[1] tokens was required for an individual to be included in the analysis. In previous leadership assessments utilizing LTA it has been recommended that at least 5,000 words be used for adequate analysis (Hermann 2003). Because of the ease, reliability, and speed of coding using an automated system, we doubled the minimum tokens required. The documents were collected through public sources, mostly from news agencies, government websites, or various regional media outlets. Appendix 8.1 contains the list of individuals, their designations, and affiliations.

Coding Variables

The documents were coded for nine indicators from the LTA and OCA approaches to leadership assessment. They include seven indicators from the LTA approach developed by Hermann (2003). The indicators for these variables were generated using Profiler Plus, an automated, text-coding software (Young 2001). The LTA coding scheme counts the presence and the absence of evidence for a certain indicator. Indicators for the following are calculated as the percentage of the positive counts (indicating the presence of a trait) out of the total positive and negative counts.

- Conceptual Complexity measures the degree to which individuals are able to see ambiguity in the environment.
- Self-Confidence measures an individual's sense of self-importance or self-worth.
- Control over Events assesses an individual's perception of the degree to which he has control over situations or is able to influence events.
- Need for Power measures an individual's desire to control or influence people or groups.
- In-Group Bias measures the importance that an individual places on his/her group.
- Distrust of Others measures whether an individual exhibits doubts or wariness of the motives of others, in particular to outsiders who do not belong to his/her group.
- Task Orientation assesses whether an individual is motivated by accomplishing goals or maintaining relationships.

Different parts of speech are the sources of evidence for different traits. Adverbs and certain phrases differentiate high and low levels of conceptual complexity. First-person pronouns indicate self-confidence. Verbs are indicators for control over events and the need for power. Favorable adjectives attributed to the leader's group and references to the group's honor and identity indicate in-group bias. Nouns and noun phrases attributed to others indicate distrust of others. Nouns are also indicators of task orientation. Dictionaries for each of these parts of speech differentiate which nouns, pronouns, verbs, adverbs, and adjectives indicate which trait (Hermann 2003, 194–203).

When coding for conceptual complexity, for example, the program looks for words that suggest whether a leader is capable of perceiving multiple dimensions in a situation, or whether the leader tends to classify events or people into dichotomous categories. In particular, words that would be coded for presence of conceptual complexity include: "generally," "alternatively," or "ambiguous"; words that would be coded for the absence of conceptual complexity include: "necessarily," "inevitably," or "obviously."

Two indicators from OCA are also employed. We are concerned with whether the leader sees the political world as threatening or friendly (View of the Political Universe), and whether individuals believe that strategies of conflict or cooperation (Strategies for Achieving Goals) will have the most success in achieving their goals. We use Profiler Plus and the Verbs in Context System (VICS) dictionary, which identifies a leader's transitive verb-based attributions (Walker, Schafer, and Young 2003). The score for View of the Political Universe is derived by subtracting the percentage of negative attributions made to others from the percentage of positive attributions made to others. A score of -1.0 indicates a highly hostile view of the political universe, and a score of $+1.0$ indicates a highly friendly view of the political universe. Similarly, the score for Strategy for Achieving Goals is derived by subtracting the percentage of negative attributions made to self from the percentage of positive attributions made to self. A score of -1.0 on this indicator suggests that the individual is likely to choose conflictual strategies for achieving goals, and a score of $+1.0$ indicates that an individual is likely to choose cooperative strategies for achieving goals (Walker, Schafer, and Young 2003).

Analysis

Our main hypothesis is that leaders of terrorist groups will have verbal characteristics, as measured by LTA and OCA indicators, that differ from those of non-terrorist political leaders. Thus, we expect that these scores can be used to classify a subject into terrorist and non-terrorist categories. In order to identify whether the scores of terrorists and non-terrorist political leaders differ, we first performed Analysis of Variance tests (all statistical analyses were done in SPSS). This test is used to determine whether these two groups are different, and on which indicators.

Table 8.1 reports the results of the one-way analysis of variance on the terrorists' and non-terrorist political leaders' scores. Three of the nine indicators (conceptual complexity, task orientation, and need for power) do not show statistically significant differences. Five indicators do show statistically significant differences at the 0.01 level: a terrorist's View of the Political Universe and Strategy for Achieving Goals are different from that of a non-terrorist as are Distrust of Others, Self-Confidence, and In-Group Bias. A sixth indicator, Control over Events, is significant at the 0.05 level.

Table 8.1   Mean Scores, Standard Deviations, and One-Way ANOVA

Operational Code/LTA Indices	Group Assessed	N	Mean	Std. Deviation	F	Sig.
Political universe	Terrorists	23	0.03	0.10	118.54	0.00
	Non-terrorist political leaders	65	0.34	0.12		
	Total	88	0.26	0.18		
Strategy for achieving goals	Terrorists	23	0.27	0.16	44.69	0.00
	Non-terrorist political leaders	65	0.48	0.12		
	Total	88	0.43	0.16		
Distrust of others	Terrorists	23	0.21	0.07	75.53	0.00
	Non-terrorist political leaders	65	0.11	0.04		
	Total	88	0.14	0.06		
Self-confidence	Terrorists	23	0.29	0.08	16.87	0.00
	Non-terrorist political leaders	65	0.37	0.08		
	Total	88	0.35	0.09		
In-group bias	Terrorists	23	0.07	0.02	14.80	0.00
	Non-terrorist political leaders	65	0.08	0.02		
	Total	88	0.08	0.02		
Control over events	Terrorists	23	0.33	0.03	5.24	0.02
	Non-terrorist political leaders	65	0.35	0.04		
	Total	88	0.35	0.04		
Conceptual complexity	Terrorists	23	0.58	0.05	0.04	0.84
	Non-terrorist political leaders	65	0.58	0.04		
	Total	88	0.58	0.04		
Task orientation	Terrorists	23	0.61	0.09	1.21	0.27
	Non-terrorist political leaders	65	0.63	0.06		
	Total	88	0.63	0.07		
Need for power	Terrorists	23	0.25	0.04	0.00	0.95
	Non-terrorist political leaders	65	0.25	0.03		
	Total	88	0.25	0.03		

Terrorists tend to score lower on View of the Political Universe, Strategy for Achieving Goals, Self-Confidence, In-Group Bias, and Control over Events, but higher on Distrust of Others.

People in the terrorist group tend to view the political universe as more threatening and hostile, choose conflictual strategies for achieving their goals, and are more distrustful of others. These indicate that terrorists are marked by more negativity toward the political environment. This profile is not surprising, given that by their nature terrorist activities are inherently characterized by violence and conflict. Similarly, the mean score on Self-Confidence is lower in the terrorist group than in the non-terrorist political leader group. This score suggests that terrorists are likely to have lower perceptions of self-value or self-worth. This negative self-image may to some degree account for their choice of violent strategies rather than participating in legitimate political processes. Moreover, the terrorist leaders have lower scores on Control over Events. These leaders are likely to believe that there is little to be done to influence what happens and that only extreme strategies will be effective.

Somewhat counterintuitively, individuals in the terrorist group have lower In-Group Bias scores than the non-terrorist political leaders. We expected the terrorist group to score higher on this indicator, because groups have immense influence on individual motivations to perform terrorist activities. Indeed, a great deal of research on terrorism has centered on the effects of group membership (Crenshaw 2000).

We have also performed Discriminant Function Analysis using the six statistically significant indicators to determine if they are sufficient collectively to distinguish the terrorists from the non-terrorists. Equal prior probabilities were selected in order to compensate for the unequal group sizes. The discriminant function analysis resulted in a function that was statistically significant ($p = 0.01$). This function correctly classified 94.3 percent of the cases: 21 of the 23 terrorists and 62 of the 65 non-terrorist political leaders.

Table 8.2 shows the Standardized Canonical Coefficients and the Structure Matrix for the Discriminant Function. From the standardized coefficients we see that the scores on the Political Universe and Distrust of Others have the greatest relative importance to the discriminant function, and the structure matrix indicates that these same scores are related the most to the discriminant function.

We conclude that the Discriminant Function Analysis (DFA) gives us a useful and highly successful function that distinguishes between terrorists

Table 8.2 Standardized Canonical Coefficients and Structure Matrix

Operational Code/LTA Indices	Standardized Canonical Discriminant Function Coefficients	Structure Matrix
Indicator	Function	Function
Political universe	0.571	0.850
Distrust of others	−0.397	−0.678
Strategy for achieving goals	0.007	0.522
Self-confidence	0.274	0.321
In-group bias	0.362	0.300
Control over events	0.257	0.179

and non-terrorists. We can also use DFA to classify and give additional insight into the more ambiguous actors who are either former terrorists or leaders of states that sponsor terrorism. Using the patterns from our original DFA to create two "prototypes"—*Terrorist* and *Non-Terrorist*—we entered 11 additional actors, all of who are either former terrorists or leaders of terrorism-sponsoring states, into DFA for classification purposes. The DFA placed the following actors in the *Terrorist* prototype: Ali Khamenei, Fidel Castro, Saddam Hussein, Muammar Qadhafi, Ali Akbar Rafsanjani, and Subcomandante Marcos. And, the following were more closely aligned with the *Non-Terrorist* prototype: Hun Sen, Abu Iyad, Martin McGuinness, Bashar al-Asad, and Mohammad Khatami. The results indicate that the more "hardline" leaders such as Ali Khamenei or Saddam Hussein have verbal behavior patterns that are similar to those of terrorists, but the more "moderate" leaders such as Mohammad Khatami or Bashar al-Asad have speech patterns that are closer to those of non-terrorist political leaders.

Based upon their mean scores and the standard deviations, former terrorists tend to resemble non-terrorist political leaders on Control over Events, Self-Confidence, Distrust of Others, and View of Political Universe, and they appear similar to terrorists on Strategy for Achieving Goals and In-Group Bias. The leaders of state sponsors of terrorism tend to resemble other non-terrorist political leaders on Control over Events, Self-Confidence, and In-Group Bias, but they look like terrorists on Distrust of Others, View of Political Universe, and Strategy for Achieving Goals.

Discussion

Overall, our hypothesis that terrorists' linguistic patterns are different from that of non-terrorists is supported. Specifically, the scores on six out of the nine LTA and OCA indicators exhibit statistically significant differences across the two groups. In addition, these indicators can be used to generate a model that correctly categorizes an individuals' likelihood to orient themselves toward terrorism in 94 percent of the cases. When we plot the OCA scores for View of the Political Universe and Strategy for Achieving Goals, a clear distinction between the terrorists and non-terrorists can be observed. Non-terrorist political leaders tend to have a positive view of the political universe and favor more cooperative strategies for achieving goals,

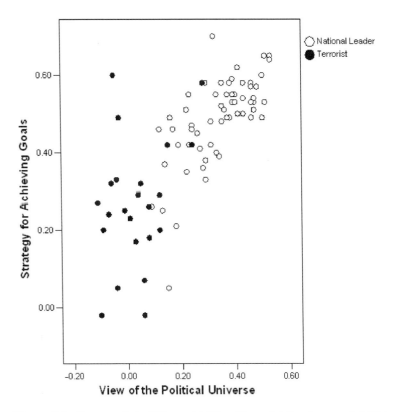

Figure 8.1   Scatter plot of Terrorist/Non-Terrorist Leaders on I-1/P-4 Indices.

while terrorists tend to have more negative views of the political universe and choose more hostile strategies for achieving goals.

The Discriminant Function Analysis gave promising results as the vast majority of the individuals were assigned to the correct group. Furthermore, these six indicators can be seen as a measure of an individual's orientation toward the world, and used as assessments of an individual's predisposition to participate in or support terrorist activities. In addition, when we take a closer look at the individuals who were misclassified by the Discriminant Function Analysis; there is often evidence to suggest that the classification offered by the Discriminant Function Analysis is appropriate. The Discriminant Function Analysis misclassified the terrorists Arnaldo Otegi and Raul Reyes as non-terrorist political leaders. Otegi, although he has had ties to *Euzkadi Ta Askatasuna* (ETA translates into "Basque Fatherland and Liberty"), has recently been the spokesperson and leader of the political party Batasuna. His increasing orientation toward the political process may account for his placement in the category of non-terrorist political leaders. Similarly, Raul Reyes, a commander of *Fuerzas Armadas de Colombia* (FARC-translates into the "Revolutionary Armed Forces of Colombia"), arguably promoted peaceful political dialogue as early as January 2002.

Of the non-terrorist political leaders Muqtada al-Sadr, Ibrahim Jaafari, and Daniel Ortega were placed in the terrorist group. Of these, al-Sadr can be considered extremely hardline, especially considering the activities of his militia forces in Iraq during the time of his speech acts (2003–2004). Indeed, al-Sadr's violent opposition to the presence of Coalition Forces in Iraq may be enough evidence for his inclusion in the original terrorist group; however, the actions of his militia men were oriented toward the military and security forces, not necessarily civilians, and thus they do not fit our definition of terrorist behavior. Ibrahim Jaafari is a current leader of the al-Dawa party in Iraq, but in the 1970s he was associated with the Islamic movement that opposed Saddam Hussein. Daniel Ortega was a leader of the Sandinista National Liberation Front and can be considered a hardline leader.

This study shows that terrorists' speech patterns differ from those of non-terrorist political leaders. Specifically, people who engage in and support terrorism score lower on View of the Political Universe, Strategy for Achieving Goals, Self-Confidence, In-Group Bias, and Control over Events, and score higher on Distrust of Others. These scores, when used in Discriminant Function Analysis, are successful in differentiating between supporters of terrorism and other non-terrorist political leaders.

Appendix 8.1

Group 1: Designated Terrorist Leaders

Individual	Organization
al-Zahhar, Mahmud Khalid	HAMAS
al-Zawahiri, Ayman	Al-Jihad
Balasingham, Anton	Liberation Tigers of Tamil Eerlam (LTTE)
Basayev, Shamil	Riyadus-Salikhin
Bin Laden, Osama	Al Qaeda
Castano, Carlos	United Self Defense Forces of Columbia (AUC).
Guzman, Abimael	Shining Path
Habash, George	Popular Front for the Liberation of Palestine (PFLP)
Hamza, Sheikh Abu	Armed Islamic Group (GIA)
Kahane, Meir	Kach
Khaled, Mishal	HAMAS
Koresh, David	Branch Davidians
Nasrallah, Sayyed Hassan	Hizballah
Ocalan, Abdullah	PKK
Rajavi, Maryam	Mujahedin e Khalq Organization
Rajavi, Massaud	Mujahedin e Khalq Organization
Rantisi, Abdel Aziz	HAMAS
Reyes, Raul	Revolutionary Armed Forces of Columbia
Rosebraugh, Graig	Earth Liberation Front
Shallah, Ramadan	The Palestine Islamic Jihad
Sison, Jose Maria	Communist Party of the Philippines/ New People's Army
Otegi, Arnaldo	Basque Fatherland and Liberty—ETA
Velazco, Isaac	Tupak Amaru

Group 2: Non-terrorist political leaders

Leader	State
al-Hakim, al-Aziz	Iraq
al-Hakim, Muhammad Baqr	Iraq
al-Sadr, Muqtada	Iraq
al-Yawr, Ghazi	Iraq
Alawi, Ayad	Iraq

Arafat, Yasir	Palestine
Barwari, Nasreen	Iraq
Begin, Menachem	Israel
Bush, George H.W.	United States
Buzek, Jerzy	Poland
Cardoso, Fernando	Brazil
Carter, Jimmy	United States
Chalabi, Ahmed	Iraq
Chavez, Hugo	Venezuela
Chen, Shui Bien	Taiwan
Chinnawat, Thaksin	Thailand
Clinton, Bill	United States
Crown Prince Abdallah	Saudi Arabia
Dean, Howard	United States
DeLaRua, Fernando	Argentina
Djukanovic, Milo	Serbia and Montenegro
Edwards, John	United States
Eisenhower, Dwight	United States
Erdogan, Recep Tayyip	Turkey
Ford, Gerald	United States
Fox, Vicente	Mexico
Fujimori, Alberto	Peru
Gandhi, Sonia	India
Georgievski, Ljubco	Macedonia
Jaafari, Ibrahim	Iraq
Jiang, Zemin	China
Johnson, Lyndon	United States
Karzai, Hamid	Afghanistan
Kennedy, John	United States
Kerry, John	United States
King Abdullah	Jordan
King Hussein	Jordan
Koizumi, Junichiro	Japan
Kostunica, Vojislav	Serbia and Montenegro
Macapagal, Arroyo Gloria	Philippines
Milosevic, Slobodan	Serbia and Montenegro
Mubarak, Hosni	Egypt
Musharraf, Pervez	Pakistan
Nazarbayev, Nursultan	Kazakhstan

Nixon, Richard	United States
Noriega, Manuel	Panama
Orban, Victor	Hungary
Ortega, Daniel	Nicaragua
Pachachi, Adnan	Iraq
Pastrana, Andres	Colombia
Peres, Shimon	Israel
Putin, Vladimir	Russia
Racan, Ivica	Croatia
Reagan, Ronald	United States
Sadat, Anwar	Egypt
Salih, Barham	Iraq
Sharon, Ariel	Israel
Shevardnadze, Eduard	Georgia
Talabani, Jalal	Iraq
Truman, Harry	United States
Vajpayee, Atal	India
Yeltsin, Boris	Russia
Zebari, Hoshyar	Iraq
Zedillo, Ernesto	Mexico
Zhu, Rongji	China

Group 3: Former Terrorists

Former terrorist	Organization
Iyad, Abu	Al Fatah
Marcos	Zapatistas
McGuiness, Martin	IRA
Sen, Hun	Khmer Rouge

Group 4: Leaders from States that Sponsor Terrorism

Leader	State
al-Asad, Bashar	Syria
Castro, Fidel	Cuba
Hussein, Saddam	Iraq
Khamenei, Ali	Iran
Khatami, Mohammad	Iran
Qaddafi, Muammar	Libya
Rafsanjani, Ali Akbar	Iran

Note

1. The total count of words and punctuation for Arnaldo Otegi is 9247. We included him in the set for the analysis because this total count is very close to the minimum. Of the other collection attempts, the scores for Farooq Kashmiri and Abu Sabaya were not included in the analysis due to the low token counts: 1802 and 2562, respectively.

PART V

APPLICATIONS: THE DOMAIN OF INTERNATIONAL POLITICAL ECONOMY

CHAPTER 9

ECONOMIC SANCTIONS AND OPERATIONAL CODE ANALYSIS: BELIEFS AND THE USE OF ECONOMIC COERCION

A. Cooper Drury

Introduction

Studies of decision making have shown that the leader's beliefs have an impact on the decision process. Most of the literature, however, has concentrated on issues that involve security matters and the potential use of military force. The possibility of military confrontation elevates the situation in which the decision must be made to a crisis. Consequently, the stress under which the leader must make decisions may fundamentally alter the decision-making process such that the leader must rely more heavily on his or her beliefs since there is less time for the decision to be made and it involves the possible use of deadly force. For example, President George H.W. Bush once commented that sending U.S. troops into harm's way was the most difficult decision he faced. During the interview, the former president had to turn away from the camera to regain his composure. Such emotional decisions made under such stressful circumstances may increase the influence the leader's beliefs have.

In addition to the increased stress and emotional aspects of a decision to use force, the leader will be intimately involved in the decision process. For example, President Kennedy's near direct control of the naval vessels as the Soviet ships approached Cuba during the missile crisis reflects how much more personal these decisions can be (Allison 1971). Trade negotiations or decisions regarding the disbursement of aid, on the other hand, tend to be more bureaucratized or influenced by a larger group of administration officials. These "lower" political issues may be less influenced by the leader's beliefs simply because he or she is less involved in the decision process (Rosati 1981).

Issues or disputes that do not involve the immediate potential use of military force, therefore, provide a robust test for the influence of beliefs on decision making. Specifically, if a leader's beliefs affect the decision process in less intense disputes, then beliefs are likely to have an important impact on all levels of decision making. In this chapter I use the U.S. president's decision to employ economic sanctions to assess whether his beliefs affect the decision to use a less intense form of coercive diplomacy. Later I discuss the process through which the president decides to employ economic coercion and then delineate hypotheses to assess the argument. The results show that decisions concerning less intense options are still significantly affected by the president's belief system as measured by his operational code. I conclude with a discussion of how beliefs affect the decision to use economic coercion.

The Decision to Use or Modify an Economic Sanction

The president's decision to use economic coercion is determined by factors that fall into three models (Drury 2005). First, international factors act as the primary driving force behind the president's choice to use an economic sanction. This model asserts a rational choice perspective that explains the president's use of economic coercion as a direct reaction to relations with the other state. Contemplating these relations, he will use sanctions when the benefit of their use outweighs the cost of their imposition. The president will apply and perhaps increase the level of economic coercion when recent history suggests that the target is intransigent toward his demands. In the simplest of terms, when the target country resists the president's demand, he will apply more pressure in the form of economic sanctions (Drury 2000, 2001, 2005; George 1991; Morgan 1990, 1994; Sislin 1994; Snyder and Deising 1977). Therefore, the president is more likely to use economic pressure to coerce the opponent when the benefits of such an attempt outweigh the costs.

However, the opponent may also take action to try to stop a president who is contemplating economic coercion. Provocative, bellicose actions by the target signal to the president that the target intends to resist the sanctions and suffer the costs they incur. Since economic sanctions cost the sender a loss of trade in goods and services, the president will tend to see belligerent actions by the target as a sign that economic coercion is doomed to fail. Consequently, the president will be less likely to sanction. In effect, the target is able to deter the White House. While previous research has shown that in a highly tense dispute even provocative actions are unable to deter the president, they tend to reduce the probability that the president will step up the pressure with economic sanctions.

According to the rationality of an international explanation, therefore, economic sanctions play a role as one form of coercion available to the sender. When the president contemplates using economic coercion, the United States and a target have already entered into a crisis or dispute—the target has taken some offensive action resulting in a demand from the president; the target resists the challenge, a move that increases the U.S.–target tension level and begins the confrontation (Drezner 2001). If the tension is sufficient, the president will decide to levy economic sanctions in an attempt to force the target to capitulate to his demands.

The second model of rationality that affects the president's decision concerns a domestic politics explanation. Because the president does not make foreign policy decisions in a vacuum that isolates him from domestic conditions, domestic political factors must be incorporated into the explanation of the decision process. Previous research has shown that the president may use economic sanctions as a means to placate public demands for action or simply to appear as a more active president in general (Kaempfer and Lowenberg 1988; Li and Drury 2004; Lindsey 1986). There is a debate over the function of that connection with some arguing that the president uses foreign affairs to divert the American public away from domestic issues and others arguing that the president prefers to use force when he has more political capital on the home front (DeRouen 1995; Levy 1989; Meernik 1994; Ostrom and Job 1986). Recent investigations of the decision to use economic coercion show that the president does have a slight preference for using economic sanctions when his approval is higher rather than lower (Drury 2001, 2005). Consistent with the conclusion that the president does not use opportunities to use economic coercion as a diversion, he also tends to use sanctions when the U.S. economy is performing well. High levels of inflation and unemployment drive down the probability that he will deploy economic coercion. Finally, Kaempfer and Lowenberg (1988, 1989) have argued that sanctions are an opportunity for trade protectionism. Cutting off imports from the target protects domestic producers and drives up the price of the product. Therefore, the president may be expected to use economic coercion to offset the trade balance with the target.

International or dyadic factors will have a greater impact on the occupant of the White House, but the president's approval, the economic situation generally, and the U.S. economic relationship with the target will affect how sanctions are used and modified. In these first two models of political rationality, there is an underlying assumption of objective or substantive rationality (Simon 1985); that is, the president is reacting to outside stimuli and making a decision to maximize his benefits and minimize his costs. For instance, the coercive diplomacy/international politics model predicts the president will enact economic sanctions when the tension between the target nation and the United States has risen—when the costs of not acting become greater than the costs of acting. The domestic imperatives model predicts that the president will be more likely to take action when there is a trade deficit with the target and when his approval is high; again the president seeks to maximize benefits and minimize costs. Both models have underlying assumptions derived from rational choice theory because they are based on previous research with hypotheses generally consistent with rational choice assumptions.

The first two models are quite reasonable in assuming that the president reacts to outside stimuli, but to stop theorizing there is myopic. As Walker and Schafer (2003, 2) point out "leaders matter in the explanation of a foreign policy decision by acting on their definition of the situation in the domain of world politics" (see also Snyder, Bruck, and Sapin 1962). The president's beliefs about the world around him affect how he processes and interprets the available information. The decision to use economic sanctions becomes bounded by these beliefs, and therefore, the last explanation rests on the assumptions of bounded rationality. Presidents with more friendly views of the world and a more cooperative approach to goals decrease the likelihood that they will resort to economic coercion.

Hypotheses

The hypotheses provided here reflect the three models that explain both the president's decision to initiate economic coercion and the decision to modify (lift, decrease, increase) the sanction policy. Beginning with the international factors, I first tap the idea that the tension between the sender and the target is positively associated with the use of sanctions. This hypothesis suggests that more intense disputes are more likely to experience the onset of sanctions. Drury (2005) showed that the *rate* of escalation of the dispute had no effect on the president's decision. Therefore, the president does not look forward to what the relations with the target are expected to be. Instead the president concentrates on the actual tension level. Specifically, *the president is more likely to initiate an economic sanction against a target when the dyadic tension between the United States and that target increases (Hypothesis 1a).* Similarly, *presidents will be more likely to increase sanctions against a target when the tension level is high (Hypothesis 1b).*

The next hypothesis taps the effect provocative actions by the target have on the president's decision to use economic coercion. A provocative, belligerent target sends a very clear signal that it is going to resist the sender even if the consequence is suffering considerable economic cost. Consequently, it seems likely that if sanctions are imposed against a belligerent target, the sanctions will be protracted. Since the United States would also suffer considerable costs in such a protracted sanction episode, there is an incentive for the president to forego economic coercion for some other policy, be it engagement, containment, or some other, more intense form of coercive diplomacy. *If the target acts in a provocative, bellicose manner toward the United States, the president will be less inclined to initiate economic sanctions (Hypothesis 2a).* When modifying a sanction already in place, *provocative actions will make the president more likely to end or limit the sanctioning effort (Hypothesis 2b).*

Three hypotheses represent the domestic political factors that are theorized to have an impact on the president's decision to sanction. The president seeks to take action when he has greater political capital, and his job approval rating is a fundamental source of that political capital. Therefore, I expect that higher polling results provide an incentive for the president to take action. In the case of a dispute with another nation, the president will be more aggressive when he has more capital to expend at home. The president's absolute approval rating is not the best indicator of his preferences, however. Since public opinion is dynamic, the president is more likely to evaluate his current approval relative to the recent past. If a president is doing better than he has in the past three months, then he has more political capital to expend. *If the president's job approval rating is above its recent average, he will be more likely to enact economic sanctions (Hypothesis 3a). A high approval rating will also make the president more likely to increase sanctions once they are already in place (Hypothesis 3b).*

The president is concerned not only with his approval but also with the U.S. economy. According to the diversionary theory of war literature, the president is expected to attempt to divert the public's attention from a faltering economy by engaging in adventurous foreign policy. Military actions draw the public's attention, and although they are expensive, costs are not the first issue raised when the military is deployed. For that reason, use of the military can distract the public's attention from economic woes. This expectation does not translate to economic sanctions because of the nature of the coercion. Economic sanctions, however, cost the economy and do not provide a distraction from it. No president prefers to be seen as putting costs on an economy that is already suffering. Therefore, *as the misery index (inflation plus unemployment) increases, the president will be less likely to use economic coercion (Hypothesis 4a)*. Additionally, *the misery index will also push the president to decrease or lift sanctions after they have been deployed (Hypothesis 4b)*.

Not all economic conditions have the same effect, and the trade balance between the United States and target provides the president with an incentive to use economic coercion. Sanctions have protectionist effects that can favorably affect the trade balance with the target. The president has an incentive to initiate a sanction against the target as cover for a protectionist policy. *A trade deficit, therefore, will increase the probability that the president will initiate an economic sanction (Hypothesis 5)*.[1]

The final two hypotheses tap the last model—bounded rationality imposed by cognitive constraints. The president's belief system will have an effect on the likelihood that sanctions are deployed. While not as hostile as military force, economic coercion is still a hostile action. If a president's belief system is more cooperative, then he will hesitate before using sanctions compared to a president with a more hostile world vision. Specifically, *presidents (1) who have a more friendly view of the political universe and (2) approach goals more cooperatively will be less likely to initiate an economic sanction (Hypotheses 6 and 7)*. Once the sanctions are in place, the president has already selected a coercive means for dealing with the target. Instead of his view of the political universe and approach to goals affecting the decision to modify the sanctions, I expect that it will be the president's belief regarding control over the dispute with the target. Thus, *as the president's belief in his ability to control historical development increases, the president will be more likely to lift or decrease the sanctions (Hypothesis 8)*.

In addition to the eight hypotheses, three control variables are included in the analysis. First, several scholars have argued that democratic dyads will be less likely to sanction one another (Cox and Drury 2002; Lektzian and Souva 2003), and if they do, the sanctions will be shorter (Bolks and Al-Sowayel 2000) and then return to pre-sanction trade levels faster (Lektzian and Souva 2001). To control for this effect, I include the target's regime score in the model. Second, the target's GDP per capita must be added to the model to control for the potential tendency to select weaker targets (Olson 1979). Finally, I include the total trade between the United States and the target/country to control for the possibility that the president will be more likely to use economic sanctions against a state with which the United States has trade. Basically, I must control for the potential tendency by the United States to sanction countries that it can sanction—those with whom there is significant trade.

Data

I now turn to a description and discussion of the data that I use to assess the models specified earlier. The data cover the period from 1966 to 2000. They are arrayed as a time-series cross-section (TSCS) where the time period is the month and the cross-section is the target/country. Also known as a pooled time-series, the method stacks or pools each unit's (in this case the target/country) time-series on top of the others. The result is a larger data set that includes both cross-section and time-series elements, which permit both greater generalization and causal inference thanks.

Since I am interested in explaining the conditions that lead the president to initiate sanctions against another country, I include all of the states that were targeted for economic sanctions by the United States and a control group of countries that were never sanctioned during the period covered by the data. Between 1966 and 2000, the White House sanctioned 29 countries at least once during the 35-year period. An additional 21 randomly selected countries were added to the data as a control group of unsanctioned states.

The first dependent variable is the president's decision to initiate economic sanctions against another nation. A presidential decision to initiate is defined as a statement or act by the president, spokesperson, or secretary-level member of the administration that (i) immediately imposes economic sanctions against another country, or (ii) imposes a sanction that will come into effect in the near future. It does not include threats of sanctions that may be deployed; instead, the economic coercion must be implemented or in the implementation process. Some cases involved Congressional action in the form of legislation that either created an economic sanction or required the president to impose a sanction. Unless the president took direct positive action toward the legislative bill, the case was dropped. Direct positive action is defined as signing a bill into law, issuing a supportive statement, or any supportive executive action on a Congressional initiative.

The second dependent variable is the president's decision to modify sanctions that are already deployed. The president has three options: he can completely lift the sanctions; he can incrementally decrease them; or he can increase the economic pressure on the target by instituting another sanction such as a new trade restriction (Drury 2005). These three options are coded on an ordinal scale. All other cases in which no sanctions were in effect are coded as missing data. Consequently, only those states that were sanctioned are included in the analysis. Falsification of the hypotheses does not come from null cases, but from variation over time and through space. The data measuring the president's decision to initiate and modify economic sanctions were gathered from a variety of sources. First, the Hufbauer, Schott, and Elliott (1990a, b) volumes provided the foundation for the cases of U.S. sanctions. For sanctions that started after the 1990 Hufbauer, Schott, and Elliott volumes were published, I used a list of all the economic sanction cases from their forthcoming third edition. These data were supplemented and completed with searches of the *Lexis-Nexis* database of newspaper and government documents and complete case studies published on the Institute for International Economics website. The news digest/archive *Facts on File* (1966–2000) also supplemented the data.[2]

The data needed to represent the first hypothesis—that more tense disputes lead to economic coercion—is a gauge of the tension between the United States and the target. To measure the magnitude of tension between the United States and the target, I use data from the World Event Interaction Survey (WEIS) and Integrated Data for Event Analysis (IDEA). The data are nominal events coded primarily from the *New York Times* concerning the interactions between nations for the years 1966–1992. For the years 1993–2000, I use IDEA. Like WEIS, IDEA codes events between states as reported in the news media, in this case, Reuters Newswires. Although coded by a machine rather than a human, the nominal codes that are generated match closely with the WEIS codes (Bond et al. 2003). As nominal data, little more than the frequency of their occurrence can be analyzed. Joshua Goldstein (1992) created a weighting scheme that converts the nominal WEIS codes to a cooperation–conflict scale. After a simple transformation, the data range from a cooperative score of zero to a highly hostile score of 18.3. Thus, as the tension variable increases, the tension level between the United States and the target also increases.[3]

To measure the provocation from Hypothesis 2, I use the difference in the U.S. and target/country tension scores to determine how much more hostile or less cooperative the target/country is toward the United States, relative to the U.S. tension directed at the target/country. To derive this variable, I subtract the WEIS/IDEA score of the United States directed at the target/country from the target's WEIS/IDEA score directed at the United States. Since I am only interested in provocation by the target/country toward the United States, I recode all negative scores (times when the United States was acting as the provocateur) to zero. All missing values are also coded as zero since a lack of data can be regarded as a lack of provocation. That is, if the target was provocative, I expect it to appear in the data. If nothing appears, then it should be safe to assume that no provocation occurred.

Turning to the domestic political variables, I begin with the measure of the president's job approval rating in Hypothesis 3. Using the standard measure of presidential approval rating from the Gallup Poll question— "Do you approve or disapprove of the way (president's name) is handling his job as president?" (Burbach 1995; Gallup Poll Monthly 2000)—I code a dichotomous variable such that a one indicates the president's approval is above its three-month moving average and a zero that it is below that level.

America's economic health is also hypothesized to affect the president's decision to initiate an economic sanction (Hypothesis 4). The economic conditions are characterized by the inflation and unemployment rates as reported by the U.S. government. To best capture the effect these variables have on the decision to initiate or modify economic coercion, I add them together to create the misery index. In addition to the domestic economic health of the United States, I hypothesize that the president will be more likely to be economically coercive when there is a trade deficit with the target/country and less so when there is a trade surplus (Hypothesis 5). I calculate the trade surplus between the United States and each target/country and standardize the variable by dividing it by the total U.S. trade.

The final three hypotheses (Hypotheses 6–8) suggest that the president's belief system will influence his decision to use and alter economic sanctions. To tap these hypotheses, I use three different measures of the operational code—one that represents the philosophical beliefs (P-1), one that represents instrumental beliefs (I-1), and one that measures the locus of control (P-4) (Walker, Schafer, and Young 1998, 2003). The data for both variables come from speeches of all the presidents using the Verbs in Context (VICS) coding scheme and the Profiler plus (version 5.1) text parser (Walker, Schafer, and Young 1998, 2003).[4]

I now turn to the data for the control variables for the model. First, democracies tend not to sanction one another. To control for this potential effect, I include the target's regime score as determined by the Polity IV data set. The Polity IV data independently measures a country's level of democracy and autocracy, subtracting the autocracy score from the democracy score to create an overall measure of regime type (Marshall and Jaggers 2000). The resulting variable ranges from −10 to 10. Second, to control for the potential preference to use economic coercion on weaker states, because they will not be able to withstand the economic pressure and make soft and attractive targets, I include the target's GDP per capita from the Penn World Tables. Finally, to control for the potential bias to sanction those countries with which the United States has significant trade, I include the total trade with the target. This variable is measured by adding U.S. imports and exports with the target and logging the values (Gleditsch 2002).

Results

The analyses proceed in two steps. First, I assess the president's decision to initiate economic coercion, and second, I analyze his decision to modify those sanctions already put in place. Because the president's decision to initiate economic coercion is a dichotomous variable, I use logit to estimate the model with P-1 and I-1 in separate equations because they are highly collinear.[5] The results in table 9.1 show that, overall, the model performs reasonably well with a pseudo-R^2 of 0.16 and 0.15, respectively, for each equation. Both equations are significant with p-values less than 0.000. The data support five of the eight hypotheses, and partially contradict one.

As expected, the tension level is the driving force behind the president's use of economic sanctions. A one standard deviation increase in the tension level changes the probability of sanctions from 50 to 62 percent, holding other variables constant. Provocation also has a strong impact on the president's decision. A one standard deviation rise in the belligerent nature of the target decreases the likelihood that sanctions will be used from 50 to 39 percent. Two domestic variables, presidential approval and the misery index, are also significant and support the hypotheses in both equations, while the trade surplus is marginally significant in only one equation and in the wrong direction.

The domestic variables have relatively marginal effects compared to the effect of the international variables. If the president is above his average approval rating, he has a 56 percent probability of using economic coercion, while only a 46 percent probability if he is below the recent average. The misery index decreases the likelihood of sanctions from 50 to 46 percent as it climbs by one standard deviation.

The results for the two operational code variables are mixed. The strategic approach to goals (I-1) is significant, but the president's view of the political universe (P-1) does not approach significance. As hypothesized, the more coercive the president's strategic orientation, the more likely he is to use economic sanctions. As I-1 increases by one standard deviation toward a more cooperative preference for tactics, the probability that sanctions will be initiated drops from 50 to 42 percent. While this impact is not huge, its overall impact is second only to the tension and provocation variables and on a par with the effect of the economy.

Table 9.1   The Decision to Initiate Economic Coercion, 1966–2000

	Coefficients (S.E.s)	
Variables	I-1 Model	P-1 Model
Tension	0.180★★★	0.201★★★
	(0.033)	(0.034)
Provocation	−0.124★★★	−0.125★★★
	(0.030)	(0.030)
Presidential approval domain	0.375★★	0.328★
	(0.187)	(0.188)
Misery index	−0.073★★	−0.032
	(0.032)	(0.032)
U.S. trade surplus as % of total trade	23.885	24.966★
	(15.582)	(14.562)
Operational code I-1	−4.168★★★	—
	(1.241)	—
Operational code P-1	—	−1.314
	—	(1.328)
Polity score	−0.030★	−0.035★★
	(0.017)	(0.017)
Target GDP per capita	−0.000★★★	−0.000★★★
	(0.000)	(0.000)
Logged total U.S. trade with target	0.134★★★	0.134★★★
	(0.039)	(0.040)
Time since last decision	−0.051★★★	−0.056★★★
	(0.010)	(0.011)
Spline 1	0.000★★★	−0.000★★★
	(0.000)	(0.000)
Spline 2	0.000★★	0.000★★
	(0.000)	(0.000)
Spline 3	0.000	0.000
	(0.000)	(0.000)
Constant	−1.007	−3.848★★★
	(1.109)	(0.818)
Observations	9130	9130
Pseudo-R^2	0.161	0.153

Notes: Robust standard errors in parentheses.
★ $p < 0.1$; ★★ $p < 0.05$; ★★★ $p < 0.01$.

Turning to the decision to modify sanctions that are already in place, I model the president's decision with an ordered logit analysis. The results appear in table 9.2 and are very similar to the decision to initiate sanctions with two exceptions. First, the model performs considerably worse

Table 9.2 The Decision to Modify
an Economic Sanction, 1966–2000

Variables	Coefficients (S.E.s)
Tension	0.272***
	(0.080)
Provocation	−0.103*
	(0.059)
Presidential approval	−0.107
	(0.284)
Misery index	−0.084**
	(0.041)
Operational code P4	−28.373*
	(16.697)
Polity score	−0.024
	(0.027)
Target GDP per capita	0.000
	(0.000)
Observations	203
Pseudo-R^2	0.085

Notes: Robust standard errors in parentheses.

* $p < 0.1$; ** $p < 0.05$; *** $p < 0.01$.

(pseudo-R^2 = 0.085), although still significant (p-value = 0.0007). Given that the model does not incorporate the actions of the target except through the tension and provocation levels, it is not too surprising that the accuracy is lower. The second difference is the job approval rating, which has no significant effect on the decision to modify sanctions. Once the sanctions are in place, the public pays even less attention to them allowing the president to act with greater freedom.

The tension, provocation, misery index, and locus of historical control (P-4) are all significant and in the expected direction. Like the decision to initiate, tension has the biggest impact on the president's choice to alter the sanctions. Although provocation clearly did not deter the president from initiating the sanctions, it still is associated with a decrease in the form of lifting the economic pressure. This effect is small compared to the decision to use sanctions, but it shows that the president still considers the position of the target when contemplating how to continue the coercive effort. The misery index also acts as expected indicating that the president prefers to limit the level of economic coercion during hard economic times. While economic sanctions do not tend to have a noticeable impact on the U.S. economy as a whole, a poorly performing economy seems to create an environment in which the president prefers to avoid or lift any limits placed on international trade.

The effects of operational code beliefs have a moderately substantive impact on the president's decision. The greater the president's sense of control over the political universe, the more likely he will be to lift or decrease the sanctions. A one standard deviation increase in P-4 decreases the likelihood that the president will increase the sanction regime from 44 to 37 percent, thereby increasing the probability that he would decrease or lift the sanction from 56 to 63 percent. Presidents with a higher sense of control seem to believe that they can get the target to compromise or even capitulate without the continued pressure of economic sanctions. This belief in greater control leads them to shorten or decrease the intensity of the sanctions.

Conclusions

Drawing from Drury's (2005) investigation, this study has focused on the impact that the president's beliefs have on the decisions to use and then alter economic coercion. The lower intensity of economic sanctions as a form of coercion makes them a hard test for the influence of cognitive constraints. That is, the decision to use economic coercion may not involve the president's beliefs because sanctions are not as stressful nor do they necessarily involve the president as directly as the use of the military. The results show that cognitive factors pass the test. The president's beliefs significantly affect both his decision first to initiate and second to modify economic sanctions. These results emphasize the power that cognitive factors have in decision making at less intense levels of coercive diplomacy.

In addition to the direct effect on the decision to use economic coercion, a president's strategic orientation (I-1) is also related to the tension level. The more cooperative the president, the lower the tension score tends to be. Although not enough to induce multicolinearity issues, this relationship suggests that the president's beliefs have a dual impact on his decisions. First, they tend to make him act more cooperatively toward the target in general, and second, they reduce the likelihood that sanctions will be used. While it is possible that the tension is affecting the president's preferences, the direction of that relationship is a question for future research. Although more operational code data must be collected to better assess the impact it has on the president's decision making, the results here are promising. The statistical significance and substantive impact on the decision to use and modify economic sanctions suggests that this is a fruitful avenue for research.

Notes

1. Because the trade balance is influenced by the sanctions, it is impossible to determine if the balance has an impact on the decision to modify sanctions.
2. See Drury (2005) for a complete description of the data.
3. Splicing these two data sets is not without concern. The two data sets overlap in the years 1991 and 1992. The correlation during these years is significant, but only reaches 0.31. However, including the post-Cold War era, and thus, the Clinton administration, increases the value of the analysis. Drury (2005) shows that significant differences exist between these periods but that the key findings hold. Because of the benefits for determining the impact of the operational code on the decision to use economic sanctions—the primary purpose of this chapter—I splice the data.
4. Multiple speeches from each presidency from Johnson through Clinton provided an average of 350 verbs-in-context per president. These were used to generate the P1, P4, and I1 variables. While the speeches provided plenty of data to calculate the operational code, there were not enough speeches to generate longitudinal data for each president. Therefore, the scores are generated for each president and remain constant throughout their tenure in office. Clearly, this is not as optimal as a monthly, quarterly, or even yearly average; however, these data are not currently available.
5. I also include the Beck, Katz, and Tucker (1998) correction for temporal dependence. For a full discussion of the statistical issues, see the appendix in Drury (2005). All models are estimated with *Stata 8.2*.

CHAPTER 10

ECONOMIC LIBERALISM AND THE OPERATIONAL CODE BELIEFS OF U.S. PRESIDENTS: THE INITIATION OF NAFTA DISPUTES, 1989–2002

Matthew Stevenson

The tariff is not an economic problem exclusively. It is a political problem as well.
—E.E. Schattschneider

Introduction

In the summer months of 1992 trade bureaucrats in Ottawa were besieged by a flurry of actions by their U.S. counterparts in the Bush administration. Working under the joint aegis of the U.S.–Canada free trade agreement and current U.S. trade law, Washington appeared to be shifting to a much more aggressive stance on many issues that had concerned the two sides on trade for the last several months. Canadian bureaucrats were not surprised. They liked to refer to any U.S. election year as "the silly season," ripe for electoral-minded trade disputes. However, once all was said and done, very few of the U.S. actions resulted in any concrete gains by the initiators. In fact, most of the public actions were outright failures to prevail over the liberal principle of free trade that informs the North American Free Trade Agreement (NAFTA).

The academic literature has characterized these free-trade relationship and dispute resolution processes in two ways. Institutional analysts argue that the free-trade agreements have precipitated the triumph of international law, showing that the Canadian Free Trade Agreement

(CFTA) and the NAFTA have not only changed the distribution of gains, but also changed the way bureaucracies have responded to such laws (Goldstein 1996). Assuming rationality on the part of all players, they see the interactions not only as a game where the rules have changed, but also where the rules (meaning the free trade treaties) change the behavior of the actors.

Another group of scholars argue that free trade disputes are part of the struggle between statist and societal actors responding to macroeconomic forces such as unemployment, inflation, and fluctuations in the gross national product (Mansfield and Busch 1995). Writ large, protectionism is seen as the response to political factors. However, analyses of societal and statist influences on trade policy and tariff levels remain inconclusive. While authors such as Epstein and O'Halloran (1996) argue in favor of statist influences, that is, the importance of political institutions in shaping policy, others show support for the theory that societal influences, such as political coalitions and pressure groups, have the greater say (Hiscox 1999). Finally, Mansfield and Busch (1995) take the middle path, arguing that a mix of both societal and statist influences are the determinants of trade policy and levels of protectionism.

These arguments raise two important questions. First, how well do institutional arguments fare when confronted by seemingly contradictory findings, such as those presented in this chapter for the analysis of dispute resolution within the U.S.–Canada free trade agreement? Do institutions "matter" in the way statist arguments would suggest, or do presidents work around institutions for their own electoral advantage? Second, does international law prevail in these instances? Or is it simply an illusory effect where the real cause of the outcome is not international law but perhaps the more lowbrow effects of domestic politics?

I argue in this chapter that these analysts are correct in their belief that actors have changed their ways of responding to institutional constraints. However, it is not in the manner that they believe. I explain instead how U.S. presidents have chosen a path between two countervailing constituencies—economic actors who wish to make gains through trade and political actors who wish to remain in office. I create a model that both explains and predicts the actions of presidents in pleasing these two constituencies within the framework of the NAFTA. I show that economic imperatives in this forum are trumped by political imperatives while being conditioned by presidential belief systems.

Institutions, International Law, and Actor Preferences

The nature and degree of influence of institutions over actors' preferences is a question that continues to perplex political scientists and pundits.

A puzzle in a particular institutional domain that has seemed to defy explanation is presidential decisions to initiate disputes within NAFTA. When the United States and Canada were negotiating their free trade agreement prior to 1988, a leading issue on the Canadian negotiator's agenda was the effort to shield domestic industries from protectionism in the United States. The negotiators came up with an institutional solution to this threat. In the last negotiating session, the Canadians demanded a dispute settlement mechanism that would provide a forum for settling differences between the two sides and hopefully nipping protectionist measures in the bud (Dymond, Hart, and Robertson 1994).

The analysis in this chapter will show how actors such as the president can frustrate institutional constraints in order to further their own preferences. The avenue that is used to explore this question is an analysis of the *timing* of trade dispute initiation since the creation of the U.S.–Canada free trade area. The actions of the U.S. government have puzzled observers on both sides of the border since the signing of the treaty in 1989 and its extension to Mexico in 1992. Canadian trade officials speculate that much of the dispute initiation is the result of U.S. electoral politics. American officials state unequivocally that they only turn to formal disputes as a last resort. The results of the disputes have been even more puzzling—the United States has initiated the vast majority but won only a small minority. Even so, they have continued to initiate them.

The explanation I propose is one that looks at trade disputes as the result of actors' preferences in the face of institutional challenges. My explanation is that trade disputes are the result of the president and his administration successfully trying to curry favor with the public. They do these actions while carefully avoiding endangering the larger trade regime as a whole. In short, even by losing trade disputes the President is winning. However, the face validity of this proposition is troublesome. How can anyone win by losing? The answer can be found by looking at the factors that predict such behavior—electoral variables, such as presidential approval ratings, the occurrence of elections, and the belief systems of U.S. presidents.[1]

First, I review the current literature that looks at institutional preferences and trade and lay out a brief explanation for actor behavior in the face of institutional preferences. I continue by testing the main hypotheses in my explanation by using an OLS regression model that attempts to predict and explain the timing of U.S. trade disputes. Finally, I discuss the implications of these findings for theory, public policy, and future research.

Institutional analysis has been widely used in the analysis of cooperation, especially in trade issues.[2] The neoliberal institutionalist school has focused on the role of institutions aiding cooperation and realizing the benefits of cooperative trade agreements (Keohane 1984). Recent research on disputes over tariff and nontariff barriers has also emphasized institutions as arbiters of disputes about trade agreements. Judith Goldstein (1996) has written the most germane study in analyzing the perceived role of institutions in the Canadian–U.S. free trade agreement. While her analysis can be seen as a complement to the statist-institutional arguments of Epstein and O'Halloran (1996), it suggests a new avenue of analysis for the trade dispute process in general, namely, the role and evolution of international law.

Goldstein's examination of the dispute settlement mechanism of the CFTA and NAFTA asks how this element of the trade agreement led to a change in the bureaucracy of the U.S. government. Moreover, she asks why the United States has remained a party to an agreement "in which the distribution of gains went to the weaker party," that party being Canada. Goldstein concludes that international institutions "can and do constrain domestic policy." In effect, the "powerful domestic actors" identified by Goldstein have utilized these institutions to bring about free trade. Institutions then constrain actors, using international law as their tool.

Instead, I argue that presidents have used the elements of free trade agreements to implement their own preferences, but not in the way that Goldstein expects. Taken at face value, the policy outcomes are counterintuitive to my argument, in that most of the decisions by NAFTA institutions have been in favor of Canada. There is a conventional wisdom that the international institutions have won—the president is constrained in his protectionist activities by limits put in place by the CFTA and NAFTA regimes. However, I contend that three U.S. presidents have used the existence of these agreements for their own ends, influenced more by their own preferences than constrained by powerful domestic actors or international law. I propose the rival hypothesis that, in fact, the actions of the president to initiate disputes have worked out to suit his preferences even though the United States has lost the disputes.

A Nested Games Model of Presidential Choice

I shall use the "nested games" approach introduced by George Tsebelis (1990) to show that the lack of face validity in the findings about economic policy outcomes is trumped by looking at a domestic electoral game with its own institutional constraints and "nested" within the game of international trade disputes associated with NAFTA institutions. How can the continued actions of the president leading to suboptimal outcomes for the United States be explained? I will first present the conventional wisdom that it is simply the power of international law constraining these outcomes, as espoused by Mansfield and Busch (1995), Goldstein (1996), and others. Then I will compare this analysis to the "nested game" explanation that I have proposed. Finally, I will draw hypotheses from this discussion of rival explanations and test them with data for U.S. trade disputes within NAFTA.

The Conventional Wisdom

A president does not enter into disputes lightly. When he does, it does not pay for him to lose. This conventional wisdom on trade dispute initiation is something upon which both scholars and policy makers agree (Destler 1992; Office of the United States Trade Representative, unattributable interview, July 1998). It further states that the a U.S. president is more likely to initiate trade disputes against Canada than vice versa, because he knows that there is very little Canadians can do about it. Canada's economy is overwhelmingly reliant upon the economy of the United States, and it cannot retaliate without serious risk of injury.

Given that he initiates a dispute, the imperative for the president is to win. The conventional wisdom, voiced by United States Trade Representative officials themselves, holds that there is no benefit in a lost dispute— "we don't gain anything by losing" (Office of the United States Trade Representative: Director of Canadian Affairs Mary Ryckman, interview, July 1998). Thus, once a trade dispute is initiated, the president should aggressively pursue his trade policy. Nice guys finish last. We can infer from this wisdom that presidents prefer to win trade disputes with an aggressive trade policy over a passive policy ending with a loss. Given these preferences, we would expect any given administration to initiate a number of disputes and work aggressively to win them. The historical record shows that trade disputes with Canada are entered upon often, but more likely than not, the United States loses. So why have U.S. presidents tended toward a "losing" strategy? Are they being lured into losing battles by crafty Canadians?

Actually, Canadian politicians are loath to "take on" the United States. As one staffer in Ottawa admits, it is too risky to challenge the United States in a trade fight and risk losing. They have no choice when the United States starts the process, but they have avoided their own initiatives. Canada is reliant on the *status quo* in a way that neither the United States nor Mexico is. Canadian actors cannot risk losing a confrontation with the United States. As figure 10.1 shows, Canada relies more on its external trade in NAFTA than the other two countries. Thus, it cannot afford to endanger its trade flows. So long as the NAFTA trade disputes with the

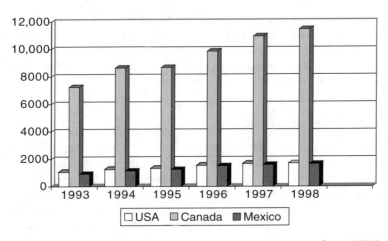

Figure 10.1   Per Capita Value of North American Trade for NAFTA Members, $US.

Sources: Department of Foreign Affairs, Government of Canada; U.S. Bureau of the Census; *The Economist.*

United States affect only a portion of its trade, as opposed to the agreement itself that would affect all its trade, it is not willing to "rock the boat."

This Canadian position is well staked out and conforms to the model of conventional wisdom that says states are constrained by their relative power and by international law in their trade policy. However, U.S. trade policy is puzzling from the vantage point of conventional wisdom. Why would a rational president initiate disputes in the absence of Canadian provocation and continue to be thwarted by institutional constraints?

Challenges to the Conventional Wisdom

I suggest we can better explain the puzzling, seemingly self-defeating behavior of U.S. presidents by looking at their actions in the light of a game nested within a larger game. This approach draws on the theoretical arguments of Putnam (1988) and Tsebelis (1990). They argue that leaders often play more than one game at a time. Putnam identifies a "two-level" application of game theory in which leaders play a domestic game and an international game and try to find a strategy that produces winning outcomes for both games. Tsebelis suggests the further possibility that a strategy resulting in suboptimal outcomes for one game may produce an optimal outcome for a more important game nested within the first game.

Let us suppose that the president has two options with which to please his constituents. On the one hand, there is the option to pursue protectionist activities, such as trade disputes that have their roots in tariffs or nontariff barriers, attracted by the short-term gains in electoral popularity that a dispute will give him and discounting the possible economic dislocation that such a dispute may cause. His short-term strategy may be primarily to win an election and secondarily to win a trade dispute.

This behavior is the president acting as an "opportunist," taking care of his future reelection. However, he still "plays to win." He can choose disputes among the many available that are likely to win. He can apply pressure on his foreign trade partners to get them to bow to his trade policy, such as making threats of retaliation in trade disputes. He can move his trade agenda to a national level and bring attention to it through all the means at the disposal of his office.

On the other hand, the president can also "play to lose." He can choose disputes that have shaky legal ground, or that have a past track record of failure. He might avoid putting trade into his national agenda and only publicize his trade moves in the locales in which they are salient. There are some historical precedents for this strategy, in which presidents have pursued policies that seem mainly symbolic and doomed to lose. Much of the Canadian conflict can also be characterized in this fashion, with issues being highlighted only in the communities affected (Stevenson 1999).[3]

It is possible as well for a U.S. president to pursue both strategies simultaneously within a two-level game framework in which domestic voters and Canada are the other players in each game. Ideally, he would like to gain a trade advantage over his Canadian neighbor as well as convince voters to reelect him. In the domestic game, voters may have imperfect information and cannot tell whether a dispute initiated by the president is fated to lose or win before casting their vote. If the president times the initiation of disputes right, then voters decide who wins an election before NAFTA decides who wins a trade dispute. The implication of this analysis is that it is in the interest of the president to "talk" free trade while pursuing a strategy of trade disputes that fail. He gets the best of both worlds: long-term economic growth sustained by the productivity gains of free trade and short-term political gains from disputes.

This strategy would fail if a president were to run for office a third time. He would have to explain his record of failed disputes. Due to term limits on the office, however, sitting presidents never have to face this possibility. If he should pursue a strategy of consistently winning disputes, he would risk the economic gains that are associated with his larger objective of free trade in the first place. Therefore, I conclude that while the conventional wisdom is correct—presidents will initiate disputes—it is wrong about which ones. Presidents will initiate disputes, but they will play to lose in order to boost popularity and help the chances of reelection without sacrificing the liberal ideological goal of a free trade area and its accompanying economic gains.

But is this argument credible? Is this type of behavior feasible by U.S. presidents? There are two sources of evidence for testing this argument. One is anecdotal evidence from participants in the political process who have admitted as much. In reference to a dispute initiated regarding the importation of lamb into the United States, for example, an administration official openly admitted to engaging in a play to lose strategy—with the express intention of using the proposed tariff to gain support for the president (Sanger 1999). I shall add to the credibility of this claim by considering more systematically what presidents *believe*. Two elements of presidential belief systems, beliefs about the management of risk and the role of chance, appear to be keys to identifying and predicting presidential dispute initiation.[4] Their variance explains to a large degree when presidents take a chance and risk abrogating trade agreements by initiating trade disputes.

Research Design

Here I test two rival explanations that question the conventional wisdom that U.S. free trade policy is driven primarily by calculations of economic gain and the constraints of international law. One suggests that electoral factors provide constraints and incentives that redefine rationality from the calculation of economic costs and benefits to include the consideration of political consequences.[5] The other is that presidential beliefs and calculations about the nature of the political universe and the most effective means of managing political decisions influence U.S. trade policy. This research design leads toward the larger substantive goal of this study, namely, to question and test the conventional wisdom that international law and ideological support for liberal free trade policies are predominant. Is it more accurate to say that institutional constraints and economic liberalism are at the mercy of the ingenuity of actors' preferences and their belief systems?

Cases

The period of study starts at the beginning of the first Bush presidency in 1989 and extends through the Clinton administration to the end of the first two years of the second Bush presidency in 2002. During this period presidential rhetoric espoused a liberal free trade policy (Stevenson 1999). Cases include only those initiated by the United States through the executive branch, specifically the Department of Commerce and International Trade Administration.

There is a difference between cases "filed" by the U.S. government, and those "initiated" by all entities in the United States. Using a broader criterion, it would be possible to construe all cases as being "initiated" by the United States. However, I use a narrower standard for disputes initiated by the United States, including only those cases connected to the president himself or his administration. Further, the population that I analyze in this chapter is the set of disputes initiated by the United States and judged subsequently in favor of Canada. Those cases disputing a Canadian tariff that the United States won are not considered unfair disputes, nor are they included in this study.[6]

Variables and Hypotheses

The research hypotheses in this study concern the relationships between presidential dispute initiation and changes in domestic political variables, prime economic indicators, and presidential belief systems. I operationalize the dependent variable of presidential behavior as changes in trade policy, specifically when a president (or by proxy his administration) chooses to move from a free trade position and initiates an invalid trade dispute with Canada.[7] Candidates for reelection can score points with voters long before a dispute comes to resolution. This was the case explicitly in the long-running lumber dispute with Canada, as former Oregon senator Packwood's aides have intimated (former Packwood aide Brad Figel, interview, July 1998). Thus, the critical point in these disputes is when they are *initiated*, not when they conclude.[8]

Domestic Political Imperatives

With respect to domestic approval ratings and presidential behavior, as approval ratings go down in period "a," I expect the number of "unfair" disputes in period "b" to increase (Gallup Poll 1989–2002). The lag in the dependent variable is modeled in order to control for possible causal order issues in which a decrease in approval might be a consequence of dispute initiation. This hypothesis is consistent with the explanation that candidates will take action with an eye to the voting public in order to boost their reelection chances. By extension I also expect the number of unfair disputes initiated to rise in an election year. As the proximity to a congressional or presidential election increases, the saliency of trade disputes rises as a means of gaining electoral support. A trade dispute put in action three years before an election has much less significance to the voting public than a dispute initiated three months before an election.[9]

Prime Economic Indicators

I anticipate that the relation between initiated disputes and the prime economic indicators of unemployment and inflation will be positive (Department of Commerce 1989–2002). When unemployment increases, I expect the number of initiated disputes to increase.[10] I use the Consumer Price Index (CPI) as an indicator of inflationary pressures. It tends to move opposite to the unemployment figures and has an immediate impact on all potential voters in the form of constrained consumption. I expect CPI to be directly related to the number of initiated disputes.

Presidential Beliefs

A number of operational code variables were also included for this analysis. Each month during a president's term, a public news conference or discussion by the president was coded for a number of operational code beliefs (Papers of the U.S. Presidents 1989–2002). Four of these variables are included in our final model, reflecting a president's views on risk-taking (I-3), the predictability of the political future (P-3), control over historical development (P-4), and the role of chance (P-5). Also, a dummy variable is included to control for whether the president is a Democrat or a Republican. There is little clear expectation as to whether Democrats or Republicans will tend to have beliefs that incline them toward more disputes, but it is important to include this variable to acknowledge potential differences between Bill Clinton's two administrations and the administrations of George Bush I and George Bush II.

Model Parameters

The regression equation that I propose to model the hypotheses is:

$$Y = a + b_1x_1 + b_2x_2 + b_3x_3 + b_{3a}x_{3a} + b_4x_4 + b_5x_5 - b_6x_6 + b_7x_7 + b_8x_8 + b_9x_9 + b_{10}x_{10} + e$$

Where the variables are defined as follows:

Y: The amount of unfair trade disputes initiated in period $t + 1$.
a: Constant term.
$b_1 - b_{10}$:   Unstandardized partial regression coefficients.
x_1:   Binary dummy variable for political party of the incumbent president.

x_2:   CPI in month t.
x_3:   Dummy variable for presidential incumbent election year.
x_{3a}:   Dummy variable for nonincumbent presidential election year.
x_4:   Unemployment rate during month.
x_5:   Dummy variable for congressional election year.
x_6:   Approval rating of the president during month.
x_7:   I-3 score from trade-related speech in month.
x_8:   P-5 score from trade-related speech in month.
x_9:   P-4 score from trade-related speech in month.
x_{10}:   P-3 score from trade-related speech in month.
e: Residual

The design for this analysis is a panel of observations between independent and dependent variables. Each observation period is a month. I examine the relationship between the next period's number of disputes and the independent variables in the preceding period.

Results

The analysis of the model of presidential dispute initiation in response to fluctuations in political, economic, and cognitive indicators reveals that some political and operational code variables are statistically significant, while economic variables are not. The results in table 10.1 show that for every unit decrease in presidential popularity, we can expect a 0.01 increase in the number of disputes initiated by the president in the three-month period of study. This is a small effect, but the direction is as expected. The second political effect, election years, shows the expected relationship for presidential elections (even for nonincumbents). It does not show a relationship for congressional election years, indicating minor influence by the legislative branch.

The expected relationship between dispute initiation and levels of unemployment in the United States does not appear. The same is noted for the CPI economic indicator. These findings reinforce the primacy of political considerations over economic concerns regarding dispute initiation. When specified in a model without operational code variables, the economic indicators are statistically significant and in the expected direction. But their influence drops out with the introduction of operational code beliefs as variables. This effect will be discussed further later. Here I simply note that unfair disputes also have no long-term benefit to the economy according to neoclassical economic theory.

The binary variable for party indicates that the Democratic administration of President Clinton was less inclined to initiate disputes in comparison to the elder and younger Bushes. This may seem to be a counterintuitive

Table 10.1 Parameter Estimates for a Model of Presidential Reactions to Changes in Leading Economic, Political, and Operational Code Indicators

Parameter	Unstand. coeff.	S.E.	T	Sig. T
Constant	0.52	1.19	0.44	0.65
Party (Democratic)	−0.34	0.16	−2.15	0.03
Approval rating	−0.01	0.006	−2.09	0.04
Congressional election year	−0.01	0.14	−0.02	0.99
Incumbent presidential election year	0.33	0.16	2.01	0.05
Nonincumbent presidential election year	0.46	0.24	1.94	0.05
Unemployment rate	−0.02	0.08	−0.25	0.80
CPI	−0.004	0.005	−0.71	0.47
I-3	−0.72	0.36	−1.98	0.05
P-3	−0.50	0.73	−0.68	0.49
P-4	0.69	0.64	1.09	0.27
P-5	1.52	0.76	2.00	0.05

R-square = 0.175;	N = 148;	F = 2.79.

finding, but given the context of the various administrations, it is possible to suggest several explanations. For instance, Republican administrations, which are generally pro-trade, may have more leeway to play fast and loose with disputes than their Democrat counterparts. A number of other factors, such as differing United States Trade Representatives, the relative autonomy of the Commerce Department, and ideological differences between cabinet-level decision makers in the three administrations offer other avenues of explanation that present fertile ground for further studies.

The most fascinating results are the overwhelming influence of change in operational code beliefs as a predictor for explaining trade dispute initiation. Not only do these indices substantially dampen the influence of variables in the economic and political hypotheses, they are by far the best predictors of presidential trade disputes. The negative sign of the I-3 coefficient indicates that as presidents become less risk-acceptant, their propensity to initiate trade disputes increases. The positive sign of the P-5 coefficient indicates that as presidents increase their estimates of the role of chance, they are more likely to initiate trade disputes with their two partners.

To untangle the meaning of the I-3 relationship, we examine the correspondence between the leaders' risk orientation (I-3) scores and their strategic orientation (I-1) scores. I-3 is a positive, linear function of I-1 in these cases, indicating that the less cooperative the president's strategic orientation, the less acceptant he is of a cooperative strategy and the accompanying risk of domination by others. This analysis yields the following interpretation of the I-3 finding: *as presidents become less acceptant of the risk of being dominated by others, they are more likely to increase the number of trade disputes they initiate.* The increase in trade disputes is their way of managing an aversion to the risk of domination. This interpretation corresponds with the findings of the other variables in the model—as electoral balloting approaches and as approval ratings (a measure of the capability of winning the election) decline, presidents become more diversified in their efforts to win elections. They look for novel tactics in avoiding electoral losses, including initiating trade disputes to rally electoral support.

Interpreting the robust finding for the role of chance (P-5) indicator also raises questions, as P-5 represents the interaction of two other indicators (P-3 and P-4) in the model. The influence of the leader's belief in the predictability of the political future (P-3) and the degree of control over historical development (P-4) separately drop out from the model when electoral variables are introduced. The effect of P-5 is predominant, even when controlling for P-3 and P-4, indicating that the interaction effect is most important. Increases in the P-5 score represent the presidents' belief in the role of chance in human affairs and historical development, stemming from the interaction between his beliefs in the predictability of the political future (P-3) and control over historical development (P-4).[11]

Driven by beliefs that the future is relatively unpredictable and uncontrollable, *if the president sees the "role of chance" as high, he may be more willing to take risks on the initiation of high-profile trade disputes.* This interpretation of the results for the role of chance (P-5) variable dovetails nicely with the declining tolerance for the risk of being dominated represented by the leader's risk orientation (I-3) variable. Trade disputes appear to be a useful policy outlet for presidents who are looking for actions to improve their electoral chances—especially those presidents who are relatively intolerant of losses and view the predictability of the future as low.[12]

These findings give pause to the conventional wisdom of institutional and statist theories of presidential behavior, which emphasize the constraints of international law and economic forces on presidential actions. The results indicate that a president's commitment toward an institution and a stated liberal ideological bent toward free trade are somewhat Machiavellian. When their belief systems dispose them toward taking a chance, they are willing to abrogate signed international agreements in order to achieve their ends.

Finally, the R-square of 0.17 leaves much of the variance within the model unexplained. I attribute this gap partly to many of the relationships between the president and various individuals, which are not factored into an analysis of this sort. This model assumes a rational president reacting to macro-level occurrences, such as fluctuations in the prime economic indicators or rising electoral concerns. With the exception of presidential beliefs, it takes little account of micro-level variables. Lobbying by individuals or interest groups and congressional influences are left out, that is, the influence of commercial interests when corporations receive a "break" from Congress for whatever reasons.

Conclusions and Implications

Goldstein (1996) ends her treatment of Canada–U.S. trade institutions by noting that the agreement is "an international solution to a domestic problem." The problem, she explains, is protectionist leanings in the U.S. Congress. The main argument in this chapter refutes that claim. The initial impetus for the NAFTA institution was Canadian, and if one accepts my nested game argument, the perceived benefits of the dispute resolution process have accrued to the president. Thus, the actions of presidents are more opportunistic than anything else. They serve to remind us of actors' capabilities to prevail in the face of institutional constraints.

Moreover, the findings of the Machiavellian empirical analysis show the convergence of domestic and international politics as a two-level game. The role of domestic politics in international relations is hotly debated, and these findings point toward a strong influence on the part of domestic political imperatives. While the economic policy outcomes of these actions are *ad hoc* and not to be confused with the larger policy objectives of the government (trade liberalization), there is some reason to believe that such actions can undermine such larger policy objectives. If the domestic imperatives become strong enough for administrations to desire concrete results from all their trade actions, then the long-term benefits of such institutions may be threatened. It is the fate of institutions, especially those that constrain profit-seeking behavior, to be besieged eternally by the ingenuity of humankind whose successes in circumventing institutional constraints may often escape notice.

The findings of this study do not lend much support to the societal or the statist explanations for U.S. foreign economic policy. The results do put a new twist on the societal explanation. Trade disputes are not a result of societal pressures, but they do anticipate the pressures that the electoral cycle might bring. They are proactive in nature, as opposed the reactive assumption made by traditional approaches. International law is ascendant, but not for many of the reasons its proponents claim. It succeeds for the wrong reasons in NAFTA cases—its test cases are designed to lose. The great success of the NAFTA panels in reaffirming the NAFTA statutes are not an indication of the primacy of either approach or the growing influence of international law. NAFTA's success in dispute resolution without undermining free trade has occurred mostly as the result of domestic actors using existing laws to achieve their own ends.

This study shows that domestic politics trump economic policy. Presidents are influenced by institutions, but this influence is circumvented to satisfy electoral goals. In support of this interpretation, I have introduced as evidence the conditioning effects of presidential belief systems. The economic and political imperatives that inform the statist and institutional arguments are strongly influenced by the beliefs of presidents regarding the management of risk and the role of chance in historical development. In a systems model of dispute initiation as a response to electoral and economic imperatives, this agent-centered dimension provides a powerful additional avenue for future research.

Notes

1. In making this argument, I assume that trade disputes are the prerogative of the executive branch. As Goldstein (1996) points out, the law is designed to allow the president discretion in trade action. Other scholars suggest that protectionism writ small, such as discrete trade disputes (as opposed to general tariff levels), are the result of interest groups channeling their preferences through the executive branch. While many of the disputes represent the preferences of congressmen, firms, and the like, there is no reason the president cannot pick and choose among the options presented to him for those disputes that serve his electoral purposes. For a good summary of this literature and the debates surrounding preferences and general tariff levels, see Milner and Yoffie (1989) and Epstein and O'Halloran (1996).

2. Peter Gourevitch (1996) explains that "Institutional models explain public policy as the output of process defined by institutions." If institutions define the process, then we can suppose that actors will work within institutions when the preferences of those institutions suit their needs, but when actor's preferences change, they will seek to work outside those institutions, or change their behavior to subvert the original preferences of the institutions themselves.

3. Conversely, other trade issues have been the subjects of "efforts to win," and infinitely more resources have been poured into the fight despite much smaller potential rewards. One need only look at the salience of trade conflict with Japan over agricultural issues, which have small real value to the

economy of the United States as a whole, in comparison to trade in primary resources with Canada, the value of which to the United States is immense.

4. Risk Orientation and the Role of chance are two beliefs in a decision maker's "operational code," which are the leader's beliefs about the nature of the political universe and the most effective means of political action. For a discussion of these beliefs and their indicators retrieved from public statements of U.S. presidents and other world leaders, see Schafer (2000); Walker (1990); Walker, Schafer, and Young (1998, 2003).

5. The existence of a political–business cycle is not a new idea. Neither is the application of policy to influence elections. However, extending this analysis to trade disputes is relatively novel. For treatments of the electoral economic cycle, and policy effects therein, see Alesina and Rosenthal (1995); Clarke et al. (1992); Tufte (1978).

6. There exists only one of these types of disputes in the 1989–2002 period.

7. This dependent variable is the number of disputes brought by the United States before the bi-national trade secretariat each month period, which are subsequently judged "unfair" by the NAFTA secretariat's panels. The data were obtained by coding the judgments themselves in conjunction with secondary sources. The determination of "fairness" was left to the decision of the secretariat's panels that judged the merits of the U.S. claims.

8. Many other points within the dispute process could conceivably be "critical" points for the president to gain maximum benefit for his reelection chances. Choosing which point in the dispute process is critical deserves some explanation. Suppose that we say that the time when the dispute is formally resolved is the critical point for the initiating party; the results are in hand, and the president and his functionaries can reap the political benefits of their earlier actions. It would be tempting to allocate this particular point as the critical juncture in the process, but I reject this coding choice for two reasons. First, I assume that the president and those in his party are aware that most trade disputes fail. This conclusion can be drawn simply from the historical record. Second, interviews with those in the campaign organizations of the dispute-initiating parties have said frankly that the fact that disputes "were on the table" was used as a selling point on the campaign trail.

9. There then arises the question of non-returning presidents. Presidents are limited to two terms. Why would presidents continue such actions if they were not in line to be reelected? There is only one instance in the panel where a nonincumbent ran—2000. A dummy variable is included to account for this effect.

10. I chose the unemployment variable rather than GNP as the one that would have the most salience to a sitting president. Unemployment levels and GNP both have support in the current literature as being salient to

the president, but the literature on retrospective voting notes that the impact of unemployment has the greatest influence on voting choice. Presidents know that voters vote their pocketbook, and of the two figures, unemployment has the greatest immediate effect on the pocketbook. GNP figures correlate with unemployment, though they lag by months (Stevenson 1999).

11. When examined separately, the index for the predictability of the political future (P-3) is found to be a better predictor than the control over historical development (P-4) index is for the role of chance (P-5) index in presidential trade-related text. P-5 is mainly a function of P-3, which has a negative relationship with P-5.

12. These findings are also broadly consistent with prospect theory, which predicts that decision makers will be more likely to make risky decisions when they see themselves as operating in the domain of losses rather than in the domain of gains (Levy 1997). If U.S. presidents see themselves as operating in the domain of losses in the nested election game, then they risk initiating an unfair trade dispute in order to win the election game. Conversely, if they see themselves operating in the domain of gains in the wider trade game, they are risk-averse about losing the gains of free trade by initiating and aggressively pursuing protectionist disputes. So they initiate disputes that are unfair and play to lose in the electoral game in order to avoid losing economic gains in the trade game while making political gains in the election game.

CHAPTER 11

BANKERS AND BELIEFS: THE POLITICAL PSYCHOLOGY OF THE ASIAN FINANCIAL CRISIS

Cameron G. Thies

Introduction

The Asian Financial Crisis is commonly dated to July of 1997, when the Thai central bank authorities, under relentless speculative pressure, allowed the baht to float freely. Most accounts of the crisis take the constitution of the crisis as a given and focus on either the structural economic conditions that "caused" it or on the outcomes that resulted from it. In this chapter I build on a small, but growing literature on constructivist international political economy (IPE) that no longer takes the global economy and its crises as a given. Instead, constructivist IPE examines the processes whereby features of the global economy, including its periodic crises, are constituted. The constitutive aspects of economic crises then enable us to further understand how key agents operating within these crises respond to mutually shared understandings about the causes of events and processes.

I build on the work of Hall (2003) and Widmaier (2004) to argue that the Asian Financial Crisis was constituted out of a clash of monetary cultures. The dominant culture of the East Asian region was a Keynesian Kantian culture that emphasized cooperation to achieve wage, price, and currency stability. This culture informed the beliefs of key actors in the region, including the central bankers who form the basis of this study. However, ideas associated with this culture, such as the Asian development model, which were once seen in a positive light by the core economic powers of the world, later were reconstituted as being the cause of the crisis. The International Monetary Fund (IMF), at the behest of the United States, began to attack the Keynesian Kantian culture of East Asia that it had itself discarded in the 1980s. This intervention was designed to install a Neoclassical Lockean monetary culture that emphasized more conflictual interstate and intrastate relations to achieve the same goals of wage, price, and currency stability. The institutional manifestations of the Neoclassical Lockean culture, namely legally independent central banks on the domestic level, and IMF intervention at the international/regional level, operated to import aspects of this culture into the region, thereby constituting a crisis.

Consistent with this theoretical model of the Asian Financial Crisis as a clash of monetary cultures, I find that Asian central bankers with more cooperative philosophical and strategic beliefs were able to reduce exchange rate volatility during the crisis years. Central bank institutions and IMF interventions on behalf of the Neoclassical Lockean culture produced the opposite. I also consider the interaction of central banker beliefs with their central bank institutional environments and the wider political systems they inhabit with some interesting results. Finally, all of these factors are considered in a cross-sectional time-series model alongside commonly identified structural economic variables known to affect exchange rate volatility during the Asian Financial Crisis.

The Socio-Cognitive Construction of Financial Crises

In the relatively short time that has passed since the Asian Financial Crisis was in full swing, a great deal of literature has emerged attempting to explain both its genesis and the varying outcomes experienced by the states of the region (e.g., Jackson 1999; Lee 2003; MacIntyre 2001; Noble and Ravenhill 2000; Pempel 1999; Tsurami 2001; Van Hoa and Harvie 2000). Most of these contributions seek to explain individual country outcomes in terms of general precipitating conditions for the region as a whole. This chapter moves away from this type of structural economic analysis toward an understanding of how individual agents participated in the construction of the Asian Crisis as a crisis, and how their beliefs affected the trajectory of the crisis. Constructivist approaches to international political economy have begun to examine these issues (see Burch and Denemark 1997, for an introduction). In particular, the work of Hall (2003) and Widmaier (2004) can assist in building a theoretical model of the Asian Crisis that allows us to consider the impact of key individuals as well as political and economic institutions and underlying structural economic factors operating in the intersection of two monetary cultures.

Hall (2003, 71) draws attention to a fact repeated by most analysts of the Asian Crisis: the Asian development model, characterized by strong government intervention to promote industrial development and export-led growth, was first heralded by the IMF as producing the "East Asian miracle" of the 1980s, then thoroughly trashed by the same in the aftermath of the crisis as a form of "crony capitalism" itself responsible for the financial crisis. Hall's project becomes a reconstruction of the discursive practices that enabled representations of the " 'causes' of the crisis" to "constitute and reconstitute the social meanings by which past and current social and economic practices are legitimated and delegitimated." The narrative structures produced during this process "recreate and reconstitute the present and future conditions for strategic action." Hall's analysis demonstrates how the U.S. Treasury Department under Robert Rubin and Lawrence Summer, the IMF under Michel Camdessus, and the South Korean government under Kim Young-sam and Kim Dae-jung participated in shaping the narrative structures that effectively "demolished" the Asian development model in the context of the Asian Financial Crisis.

Hall's work draws attention to several important factors for the present study. First, objective economic (material) conditions are not solely responsible for the production of crises, not even economic and financial crises. Second, though states may be considered to "act" in the international political economy, focusing on the individual agents of the state moves us closer to understanding the constitutive and causal mechanisms at work in the production of a crisis. Third, the ideas and beliefs of individual agents matter, especially if they are in positions of influence in key institutions such as treasury departments, international organizations, and the executive branch of government. Finally, those ideas and beliefs matter not only for the constitution of an event or series of events as a crisis, but in terms of the actual practices of agents operating within the crisis.

The dominant narrative that emerged out of the narratives of the key actors in this crisis focused on issues of transparency, good governance versus crony capitalism, the root (structural) causes of the crisis, the need for further liberalization, retribution by the hidden hand of the market, and the Washington Consensus on the need for neoliberal reforms throughout the developing world. Thus, the Asian development model that produced the East Asian miracle was reconstituted as the source of the Asian Financial Crisis. The dominant narrative forming during the crisis years can also be seen as the assault of one system or culture of shared monetary understandings and its expected policy behaviors on another system, including the replacement of some elements from the other system. The discursive shift that Hall (2003) documents can therefore also be seen as a cultural shift (Widmaier 2004).

Widmaier (2004) documents a general shift in the post–World War II international political economy away from cooperation to achieve monetary stability to the primary use of austerity to achieve the same end. He accomplishes this by examining the shared monetary understandings of government officials (e.g., chief executives, advisors, and central bankers), intergovernmental organization officials (e.g., IMF and World Bank), and economists as they changed over time. In the aftermath of World War II, these key individuals were all operating upon the principles of Keynesianism, which argued that state and societal cooperation was crucial to achieving wage, price, and currency guidelines. According to Keynesianism, expectations are just as important as "real" economic forces in achieving stability in these areas, such that "speculation" and the "psychology of the market" become important factors for policy makers to consider. "Spontaneous optimism" concerning the future can produce economic expansion and stable prices, while "spontaneous pessimism" can just as easily (or perhaps more so) bring the opposite. Widmaier (2004, 438) suggests that these Keynesian ideas produce a culture of Kantian friendship in terms of Wendt's (1999) classification of cultures of anarchy.

A Kantian culture arises when states and societal interests act to coordinate their expectations to produce wage, price, and exchange rate stability (similar to Wendt's rule of nonviolence), and aid each other in these efforts (similar to Wendt's rule of mutual aid). Widmaier (2004) argues that this Keynesian Kantian culture prevailed in the international political economy among the core economies well into the 1970s. The movement away from this culture was not the result of stagflation or the end of the dollar-based fixed exchange rate system, but of a change in ideas among economists and other key individuals. I suggest that a similar Keynesian Kantian culture was in operation among the East Asian states prior to and during the Asian Financial Crisis. Most of the states in the region maintained some type of peg to the U.S. dollar, and rather than engage in competitive devaluations, most maintained an overvalued peg. Government officials maintained very close links with business leaders as expected in the Asian development model. Labor was often actively repressed under this model, which differs from the type of cooperation experienced by the core economies after World War II. However, even successful labor movements in East Asia often gave way to cooperative arrangements with governments to restrain wage growth. As a result, the situation in East Asia represents a type of Keynesian Kantian culture of cooperation both within and between states to achieve relative exchange rate stability.

Not only did the Asian development model clash with the current ideas of the U.S. Treasury and the IMF, but its underlying Kantian culture had also been eclipsed among core economies. Neoclassical monetary understandings had become standard in the United States by the 1980s, combining classical monetarism with Keynesianism. Classical views suggested that monetary crises were caused by state failures and any macroeconomic adjustment by the government or outside assistance would further encourage situations of "moral hazard" whereby investors would make risky decisions knowing they were insured against complete failure. Classical monetarists believed that self-help policies were the only solutions to monetary crises. As a result, states should engage in competitive devaluations or the accumulation of balance of payments surpluses, and end cooperation in currency stabilization, thus forcing domestic adjustments in wages and prices. Classical views represent a type of Hobbesian culture, in which states do not cooperate with each other in the attempt to ward off speculative attacks on their currencies.

Neoclassical monetary understandings view monetary crises as reflections of long-term state failures, though they recognize that markets can make mistakes in the short-run due to "sticky prices" or "exchange rate overshooting." These short-term failures allow for intermittent cooperation in the form of outside assistance or macroeconomic stabilization. States therefore cooperate to avoid competitive devaluations and the contagion of speculative attack in a type of Lockean culture. The U.S. and IMF response to the onset of economic instability in Asia represents a blend of classical and neoclassical monetary understandings. Ultimately, the IMF usually recommends a floating currency, which in most cases in Asia would represent a competitive devaluation, as well as domestic austerity. The IMF loaned huge sums of money to countries in the region that would submit to these demands. The clash of monetary cultures that played out during the construction of the Asian Financial Crisis still plays out in repeated and reconstituted narratives outlining the purported causes of the crisis to this day.

The clash of these cultures can help us understand how key agents constructed the Asian Financial Crisis as it unfolded. In previous work, I have demonstrated how central bankers in the developed countries were critical in steering their countries to reach their respective inflation targets in the aftermath of the Asian Financial Crisis (Thies 2004). I further suggested that an analysis of Asian central bankers during the Asian Financial Crisis would help us to understand the role that these key agents play in achieving macroeconomic stability in both the developing and developed world. Therefore, this chapter focuses on the impact of Asian central bank governors in shaping the Asian Financial Crisis.

I expect that the Keynesian Kantian culture informed the belief systems of these central bankers during the crisis period. Central bankers should hold beliefs emphasizing cooperation in promoting exchange rate stability. To the extent that these beliefs constitute and shape the crisis, they should be successful. However, the IMF under U.S. guidance began to import classical and neoclassical monetary understandings in the attempt to displace Kantian cooperation with Lockean rivalry (or at the extremes, Hobbesian conflict) that they had already constituted as the proper culture of monetary relations among the core economies and attempted to export throughout the developing world.

Related to that culture are institutional models that have been disseminated throughout the world, without much concern about their compatibility with existing culture. The central bank institutions occupied by our central bankers have increasingly been adapted to a conflictual role, in terms of their independence from the government and from the society whose economy they attempt to control. Institutional monocropping in the form of enhanced legal central bank independence (CBI) had long been under-way in Asia and the rest of the world (Evans 2004). Therefore, we consider the culturally induced beliefs of central bankers, their counter-culturally formed institutions, alongside the larger political system within which they operate, and the usual structural economic (material) factors thought to shape exchange rate volatility in the Asian Financial Crisis.

Data and Methods

I analyze the experiences of nine East Asian countries and their central bank governors over 12 quarters between 1997 and 1999. The countries included in the analysis are China, Hong Kong, Indonesia, Japan, South Korea, Malaysia, Philippines, Singapore, and Thailand. Determining the beginning and ending points for analyzing a crisis is often arbitrary, and the Asian Crisis is a case in point. Gilpin (2000, 145) discusses this problem with regard to the Asian Crisis, noting that some analysts date the start of the crisis to the final weeks of 1996 when foreign investors were already becoming nervous about the ability of Thailand to repay its foreign debt. The most dramatic impact of the crisis occurred after the devaluation of the Thai baht in July of 1997 and throughout the following year as currency speculation ran rampant throughout the region. The crisis began to taper off in 1999, though its effects were certainly still felt throughout the region and the world, as periodic speculative attacks continued to occur in Asia, and both Russia and Brazil experienced their own crises. The 12 quarters of 1997–1999 should provide substantial variation on the dependent variable of interest, exchange rate volatility, across a time period that is conventionally defined as the crisis period.

Exchange rate volatility was chosen for analysis since it represents the main focal point for this crisis. Speculative attacks on currencies provided the material links between countries in the region and fostered the psychological contagion among investors that helped to fuel the Asian Financial Crisis. Most countries in the region maintained some type of peg to the U.S. dollar prior to the onset of the crisis. The Thai baht was the first to fall, after the central bank was unable to defend speculative attacks on its value relative to the dollar. However, the Indonesian rupiah, and the South Korean won were soon to follow. Some central banks launched successful defenses of their currencies, such as Hong Kong. As a result, tracking the ability of central banks, central bankers, and the governments of these countries in attempting to maintain currency stability provides a useful measure of variation during the crisis period. Exchange rate volatility is measured as the coefficient of variation of the nominal exchange rate, which is calculated as the standard deviation of a currency's value over its mean value on a quarterly basis. This is a fairly typical measure of exchange rate volatility (e.g., Frieden 2002), although there are others (e.g., Hays, Freeman, and Nesseth 2003; Leblang 2003). Data for the exchange rates are from the PACIFIC Exchange Rate Service hosted by the Sauder School of Business at the University of British Columbia, http://fx.sauder.ubc.ca/.

The primary independent variables of interest are several indicators of the operational code construct applied to the central bank governors of the aforementioned countries. All publicly available speeches given by these central bank governors were coded using the Profiler Plus software program for the operational code. Every attempt was made to secure at least one speech per quarter per central bank governor. When multiple speeches were available for a particular governor per quarter, the resulting operational code scores were averaged to produce one score to represent the quarter. In particular, I examine P-1, which is an indicator of an individual's philosophical beliefs about the nature of the political universe ranging from conflictual to cooperative. I also examine I-1, which represents an individual's own strategic approach to political goals, ranging from a conflictual to a cooperative strategy. As the central indicators of the operational code construct, these two indices are used to represent the impact of central bank governors' beliefs on exchange rate volatility. As stated in the theoretical section of the chapter, I suggest that in the Kantian monetary culture of the East Asian region, we should expect cooperative beliefs to be related to exchange rate stability. However, in keeping with previous research on the impact of central bank governors on macroeconomic outcomes, I also consider the mediating effect of central bankers' institutional environments (Thies 2004). Central banks represent an institutional manifestation of the Neoclassical Lockean culture.

The first institutional environment of concern in this study is the central bank inhabited by the central bank governors. Central banks have increasingly come to be seen in the Neoclassical view as the bearers of macroeconomic stability in the global economy. In particular, the legal independence of the central bank from the government is seen as an important determinant in the central bank's ability to promote price stability and exchange rate stability, among other supposed positive benefits (e.g., Bernhard, Broz, and Clark 2002). Independent central banks will not feel political pressure to induce surprise inflation in order to stimulate employment. In fact, increasingly, central bank charters are being rewritten to focus on one main goal: price stability, at the expense of other goals like full employment. However, most of the supposed benefits of legal CBI seem only to accrue to the developed states, with little evidence that these institutions are able to deliver the same kind of macroeconomic stability in the developing world (e.g., Maxfield 1997). The analysis in this chapter tests whether these institutions are effective in reigning in exchange rate volatility in Asia during the crisis period.

I use Cukierman's (1992) measure of the legal independence of central banks (LVAU). It is one of the more commonly used measures of CBI. The central bank charters of the countries in this sample were coded based on four main aspects of CBI. The coding produces values for the independence of the bank governor, independence of the bank on policy decisions, objectives of the bank, and limitations on lending by the bank. The values from these four areas are aggregated and weighted to arrive at a final index of CBI, which ranges from 0 (dependent) to 1 (independent). Those central banks scoring at least one standard deviation above the mean on the Cukierman index are recoded as high = 1, and all others low = 0. As mentioned previously, I also interact P-1 and I-1 with CBI to produce an estimate of the marginal effect of the individual in his institutional environment, in this case, the central banker operating within a central bank.

The second institutional environment of concern is the wider political system structure. MacIntyre (2001) has made an argument that the concentration or dispersal of veto authority in a political system produced different outcomes for the countries affected by the Asian Financial Crisis. Veto players may be institutions, organizations, and/or individuals that have the power to block change from the status quo. In particular, higher numbers of veto players can lead to a problem of policy rigidity, in which the government is not able to act in a timely manner to address a financial crisis. Lower numbers of veto players may lead to the problem of policy volatility, in which the government is able to react too quickly by changing course frequently, thus exacerbating uncertainty among investors. In

MacIntyre's analysis, he examined the impact of veto players on investment reversal during the Asian Financial Crisis, but I believe they may also impact exchange rate volatility. Veto players may also reflect the transparency of the decision-making process in the political system. A higher number of veto players are likely to reflect greater transparency, while a lower number of veto players reflect lower transparency, since fewer actors are required to review and approve policy changes. According to the IMF and other participants in the dominant Neoclassical narrative of the Asian Financial Crisis, greater transparency should mitigate the effects of an economic crisis.

The veto player measure used in this chapter is based on Keefer and Stasavage's (2002, 2003) indicator of checks. Checks is created by counting the number of veto players, taking into consideration whether the executive and legislative chamber(s) are controlled by different parties under presidential systems or the number of parties in the governing coalition in parliamentary systems based on data described in Beck et al. (2001). The result is a simple count measure that ranges from 1 to 6 in our sample, with a mean score of 3. I also interact P-1 and I-1 with the measure of veto players to produce an estimate of the marginal effect of a central banker working within the wider political system.

In addition, I consider the impact of the international institution most heavily involved in the Asian Financial Crisis—the IMF. The IMF was criticized for initially failing to get involved, then misdiagnosing the source of the crisis and demanding inappropriate structural reforms. Many observers have suggested that the structural reforms required by the IMF in countries that received assistance such as Thailand, South Korea, and Indonesia may have actually exacerbated the crisis, including former senior vice president and chief economist of the World Bank, Joseph Stiglitz (2003, 217–219). IMF intervention is measured as a dummy variable with 1 = intervention and 0 = no intervention.

I also control for a variety of other factors identified by scholars of the Asian Financial Crisis as affecting its onset and severity, including the current account balance, domestic bank credit, GDP growth, inflation, and international reserves. The current account measures a country's trade in goods and services as well as official transfers, such as a country's interest payments on foreign debt. Declining exports and perceived government inability to continue debt service obligations are part of the typical explanation for the onset of the crisis and speculative attacks on currencies. In the case of the Asian Financial Crisis a surplus on the current account should promote exchange rate stability. The weak and poorly regulated banking and financial systems of many Asian countries are also seen as precipitating conditions for the crisis. Banks had helped to fuel speculation in the real estate market, leading to inflated property values, and large portfolios of nonperforming loans. Many of these loans were denominated in foreign currencies and issued for the short-term, exacerbating the effects of speculative attacks on local currencies. Higher percentages of domestic bank credit to GDP should therefore lead to higher exchange rate volatility.

Increased GDP growth should constrain exchange rate volatility. Higher rates of inflation should be associated with increased exchange rate volatility, though the overall levels of inflation during the Asian Crisis were actually quite low, and in some cases moved to deflation during the crisis. In this particular context, higher inflation may also be related to currency stability. A higher amount of international reserves as a percentage of base money will probably increase exchange rate volatility. Currency speculators may see the accumulation of reserves as part of a country's preparation to defend against speculative attacks. Finally, I control for the quarter under analysis as an indicator of the passage of time during the crisis. Over time, we expect that volatility should decline as the region emerges from the depths of the crisis.

I estimate the following pooled cross-sectional time-series models using the Beck and Katz (1995) panel-corrected standard error approach. Two models are presented, one in which central bankers' philosophical beliefs (P-1) are interacted with their central bank and political system characteristics, as well as one in which their strategic beliefs (I-1) are similarly modeled. Including both P-1 and I-1 and these interaction terms in a combined model would pose serious multicollinearity problems.

Analysis

The effects of central bankers' beliefs about the nature of the political universe are presented in table 11.1. As expected, in a Kantian monetary culture, cooperative beliefs about the nature of the political universe (P-1) are related to exchange rate stability. Thus, as Thies (2004) has previously demonstrated, key individuals clearly have important effects on macroeconomic stability. However, the present study is the first to document the significant impact of individuals on macroeconomic stability outside of the core economies. Taken together, these two studies present an interesting picture of the significant impact of central bank governors as individuals on the economies they are charged with overseeing during the Asian Financial Crisis period across the globe. The present finding that cooperative beliefs produced exchange rate stability is clearly an anathema for classical and neoclassical monetary understandings.

Table 11.1   Central Bankers' Philosophical Beliefs and Exchange Rate Volatility in the Asian Crisis

Independent Variable	Coefficient	Panel Corrected Standard Error
P-1 (nature of the political universe)	−4.7744★	2.2328
Central bank independence	2.5726★	1.1175
P-1 × CBI	1.0866	1.6369
Veto players	−1.1860★★	0.4259
P-1 × veto players	1.5182★	0.8018
IMF intervention	4.8061★★★	0.5619
Current account balance/GDP	−0.1479★★★	0.0410
Domestic bank credit/GDP	0.0059	0.0045
GDP growth	−0.0518	0.0286
International reserves/base money	2.1828★★★	0.4128
Inflation	−0.0929	0.0530
Quarter	−0.0807	0.0551
Constant	2.8624★	1.4802

N = 93
Adj. R^2 = .58
Wald χ^2 = 135.28★★★
Note: All significance tests are two-tailed: ★ p < .05; ★★ p < .01; ★★★ p < .001.

Legal CBI also has a significant effect on exchange rates, but in this case to push them toward volatility. This finding is interesting for two reasons. First, this is one of the few studies where legal CBI is significantly related to any dependent variable of interest outside of the core economies. Second, more legally independent central banks actually promote currency volatility during the Asian Financial Crisis. I suggest that this is a result of institutional monocropping, whereby an institution designed for operation in a different monetary culture is implementing policies inconsistent with the underlying intersubjective understandings of the region. Legally independent central banks are an institutional product of the Neoclassical Lockean monetary culture. The interaction of central banker beliefs with the central bank institution has a positive sign, but is not significant.

The greater the number of veto players the lower the amount of exchange rate volatility. However, the interaction of central banker beliefs with the number of veto players actually produces a positive, significant impact on exchange rate volatility. This may reflect the possibility that the veto player concept captures both aspects of transparency in the former case and policy rigidity in the latter, though it is impossible to sort this out given the operationalization of the concept. Neoclassical ideas about the benefits of transparency in the political system seem to be born out in this analysis. Yet we also find that cooperatively minded central bankers in political systems characterized by high numbers of checks and balances end up adding to exchange rate volatility, though we should keep in mind that this is a marginal effect.

IMF intervention in countries such as Thailand, Indonesia, and South Korea served to increase exchange rate volatility. As mentioned previously, the IMF was roundly criticized for its initial inaction, perhaps reflecting classical monetary understandings, then for its requirements of domestic austerity in return for financial assistance, reflecting a neoclassical monetary understanding. The clash of monetary cultures is clearly part of what constitutes the Asian Financial Crisis as a crisis. The structural economic control variables exert the expected effects, and two of them, current account balance as a percentage of gross domestic product (GDP) and international reserves as a percentage of base money, are both highly significant.

I next examine the impact of the central bankers' strategic beliefs (I-1) on exchange rate volatility in table 11.2. Although central bankers' philosophical beliefs about the cooperative nature of the political universe (P-1) were significantly related to exchange rate stability, their strategic beliefs (I-1) were not. As an independent measure of central bankers' cooperative strategies, I find that I-1 yields a positive, though insignificant effect on exchange rate volatility. CBI again produces significant, increased exchange rate volatility. However, the interaction of I-1 and CBI just misses our conventional level of statistical significance for a two-tailed test in promoting exchange rate stability. Substantively though, it appears that Asian central bankers working within a Kantian culture may have adapted a Lockean-inspired institution to work for their benefit. Thus, rather than the Lockean institutions undoing the Kantian culture, the agents of a Kantian culture may have harnessed the Lockean institutions to their own ends.

Veto players and the interaction of veto players with central bankers' cooperative strategies yield no significant results, though the signs are in the same direction as in the previous model. IMF intervention and the structural economic control variables all affect exchange rate stability in the same direction, and some of the additional controls become significant in this model. It is important to mention that there is some degree of multicollinearity at work in both models due to the interaction terms, though the variance inflation factor (VIF) scores are higher in the first model than in the second. Gujarati (2003, 362–369) notes that VIF scores and other means of assessing the impact of multicollinearity are imperfect at best. Often, the remedies are worse than the cure, as dropping the offending variables may lead to omitted variable bias and improperly

Table 11.2 Central Bankers' Strategic Beliefs and Exchange Rate Volatility in the Asian Crisis

Independent Variable	Coefficient	Panel corrected standard error
I-1 (strategic approach to goals)	0.1093	1.0686
Central bank independence	4.0127★★★	0.7677
I-1 × CBI	−1.2565	0.7628
Veto players	−0.3722	0.2371
I-1 × veto players	0.0695	0.2922
IMF intervention	4.9304★★★	0.5815
Current account balance/GDP	−0.1637★★★	0.0405
Domestic bank credit/GDP	0.0025	0.0038
GDP growth	−0.0663★	0.0282
International reserves/base money	2.2029★★★	0.4138
Inflation	−0.1288★	0.0542
Quarter	−0.0788	0.0563
Constant	0.8525	1.1479

N = 93
Adj. R^2 = .57
Wald χ^2 = 128.19 ★★★
Note: All significance tests are two-tailed: ★ p < .05; ★★ p< .01; ★★★ p < .001.

specified models. A number of factors influence the size of the standard errors in addition to multicollinearity. The best solution would probably be more data, but the number of central banker speeches that are available for the time period is limited. Overall, I believe that the results indicate that central bankers have important effects on exchange rate stability during the Asian Financial Crisis, even considering their economic and political institutional environments, and the normal range of structural economic control variables.

Conclusion

The Asian Financial Crisis is one of the most studied economic crises in recent memory. The reasons for this are relatively simple: it was one of the most dramatic reversals in economic success in modern times, and it was the first regional crisis that threatened to derail the entire global economy. The East Asian miracle based on the Asian development model became the Asian Financial Crisis based on the Asian development model in an interesting discursive reconstitution by the IMF, U.S. Treasury, and other actors operating within a Neoclassical Lockean monetary culture. The threat posed by the Asian Financial Crisis to the core economies necessitated action by the agents of the core to supplant the Keynesian Kantian monetary culture characteristic of East Asia. The very crisis itself was in part constituted by this clash of cultures.

The analysis presented in this chapter allowed us to observe this clash of cultures. Central bankers operating on their Kantian-inspired philosophical beliefs of cooperation were able to reduce exchange rate volatility during the crisis period. Central bank institutions and IMF interventions served as Neoclassical Lockean assaults on the Kantian culture, thus exacerbating the crisis by stimulating exchange rate volatility. The one-size-fits-all approach employed by the IMF to reform its subject states seems to have failed in East Asia, at least for now. Future research should consider cultural evolution in the region in the aftermath of the crisis. Has the Keynesian Kantian culture been supplanted by the Neoclassical Lockean culture? What beliefs do central bankers hold now? How would they respond to a similar crisis in the future?

This analysis also demonstrates the utility of the operational code construct in accessing the beliefs of individuals. Although the operational code has typically been used to study foreign policy decision makers concerning security issues, this chapter demonstrates that it may be profitably applied in the economic realm as well. Future research should expand the application of the operational code to other economic actors and in noncrisis periods. Hall's (2003) discursive analysis could be replicated using the operational code construct to code the speeches of Rubin, Summer, Camdessus, Kim Young-sam, and Kim Dae-jung in the context of the Asian Financial Crisis. The findings of the operational code analysis could be compared to the interpretive analysis. I would expect the findings to be mutually supportive. However, as Hays Freeman, and Nesseth (2003) have noted, we need to look beyond those years constituted and identified as "crisis" in order to know whether our general explanatory variables operate as we expect from theory.

In terms of theory, constructivism and the operational code construct appear to be a good match. Walker (2004b) and Walker and Schafer (n.d.) have both demonstrated that constructivist theory can be investigated fruitfully with the operational code. The operational code construct expects beliefs to have mirroring, steering, and learning effects, thus serving as causal mechanisms that link macro and micro-structural levels in the constitution of identity. In this chapter, I have posited that central bankers' beliefs both mirror their monetary culture to produce effects on exchange rate stability, and possibly steer action in the face of the imposition of a foreign monetary culture. Future research could be designed to more clearly separate out these effects, as well as test for learning effects. This type of analysis could demonstrate the processes that produce, reproduce, or transform a monetary culture.

Finally, this chapter demonstrates that individuals are important to the operation of the international economy. The choice of individuals to fill central banker roles throughout the world have important consequences to the economies they are charged with managing. The current IPE literature tends to be either structural or institutional, but little intellectual space is assigned to the role of individuals. This chapter should demonstrate that a great deal of intellectual purchase is gained by adding central bankers and other key individuals to the analysis of the international political economy.

PART VI

CONCLUSION

CHAPTER 12

STRUCTURAL INTERNATIONAL RELATIONS THEORIES AND THE FUTURE OF OPERATIONAL CODE ANALYSIS

Stephen G. Walker and Mark Schafer

> *Operational code analysis is a research program and not a theory, and it employs theories unfamiliar to me.*
>
> —Waltz 1999

It is relatively easy to respond to Waltz (1999) by making the claim that models and methods from the general cognitivist research program in world politics can strengthen structural theories of international relations (Hagan 2001; Tetlock 1998). It is harder to demonstrate that the additional effort to become familiar with cognitive theories is worth it for several reasons. Beliefs and other individual-level mechanisms have not always been easily accessible inside the "black box" of decision-making processes by states, groups, and individuals, and they often need to be observed with "at-a-distance" methods (Hermann 2002; Post 2003; Schafer 2000). It has also been very time-consuming to do the process-tracing necessary to reach the microfoundations of complex processes generated inside a political system.

Over the past decade the operational code research program has begun to tackle these tasks of retrieving and coding beliefs from public and private sources into VICS indices (Schafer and Walker 2001b; Walker and Schafer 2003; Young 2001). In the past few years some operational code studies have also self-consciously attempted to bridge the gap between agent-oriented and structure-oriented explanations of foreign policy and world politics (Feng 2005; Malici 2005; Schafer and Walker n.d.; Walker 2004b; Walker, Schafer, and Young 1999). The examples set by the studies of international security and international political economy in this volume offer further support for our contention that beliefs are important causal mechanisms in world politics, which can be studied with precision and economy of effort.

All of the chapters include agents as basic units of analysis. Many of the studies proceed from the "inside-out" by beginning with a focus on the definition of the self-in-situation as the immediate cause of foreign policy preferences and decisions. The diverging and overlapping beliefs of leaders and advisors within Britain and the United States reveal explanations for conflict and consensus in policy preferences between members of the British cabinet and among members of the American executive branch. Differences in images of self and other among various types of leaders, such as terrorists, former terrorists, leaders of rogue states, leaders of divided states, and ordinary national leaders account for different patterns of likely behavior in conflict situations. Several other studies proceed from the "outside-in" in explaining the actions of agents by identifying the external context as a constraint on the actions of these agents and then incorporating the beliefs of these agents into their analyses. International economic institutions, for example, the World Bank and NAFTA, constrained the actions of central bankers in Asia and presidents of the United States. The cold war tensions between the superpowers constrained relations between Mikhail Gorbachev and Ronald Reagan, and dyadic tensions between the United States and other countries constrained American presidents in their use of economic sanctions.

At the core of these efforts is a common puzzle—whether and how do the beliefs and interests of agents matter? While the authors in this volume do not seek necessarily to explain the origins of beliefs and interests, neither do they simply assume that beliefs are determined by situations, institutions, or roles, that is, beliefs are not merely endogenous variables. The analyses in these chapters also allow beliefs to act independently as exogenous variables and to interact with material circumstances, institutional rules, or socially constructed norms to explain variations in behavior.

What do the results of these analyses tell us? Beliefs act as *causal mechanisms* in various ways within the analytical frameworks offered by different schools of foreign policy analysis and international relations theory. A causal mechanism is a process of interaction among variables, which contributes to the production of effects in the form of an agent's action or a social outcome between agents (Elster 1993; Hedstrom and Swedberg 1998). Causal mechanisms may be conceptualized separately from a general theory or be one of its components. The location and role of belief systems as causal mechanisms varies in these studies and is also tested empirically by the fit between the cases under analysis and different causal models.

The effects of beliefs in these chapters embody mirroring, steering, or learning processes. Beliefs can represent (mirror) information from the external context that influences the decisions of states to take actions that maintain or change strategies of conflict management, initiate trade disputes or economic sanctions, adopt or obstruct institutional reforms, support or change international exchange rates. Beliefs can exercise steering effects wherein old information from preexisting beliefs competes with new information from the external environment to influence decisions by introducing motivated or cognitive biases. Beliefs may also change over time to more accurately represent the environment and reverse the steering effects of biases, thereby exhibiting learning effects as a change in behavior that follows a change in beliefs.

Thies's study of the Southeast Asian financial crisis finds that the philosophical beliefs of Asian central bankers mirrored in varying degrees the initial cultural context of the Asian development model represented as a Kantian Keynsian culture of cooperation. While controlling for key economic factors and domestic and international institutional variables, Thies finds that more cooperative beliefs about the nature of the political universe (P-1) resulted in steering effects that produced less volatility in exchange rates during the Asian financial crisis.

Drury's analysis of U.S. sanctions decisions finds that operational code beliefs of U.S. presidents exerted steering effects on decisions regarding economic sanctions. Controlling for the effects of international tension, target provocation, domestic approval rating, economic misery, and other variables, Drury shows that the less cooperative/more conflictual the president's strategic orientation (I-1), the more likely he is to initiate sanctions. In addition, the greater the president's belief in control over historical development (P-4), the more likely he is to lift or decrease sanctions once they are imposed. Stevenson's study of NAFTA trade disputes shows that a U.S. president's risk orientation and his belief in the role of chance affect the decision to initiate trade disputes. When these variables are considered, moreover, they reduce the effects of economic constraints and incentives to statistically insignificant levels. They are also more strongly related to the leader's decision than domestic political constraints are.

Malici's investigation of cold war dynamics demonstrates that Gorbachev's altercasting strategy produced complex learning effects on

Reagan's beliefs leading to a change in Reagan's strategy toward the USSR. The nature of these changes was a convergence between Reagan's beliefs and Soviet actions so that his belief system more accurately mirrored external realities. This led to a shift in Reagan's strategies, tactics, and moves from confrontation to cooperation, and his responses together with Gorbachev's initiatives ended the cold war between the superpowers.

These examples show the potential importance of incorporating beliefs into structural explanations of international relations represented by realist, liberal, and constructivist accounts applied to the issue areas of security and economy. The microfoundations of actions and interactions between states do not undermine macro-theories of world politics so much as enrich them. Without bringing agents into their analyses, they remain problematic, in that they are underspecified and relatively incapable of taking more than a "first cut" at explaining what puzzles them. Operational code analysis offers one set of methods and models to address this problem with more robust results.

A related approach is agent-based modeling from the inside-out represented by profiling leaders and inferring likely patterns of behavior. The studies by Crichlow, Robison, Lazarevska et al., and Feng show that decisions and outcomes can be anticipated or explained by the beliefs of different agents. The types of agents that interact to generate policy outcomes and strategic interaction processes are imaginatively and clearly specified in these studies, and the results are intuitively appealing. It is also clear that these studies speak to the needs of policy makers who want advice about specific strategies and realistic expectations regarding the prospects for changes in the policy orientations and relations of other states.

No matter whether the analyst begins with an agent-centered orientation or proceeds within the framework of a structural theory of international relations, beliefs in these studies make contributions to the explanation of actions by states and to political outcomes in the domains of international security and political economy. On a level playing field, in which the effort to investigate puzzles in world politics engages theories from both levels of analysis, the results are enriched solutions of the puzzles. We would like to reenforce this argument in the following discussions of three recent operational code studies, which underscore the variety of contributions that beliefs can make to the explanatory power of neorealist, neoliberal, and constructivist international relations theories. Then we shall conclude with a brief assessment of the prospects for future collaboration and joint progress across actor-centered and structure-oriented research programs in world politics.

Neorealism and Strategic Adjustment

One such study is an analysis of the crisis management strategies of the United States in the post–cold war era (Walker, Schafer, and Young 1999). The authors test Kupchan's (1994) realist theory of strategic adjustment and the use of force by great powers in the face of rapid changes in their security environment. He relegates the operational codes of elites to the role of an intervening variable in a causal chain driven by the external condition of vulnerability and whether the state's power position is ascending or descending. Beliefs in this account do not escape the endogeneity trap posed by an outside-in structural theory (Keohane and Martin 2003). However, an inside-out, psychologically oriented approach to foreign policy decisions offers a rival account. It emphasizes the influence of boundaries on decisions imposed by cognitive mechanisms and personality structure even in the absence of the environmental constraints represented by the contextual variables of power, interests, or public opinion.

Kupchan's theory specifies a "severe test" for foreign policy theories in the form of crucial test situations when a psychological theory is expected to fail and a structural theory of world politics is supposed to succeed (Dessler 2003). Under the condition of low vulnerability (when a state's resources are sufficient to deal with security threats), beliefs should be less autonomous and shift readily in response to changes in the strategic environment. As the last superpower at the end of the 20th century, the vulnerability of the United States was low. To escape the "endogeneity trap" and survive a severe test, the operational codes of post–cold war presidents Bush and Clinton needed to be relatively autonomous from the strategic environment and have had a demonstrated impact on U.S. conflict behavior. If differences in their beliefs remained stable over time, indicated low vulnerability, and were consistent with the U.S. exercise of power during the foreign policy conflicts with Iraq, Panama, Bosnia, and Haiti, then such results would support a psychological explanation of foreign policy decisions for cases in which a more context-oriented explanation would expect autonomous beliefs to be both unlikely and unimportant (Walker, Schafer, and Young 1999).

The results of an operational code analysis of these foreign policy conflicts showed that: (a) Bush's and Clinton's beliefs were stable during their respective administrations; (b) their contents were consistent with a condition of low vulnerability; (c) differences in their beliefs were consistent with corresponding differences in U.S. foreign policy. Whereas the condition of high vulnerability is characterized by a threatening environment and a pessimistic assessment of the prospects for achieving fundamental political goals (Kupchan 1994, 86), Bush and Clinton shared the belief that the political universe was relatively friendly and were modestly optimistic about their goals. While the belief systems of the two presidents were stable over time and shared several common properties, Bush and Clinton also differed in their choice propensities to use promises and rewards and in their shift propensities between words and deeds. If beliefs were consistent with behavior, therefore, then the Bush administration should have been less cooperative and less flexible than the Clinton administration in foreign policy conflict situations (Walker, Schafer, and Young 1999).

A context-oriented analysis of these cases predicts that under the condition of low vulnerability, the distributions of power and interests (rather than the leader's beliefs) influence the behavior of a state in response to an opponent's moves. A three-factor multivariate analysis of variance showed that one main effect and two interaction effects were significant. The United States responded to the stimulus from the opponent's move. However, the intensity of the response was conditioned by the two-way interaction between the stimulus and the president's operational code and by the three-way interaction among the opponent's move, the leader's operational code, and the conflict type (Walker, Schafer, and Young 1999).

In this account, neither the leader's beliefs and propensities for action nor external constraints and incentives accounted by themselves for the pattern of moves taken by the United States in the four conflicts. However, the beliefs of leaders did escape the endogeneity trap, because they were autonomous and had an impact in the causal analysis of foreign policy decisions, even when the context indicated that the vulnerability of the state was low. When the stakes were lowest and the balance of power was most favorable, autonomous and idiosyncratic leadership differences were most influential (Walker, Schafer, and Young 1999).

Neoliberalism and the Democratic Peace

In another study of conflict behavior between states, the authors explored whether leaders matter in reenforcing, qualifying, or refuting the cultural explanation for the democratic peace. Do the operational code beliefs of leaders make a significant difference as causal mechanisms in determining if democracies are more pacifistic than non-democracies and in explaining why democracies (almost) never fight one another (Schafer and Walker n.d.)?

The cultural explanation of the democratic peace implies that the beliefs of democratic leaders are theoretically insignificant on one of two grounds. Either the beliefs conform to democratic norms as endogenous variables or those norms override the exogenous deviant beliefs of leaders as determinants of a state's conflict behavior. The monadic version of the democratic peace argument claims that cultural norms make democracies generally more peaceful/less war prone than non-democracies. The dyadic version recognizes that democracies are generally as war prone as non-democracies, but that shared cultural norms account for why democracies never (or rarely) fight one another (Elman 1997a, b; Maoz 1998).

Moreover, institutional differences between presidential and parliamentary democracies may favor one style of leadership over another. For example, a style of legalistic-moralism is attributed to the United States in contrast to a muddling-through style attributed to the United Kingdom. Although both dogmatists and pragmatists may be found within the same political culture, a legalistic-moralistic culture implies more dogmatism in a leader's beliefs while a muddling-through culture suggests more pragmatism in a leader's beliefs about diagnosing situations and prescribing political actions (Hennessey 1996; Kennan 1984; Stoessinger 1979; Waltz 1967).

A comparison of President Bill Clinton and Prime Minister Tony Blair revealed evidence that undermines the monadic version and supports the dyadic version of the democratic peace argument. Both leaders viewed democracies as more friendly than non-democracies, and they had significantly less cooperative orientations toward non-democracies. The operational codes of both leaders mirrored the cultural norms associated with democracies when the target of attributions in their public statements was another democracy, but individual differences appeared when the target was not a democracy. The President's operational code beliefs were significantly less conflict-oriented than the Prime Minister's toward non-democracies, a difference that was supported by corresponding differences in the behavior of their respective states toward democracies and non-democracies during the Kosovo conflict (Schafer and Walker n.d.).

The authors conclude that individual differences in the operational codes of the two leaders matter more in the management of conflict with non-democracies while cultural norms matter more in conflicts with democracies. As in the case of neorealist theory and strategic adjustment, the link between structural explanations and conflict behavior needed to be qualified in the case of neoliberal theory and the democratic peace. Both context and beliefs matter and, depending on the leader, they interact to produce differences in conflict behavior.

Constructivism and the Agent–Structure Problem

A final example of synergistic and complementary relationships between structure-oriented theories of international relations and agent-oriented theories of foreign policy is a recent study that examined the theoretical links between Wendt's (1999) constructivist theory of world politics and the emphasis on beliefs as causal mechanisms in operational code analysis (Walker 2004b). Wendt argues that states interact with one another at two levels: symbolic and strategic. At the level of symbolic interaction, states construct role identities and at the level of strategic interaction they negotiate or fight over interests. Role identities are shared images of self and other that also define interests and expectations about one another's behavior. His theory of identity construction and interest formation is summarized by the phrase, "Anarchy is what states make of it" (Wendt 1992).

It is also a structural theory, because Wendt argues that states learn who they are by taking cues from others and through socialization mechanisms for selecting among a repertoire of identities. He argues that there is a dominant culture (Hobbesian, Lockean, or Kantian) established and represented among states over time. These cultural systems are formed, maintained, or transformed by frequency-dependent interactions among states that reach a tipping point at which one of these representations takes over the logic of the system of states (Wendt 1999).

Processes of coercion, instrumental compliance, and legitimate obedience internalize the formation of each cultural system: a Hobbsian world of enemies, a Lockean world of rivals, or a Kantian world of friends (Wendt 1999, 246–263). Structural change is an extension of these processes of internalization. Symbolic interaction between states becomes an exercise in power that precedes and defines the strategic interaction between states. In Wendt's (1999) words:

> The basic idea is that identities and their corresponding interests are learned and then reinforced in response to how actors are treated by significant Others. This is known as the principle of "reflected appraisals" or "mirroring" because it hypothesizes that actors come to see themselves as a reflection of how they think Others see or "appraise" them, in the "mirror" of Others' representations of the Self. If the Other treats the Self as though she were an enemy, then by the principle of reflected appraisals she is likely to internalize that belief in her own role identity vis-à-vis the Other. Not all Others are significant, however, and so power and dependency relations play an important role in the story. (327)

Wendt (178–190) recognizes some slippage and resistance between agent responses and system imperatives and thereby leaves an opening for a dialogue between his social theory of world politics and a social–psychological theory of foreign policy based on operational code analysis. Their conjunction is most fruitful at what Wendt recognizes as a level of analysis between structure and agent. He proposes to "treat interaction as a distinct level of analysis between the unit and structural levels and locate it firmly within the purview of systemic theorizing" (147). The most important analytical work within Wendt's social theory of international relations occurs at this intermediate level of analysis. Here reside the processes that establish and connect collective beliefs at the macro-structural level with the foreign policy decisions of states and leaders. The processes of slippage and resistance operate to modify and transform the identities and interactions between states (Walker 2004b).

Because Wendt's theory is ultimately structure-oriented, he emphasizes the role positions embodied in systemic norms rather than the role identities articulated by the agents who are members of the system. At the same time, he recognizes no satisfactory account of the emergence of systemic norms is possible without actions by agents (Wendt 1999, 264). The application of Wendt's theoretical perspective to the study of Israeli–Egyptian relations following the 1973 Yom Kippur War revealed evidence consistent with Wendt's account of identity construction and alteration between the two states (Walker 2004b). The role identities for Self and Other embedded in the operational codes of Yitzak Rabin and Anwar Sadat both attributed a rival role to a generalized Other. However, they differed in the identity attributed to Self with Rabin assigning a collaborator identity to Israel and Sadat vacillating at the tipping point between an enemy and a collaborator identity for Egypt,

The analysis of the subjective games in their respective operational codes with Brams's (1994) sequential game theory suggests that Sadat resisted the role identity of rival for Egypt projected by Israel, and his subsequent decision to adopt the role of collaborator rather than enemy was crucial in leading to an Egyptian–Israeli peace treaty. He appeared to reconfigure his subjective game so that the identities attributed to Self and Other overlapped enough with the ones in Rabin's subjective game to permit the negotiation of conflicting interests between Israel and Egypt (Walker 2004b).

These likely processes of slippage and resistance are what a psychological analysis of the mirroring, steering, and learning effects of beliefs as causal mechanisms would anticipate within the operational code analysis research program. Beliefs are once again not merely endogenous variables in a structural theory of world politics. They have the power to have autonomous effects as well as simply mirroring the causal mechanisms associated with socialization and structural adjustment (see also Brams 1997, 2002; Maoz and Mor 2002). In the end, leaders and beliefs matter in a variety of ways as causal mechanisms in explanations of international relations.

The Future of Operational Code Analysis

The future dimensions of the operational code research program are foreshadowed by the preceding examples of synergism between agent-centered and structure-oriented research programs and by the studies in this edited volume. One dimension is to be the core of a cognitive research program that offers an agent-centered account of foreign policy and world politics. The focus is on profiling world leaders and extending the decision-making approach to puzzles in the domains of bureaucratic politics, security studies, and international political economy (Malici 2005; Marfleet and Miller 2005; see also Hermann 2002; Post 2003). Another dimension is to provide a method for systemic-level research programs to augment and enrich their structure-oriented explanations of world politics by incorporating beliefs as intervening causal mechanisms that either enhance or disrupt the influence of external conditions and institutions on processes of cooperation and conflict in the international system (Keohane and Martin 2003; Schweller 2003). A third dimension is to offer alternative or complementary accounts of strategic interactions between states generated by other research programs operating at the dyadic level of analysis (DiCiccio and Levy 2003; Doran 1991, 2003; Kugler and Lemke 1996; Organski and Kugler 1980). A fourth dimension is to focus on identifying nonlinear and emergent processes of complex systems with agent-based simulations of strategic interactions (Axelrod 1984, 1997; Jervis 1997; Maoz and Mor 2002).

The early returns from the efforts illustrated in this volume appear to make it worthwhile for agent-oriented and structure-oriented research programs to consider collaborative efforts and recognize that "theory complexes" of macro-level and micro-level causal mechanisms both complement and qualify one another (Hedstrom and Swedberg 1998; Laudan 1977; Little 1998; Russett and Starr 2000; Walker 2003).

Operational code analysis may make more contributions to foreign policy theory in the next decade than in the last one. The same can be said for the general cognitivist research program and maybe as well for the prospects of enhanced theoretical and empirical collaboration between foreign policy and international relations research programs (Lepgold and Lamborn 2002; Tetlock 1998). However, there are some institutional and intellectual obstacles that need to be overcome in order to fulfill this vision of the future (Geva and Mintz 1997; Lake and Powell 1999a). In order to fulfill this promise, it is desirable to expand the number of members in the general cognitivist research program within the research community of scholars who subscribe to the decision-making approach to the study of foreign policy and international politics (Snyder, Bruck, and Sapin 1954).

Missing in the past has been a way for research methods to be disseminated easily to these constituencies. There are relatively few universities with graduate programs that offer a focus in political psychology or foreign policy decision making. However, other institutional channels have opened up. There is a summer institute in political psychology at Stanford University that offers training to interested graduate students and junior faculty and a winter institute in foreign policy decision making at Texas A & M. The International Society of Political Psychology sponsors the former, and the Foreign Policy Section of the International Studies Association offers a large potential constituency for the latter.

The interest is clearly there within these organizational settings for formal training in the research methods practiced by members of the cognitivist research program. Two useful sources for this information have become available within the last five years. One is the publication of edited volumes that present different methodological innovations in content analysis for measuring the beliefs and personality traits of leaders at a distance along with their applications to a variety of world leaders (Feldman and Valenty 2001; Post 2003; Valenty and Feldman 2002). The other is the inauguration of two yearbooks that publish essays on theory and methods as well as particular research programs (Hermann 2004; Mintz n.d.).

It is also becoming more feasible to learn these methods "off the shelf" either by hand or with software tools from edited volumes such as the present one. Many are presented for use in a handbook edited by Smith (1992) and in the Post (2003) volume. Some of the content analysis methods in the latter volume have now been automated with dictionaries for use with a software program that identifies parts of speech in text files (Young 2001). These software programs are available from Social Science Automation, Inc., for purchase by individuals and institutions to do automated content analysis of public and private statements by political leaders. The advantages of reproducibility and the potential expansion of data archives with the use of desktop computing power make them likely technological engines for expanding membership within this research community and forging links with others (Dille and Young 2000; Schafer and Walker 2001a; Walker 2000).

The final missing ingredient is launching joint projects across research programs in foreign policy and international relations and overcoming some outdated stereotypes that have long divided cognitivist, rationalist, and structural research programs in foreign policy and international relations (Baldwin 1993; Geva and Mintz 1997; Lake and Powell 1999a; Tetlock 1998). This rivalry was institutionalized to some extent by a philosophy of science that emphasizes competition among theories rather than the view that the concepts and methods of different theories may complement one another. Will theories continue simply to compete and replace one another in a setting of competition across general research programs? Or will theory complexes begin to work together in a network of complex interdependence among research programs (Elman and Elman 2003; Russett and Starr 2000; Walker 2003; see also Kuhn 1970; Lakatos 1970; Laudan 1977)?

Only time will tell, but the developments chronicled earlier suggest that the barriers to collaboration are eroding in the face of intellectual and institutional innovations across a variety of fronts. The operational code studies in this book also provide preliminary evidence of the potential relevance of joint efforts across research programs to incorporate beliefs in explanations of foreign policy and world politics. Our hope is that this volume has contributed in a modest fashion to this enterprise by showing how agent-centered and structure-oriented approaches can learn from each other and solve puzzles of mutual interest and substantive importance.

BIBLIOGRAPHY

Abelson, Robert and Milton Rosenberg. 1958. "Symbolic–Psycho-Logic: A Model of Attitudinal Cognition." *Behavioral Science* 3: 1–13.

Abelson, Robert, E. Aronson, W. McGuire, T. Newcomb, and M. Rosenberg, eds. 1968. *Theories of Cognitive Consistency: A Sourcebook*. Chicago: Rand McNally.

Achen, Chris and Duncan Snidal. 1989. "Rational Deterrence Theory and Comparative Case Studies." *World Politics* 41: 143–169.

Adelman, Murray. 1973. "Crisis Decision-Making and Cognitive Balance." *Sage Professional Papers in International Studies*. Vol. 1. Beverly Hills, CA: Sage, pp. 61–94.

Alesina, Alberto and Howard Rosenthal. 1995. *Partisan Politics, Divided Government, and the Economy*. Cambridge: Cambridge University Press.

Allen, David. 1988. "British Foreign Policy and West European Cooperation." In *British Foreign Policy Under Thatcher*. Ed. Peter Byrd. New York: Philip Allan/St. Martin's Press, pp. 35–53.

Allison, Graham. 1971. *Essence of Decision*. Boston. Little, Brown.

Armitage, Richard. 2004. "Deputy Secretary Armitage." *U.S. Department of State*. Accessed September 2004. Available http://www.state.gov/r/pa/ei/pix/events/d/.

Ashley, Richard. 1986. "The Poverty of Neorealism." In *Neorealism and Its Critics*. Ed. Robert Keohane. New York: Columbia University Press, pp. 255–300.

Atick, Joseph. 2001. "How the facial recognition security system works." *CNN. com*. Accessed May 5, 2005. Available http://edition.cnn.com/2001/COMMUNITY/10/01/atick.

Axelrod, Robert. 1976. "The Analysis of Cognitive Maps." In *Structure of Decision: The Cognitive Maps of Political Elites*. Ed. Robert Axelrod. Princeton: Princeton University Press, pp. 55–73.

———. 1984. *The Evolution of Cooperation*. New York: Basic Books.

———. 1997. *The Complexity of Cooperation*. Princeton: Princeton University Press.

Azar, Edward E. 1980. "The Conflict and Peace Data Bank (COPDAB) Project." *Journal of Conflict Resolution* 24 (1): 379–403.

Azar, Edward E. and Joseph D. Ben-Dak. 1975. *Theory and Practice of Event Research: Studies in Inter-Nation Actions and Interactions.* New York: Gordon and Breach Science Publishers.

Bailey, Thomas. 1958. *A Diplomatic History of the American People.* 6th Ed. New York: Appleton-Century Crofts.

Baldwin, David. 1971. "The Power of Positive Sanctions." *World Politics* 24: 19–38.

———. 1978. "Power and Social Exchange." *American Political Science Review* 72: 1229–1242.

———. 1980. "Interdependence and Power: A Conceptual Analysis." *International Organization* 34: 471–506.

———. 1993. *Neoliberalism and Neorealism.* New York: Columbia University.

Barber, James. 1988. "Southern Africa." In *British Foreign Policy Under Thatcher.* Ed. Peter Byrd. New York: Philip Allan/St. Martin's Press, 96–116.

Barnett, Michael. 1998. *Dialogues in Arab Politics.* New York: Columbia University Press.

Beck, Nathaniel and Jonathan N. Katz. 1995. "What to Do (And Not to Do) With Time-Series Cross-Section Data." *American Political Science Review* 89: 634–647.

Beck, Nathaniel, Jonathan N. Katz, and Richard Tucker. 1998. "Taking Time Seriously: Time-Series-Cross-Section Analysis with a Binary Dependent Variable." *American Journal of Political Science* 42 (3): 1260–1288.

Beck, Thorsten, George Clarke, Alberto Groff, Philip Keefer, and Patrick Walsh. 2001. "New Tools in Comparative Political Economy: The Database of Political Institutions." *World Bank Economic Review* 15 (1): 165–176.

Becker, G. 1996. *Accounting for Tastes.* Cambridge, MA: Harvard University Press.

Beer, F.A., J.F. Ringer, A.F. Healy, G.P. Sinclair, and L. Bourne. 1992. "Ranking International Cooperation and Conflict." *International Interactions* 17 (4): 321–348.

Bennett, Andrew. 1999. *Condemned to Repetition.* Cambridge: MIT Press.

Berger, Peter. 1966. "Identity as a Problem in the Sociology of Knowledge." *European Journal of Sociology* 7: 105–115.

Bernhard, William, J. Lawrence Broz, and William Roberts Clark. 2002. "The Political Economy of Monetary Institutions." *International Organization* 56 (4): 693–723.

Bhaskar, Roy. 1979. *The Possibility of Naturalism.* Brighton, UK: Harvester Press.

Biersteker, Thomas. 1989. "Critical Reflections on Post-positivism in International Relations." *International Studies Quarterly* 33: 263–267.

Blacker, Coit. 1991. "Learning in the Nuclear Age: Soviet Strategic Arms Control Policy, 1969-1989." In *Learning in U.S. and Soviet Foreign Policy.* Eds. George Breslauer and Philip Tetlock. Boulder, CO: Westview Press.

Blumer, Herbert. 1969. "The Methodological Position of Symbolic Interactionism." In *Symbolic Interactionism: Perspective and Method.* Ed. Herbert Blumer. Englewood Cliffs, NJ: Prentice-Hall, pp. 1–60.

Bolks, Sean M. and Dina Al-Sowayel. 2000. "How Long Do Economic Sanctions Last? Examining the Sanctioning Process through Duration." *Political Research Quarterly* 53 (2): 241–265.

Bond, Doug, Joe Bond, Churl Oh, J. Craig Jenkins, and Charles Lewis Taylor. 2003. "Integrated Data for Events Analysis (IDEA): An Event Typology for Automated Events Data Development." *Journal of Peace Research* 40: 733–745.

Bonham, G. Matthew. 1993. "Cognitive Mapping as a Technique for Supporting International Negotiation." *Theory and Decision* 34: 255–273.

Bonham, G. Matthew and Michael J. Shapiro. 1986. "Mapping Structures of Thought." In *Different Text Analysis Procedures for the Study of Decision Making.* Eds. Irmtraud N. Gallhofer, Willem E. Saris, and Marianne Melmen. Amsterdam: Sociometric Research Foundation, pp. 125–139.

Brams, Steven. 1994. *Theory of Moves.* Cambridge, UK: Cambridge University Press.

———. 1997. "The Rationality of Surprise: Unstable Nash Equilibria and the Theory of Moves." In *Decisionmaking on War and Peace: The Cognitive-Rational Debate.* Eds. Nehemia Geva and Alex Mintz. Boulder: Lynn Rienner, pp. 103–129.

———. 2002. "Game Theory in Practice: Problems and Prospects in Applying It to International Relations." In *Millennial Reflections on International Studies.* Eds. Michael Brecher and Frank Harvey. Ann Arbor: University of Michigan Press, pp. 392–404.

Brecher, M. and J. Wilkenfeld. 1997. *A Study of Crisis.* Ann Arbor, MI: University of Michigan Press.

Brecher, Michael. 1977. "Toward a Theory of International Crisis Behavior: A Preliminary Report." *International Studies Quarterly* 21 (1): 39–74.

Brooks, Stephen. 1997. "Dueling Realism." *International Organization* 51: 445–477.

Brown, Harold, Joseph Prueher, and Adam Segel. 2003. *Chinese Military Power.* New York: The Council on Foreign Relations.

Brown, Justin. 2001. "Bush's Foreign-Policy Focus Closer to Home." *Christian Science Monitor* 93 (57): 2.

Bueno De Mesquita, Bruce and David Lalman. 1992. *War and Reason.* New Haven: Yale University Press.

Burbach, D. 1995. *Presidential Approval, 1949–1994.* Accessed: October 13, 1995. Available http://burbach.mit.edu/pubs/pubs.htm.

Burch, Kurt and Robert A. Denemark, eds. 1997. *Constituting International Political Economy.* Boulder: Lynne Rienner.

Burke, John and Fred Greenstein. 1989. *How Presidents Test Reality.* New York, NY: Russell Sage.

Buruma, Ian. 1996. "Mrs. Thatcher's Revenge." *The New York Review of Books*, 21 (March): 22–27.

Bush, George W. 2004. "Presidential News and Speeches." *The White House Online.* Accessed September 5, 2004. Available http://www.whitehouse.gov/news/releases/2001/01/.

Buzan, Barry, Charles Jones, and Richard Little. 1993. *The Logic of Anarchy.* New York: Columbia University Press.

Callahan, Patrick, Linda Brady, and Margaret Hermann. 1982. *Describing Foreign Policy.* Beverly Hills: Sage.

Campbell, David. 1998. *Writing Security: United States Foreign Policy and the Politics of Identity*. Minnesota: University of Minnesota Press.

Carlsnaes, Walter. 1992. "The Agency-Structure Problem in Foreign Policy Analysis." *International Studies Quarterly* 36: 245–270.

Carpenter, Ted Galen. 2005. "The Coming War with China over Taiwan: Inevitable or Avoidable?" *The Cato Institute*. Accessed May 2005. Available http://www.cato.org/dailys/08-.

Carter, Richard. 2000. "What Should We Expect in the Presidential Election?" *New York Amsterdam News* 91 (44): 20–21.

Checkel, Jeffrey. 1998. "The Constructivist Turn in International Relations Theory." *World Politics* 50: 324–348.

Cheney, Dick. 2001. "Cheney Discusses Patients' Rights, ANWR, and Kyoto." *Fox News Interview*. Accessed March 28, 2004. Available http://www.foxnews.com/story/0,2933,31241,00.html.

———. 2004. "Inside the Vice President's Office." *The White House Online*. Accessed September 7, 2004. Available http://www.whitehouse.gov/vicepresident/news-speeches/.

"China's National Defense in 2004." *People's Daily Online*. Accessed May 2005. Available http://english1.people.com.cn/whitepaper/defense2004/defense2004.html.

Christensen, Thomas and Jack Snyder. 1990. "Chain Gangs and Passed Bucks: Predicting Alliance Patterns in Multipolarity." *International Organization* 44 (2): 137–168.

Clark, William. 1998. "Agents and Structures: Two Views of Preferences, Two Views of Institutions." *International Studies Quarterly* 42: 245–270.

Clarke, H.D., E.W. Elliot, W. Mishler, M.C. Stewart, P.F. Whiteley, and G. Zuk. 1992. *Controversies in Political Economy: Canada, Great Britain, the United States*. Boulder: Westview Press.

Cohen, Michael and Robert Axelrod. 1984. "Coping with Complexity: The Adaptive Value of Changing Utility." *American Economic Review* 74: 30–42.

Cottam, Martha L. 1985. "The Impact of Psychological Images on International Bargaining: The Case of Mexican Natural Gas." *Political Psychology* 6: 413–439.

———. 1986. *Foreign Policy Decision Making: The Influence of Cognition*. Boulder, CO: Westview Press.

———. 1992. "The Carter Administration's Policy toward Nicaragua: Images, Goals, and Tactics." *Political Science Quarterly* 107 (1): 123–146.

———. 1994. *Images and Intervention: U.S. Policies in Latin America*. Pittsburgh: University of Pittsburgh Press.

Cox, Dan and A. Cooper Drury. 2002. "Democratic Sanctions: The Connection between the Democratic Peace and Economic Sanctions." Presented at the Annual Meeting of the International Studies Association, New Orleans.

Cox, Robert. 1986. "Social Forces, States and World Order: Beyond International Relations Theory." In *Neorealism and Its Critics*. Ed. Robert Keohane. New York: Columbia University Press, pp. 204–254.

Crenshaw, Martha. 2000. "The Psychology of Terrorism: An Agenda for the 21st Century." *Political Psychology* 21 (2): 405.

Crichlow, S. 1998. "Idealism or Pragmatism? An Operational Code Analysis of Yitzhak Rabin and Shimon Peres." *Political Psychology* 19: 683–706.

Crockatt, Richard. 1995. *The Fifty Years War*. New York: Routledge.

"Cross-Straight Tensions May Continue Despite Elections." *China Daily*. Accessed May 2005. Available http://www.chinaembassy.org.in/eng/ssygd/twwt/t174747.htm.

Cukierman, Alex. 1992. *Central Bank Strategy, Credibility, and Independence: Theory and Evidence*. Cambridge: MIT Press.

Dahl, Robert. 1957. "The Concept of Power." *Behavioral Science* 2: 201–215.

Deats, Richard. 2002. "Bush 'Doctrine' Too Narrow." *USA Today*, February 1.

Department of Commerce. Bureau of Economic Analysis. 1989–2002. *Economic Indicators*. Washington, DC: United States Government Printing Office.

DeRouen, Karl, Jr. 1995. "The Indirect Link: Politics, the Economy, and the Use of Force." *Journal of Conflict Resolution* 39 (4): 671–695.

Dessler, David. 1989. "What's at Stake in the Agent-Structure Debate?" *International Organization* 43: 441–473.

———. 2003. "Explanation and Scientific Progress." In *Progress in International Relations Theory*. Eds. Colin Elman and Miriam Elman. Cambridge: MIT Press, pp. 381–404.

Destler, I.M. 1992. *American Trade Politics*. 2nd Ed. Washington: Institute for International Economics.

Deutsch, Karl. 1963. *The Nerves of Government*. London: Free Press.

DiCiccio, John and Jack Levy. 2003. "The Power Transition Research Program." In *Progress in International Relations Theory: Appraising the Field*. Eds. Colin Elman and Miriam Elman. Cambridge: MIT, pp. 109–150.

Dille, Brian. 2000. "The Prepared and Spontaneous Remarks of Presidents Reagan and Bush: A Validity Comparison for At-A-Distance Measurements." *Political Psychology* 21(3): 573–585.

Dille, Brian and Michael Young. 2000. "The Conceptual Complexity of Presidents Carter and Clinton: An Automated Content Analysis of Temporal Stability and Source Bias." *Political Psychology* 21 (3): 587–596.

Doran, Charles. 1991. *Systems in Crisis*. New York: Cambridge University Press.

———. 2003. "Introduction: Power Cycle Theory and the Practice of International Relations." Special Issue of *International Political Science Review* 24 (1): 5–12.

Drezner, Daniel W. 1999/2000. "The Trouble with Carrots: Transaction Costs, Conflict Expectations, and Economic Inducements." *Security Studies* 9 (Autumn/Winter): 188–218.

———. 1999. *The Sanctions Paradox: Economic Statecraft and International Relations*. Cambridge, UK: Cambridge University Press.

———. 2001. "Outside the Box: Explaining Sanctions in Pursuit of Foreign Economic Goals." *International Interactions* 26 (4): 379–410.

Drezner, Daniel W. 2003. "The Hidden Hand of Economic Coercion." *International Organization* 57 (3): 643–659.

Drury, A. Cooper. 2000. "U.S. Presidents and the Use of Economic Sanctions." *Presidential Studies Quarterly* 30: 623–642.

———. 2001. "Sanctions as Coercive Diplomacy: The U.S. President's Decision to Initiate Economic Sanctions." *Political Research Quarterly* 54 (4): 485–508.

———. 2005. *Economic Sanctions and Presidential Decisions: Models of Political Rationality.* New York: Palgrave.

Dymond, Bill, Michael Hart, and Colin Robertson. 1994. *Decision at Midnight: Inside the Canada-US Free Trade Negotiations.* Vancouver: UBC Press.

Earle, W. 1986. "International Relations and the Psychology of Control: Alternative Control Strategies and Their Consequences." *Political Psychology* 7: 369–375.

Easton, David. 1953. *The Political System.* New York: Alfred A. Knopf.

Elliott, Kimberly Ann and Gary Clyde Hufbauer. 1999. "Same Song, Same Refrain? Economic Sanctions in the 1990s." *American Economic Review* 89 (2): 403–408.

Elman, Colin and Miriam Elman. 2003. *Progress in International Relations Theory: Appraising the Field.* Cambridge: MIT Press.

Elman, Miriam. 1997a. "The Need for a Qualitative Test of the Democratic Peace Theory." In *Paths to Peace: Is Democracy the Answer?* Ed. Miriam Elman. Cambridge: MIT, pp. 1–58.

———. 1997b. "Testing the Democratic Peace Theory." In *Paths to Peace: Is Democracy the Answer?* Ed. Miriam Elman. Cambridge: MIT, pp. 473–506.

Elster, Jon. 1982. "Sour Grapes-Utilitarianism and the Genesis of Wants." In *Utilitarianism and Beyond.* Eds. Amartya Sen and Bernard Williams. Cambridge: Cambridge University Press, pp. 219–238.

Elster, Jon.1986. *Rational Choice.* New York: New York University Press.

———. 1993. *Political Psychology.* Cambridge, UK: Cambridge University Press.

Epstein, David and Sharyn O'Halloran. 1996. "The Partisan Paradox and the U.S. Tariff." *International Organization* 50 (2): 301–324.

Evans, Peter. 2004. "Development as Institutional Change: The Pitfalls of Monocropping and the Potentials of Deliberation." *Studies in Comparative International Development* 38 (4): 30–52.

Farnham, Barbara. 1994. *Avoiding Losses/Taking Risks.* Ann Arbor: University of Michigan Press.

———. 1997. *Roosevelt and the Munich Crisis.* Princeton: Princeton University Press.

Fearon, James and Alexander Wendt. 2002. "Rationalism versus Constructivism: A Skeptical View." In *Handbook of International Relations.* Eds. Walter Carlsnaes, Thomas Risse, and Beth Simmons. New York: Sage Publications, pp. 52–72.

Feldman, Ofer and Linda Valenty. 2001. *Profiling Political Leaders: Cross-Cultural Studies of Personality and Behavior.* Westport: Praeger.

Feng, Huiyun. 2005. "The Operational Code of Mao Zedong: Defensive or Offensive Realist?" *Security Studies* 14 (October): 637–662.

Finlay, David J., Ole R. Holsti, and Richard R. Fagen. 1967. *Enemies in Politics.* Rand McNally Studies in Comparative Government and International Politics. Chicago: Rand McNally & Company.

Fiske, Susan and Shelley Taylor. 1991. *Social Cognition*. 2nd Ed. New York: McGraw-Hill.

Florini, Ann. 2004. "Behind Closed Doors." *Harvard International Review* 26 (1): 18–21.

Frieden, Jeffry A. 2002. "Real Sources of European Currency Policy: Sectoral Interests and European Monetary Integration." *International Organization* 56 (4): 831–860.

Gaddis, John. 1992/1993. "International Relations Theory and the End of the Cold War." *International Security* 17: 5–58.

———. 1992. "The Cold War's End Dramatizes the Failure of Political Theory." *The Chronicle of Higher Education* 23: A44.

———. 2005. "Grand Strategy in the Second Term." *Foreign Affairs* 84 (1): 2–16.

Gallup Poll. 1989–2002. *The Gallup Report*. Princeton, NJ: The Gallup Organization.

Gallup Poll Monthly. 2000. *The Gallup Report*. Princeton, NJ: The Gallup Organization.

Garner, W. 1962. *Uncertainty and Structure as Psychological Concepts*. New York: Wiley.

Garthoff, Raymond. 1987. *Policy versus the Law: The Reinterpretation of the ABM Treaty*. Washington, DC: The Brookings Institution.

———. 1994. *The Great Transition. American-Soviet Relations and the End of the Cold War*. Washington, DC: The Brookings Institution.

George, Alexander L. 1968. "Power as a Compensatory Value for Political Leaders." *Journal of Social Issues* 24 (3): 29–50.

———. 1969. "The Operational Code: A Neglected Approach to the Study of Political Leaders and Decision Making." *International Studies Quarterly* 23: 190–222.

———. 1979. "The Causal Nexus Between Beliefs and Behavior." In *Psychological Models in International Politics*. Ed. L. Falkowski. Boulder, CO: Westview Press, pp. 95–124.

———, 1980. *Presidential Decision Making in Foreign Policy: The Effective Use of Information and Advice*. Boulder: Westview Press.

———. 1991. *Forceful Persuasion: Coercive Diplomacy as an Alternative to War*. Washington DC: United States Institute for Peace.

———. 1993. *Bridging the Gap: Theory and Practice in Foreign Policy*. Washington DC: United States Institute for Peace.

George, Alexander L. and Andrew Bennett. 2005. *Case Studies and Theory Development*. Cambridge: MIT Press.

George, Alexander L. and Juliette L. George. 1956. *Woodrow Wilson and Colonel House*. New York: John Day.

———. 1998. *Presidential Personality and Performance*. Boulder, CO: Westview Press.

George, Alexander L., David K. Hall, and William R. Simons. 1971. *The Limits of Coercive Diplomacy: Laos—Cuba—Vietnam*. Boston: Little, Brown and Company.

Geva, Nehemia and Alex Mintz, eds. 1997. *Decisionmaking on War and Peace: The Cognitive-Rational Debate*. Boulder: Lynne Rienner.

Giddens, Anthony. 1979. *Central Problems in Social Theory*. Berkeley: University of California Press.

———. 1984. *The Constitution of Society: Outline of A Theory of Structuration*. Cambridge, UK: Polity Press.

Gilpin, Robert. 1975. *U.S. Power and the Multinational Corporation*. New York: Basic Books.

———. 2000. *The Challenge of Global Capitalism: The World Economy in the 21st Century*. Princeton: Princeton University Press.

Glad, Betty. 1973. "Contributions in Psychobiography." In *Handbook of Political Psychology*. Ed. J.N. Knutson. San Franciso: Jossey-Bass, pp. 296–321.

———. 1980. *Jimmy Carter in Search of the Great White House*. New York: W.W. Norton.

Glass, D. 1968. "Theories of Consistency and the Study of Personality." In *Handbook of Personality Theory and Research*. Eds. E. Borgatta and W. Lambert. Chicago: Rand McNally, pp. 788–854.

Gleditsch, Kristian S. 2002. "Expanded Trade and GDP Data." *Journal of Conflict Resolution* 46: 712–724.

Goffman, E. 1959. *The Presentations of Self in Everyday Life*. New York: Doubleday.

Goldblatt, J. and R. Fern. 1986. "Chronology." In *Stockholm International Peace Research Institute, World Armaments and Disarmament*. New York: Oxford University Press, pp. 598–594.

Goldmann, Kjell. 1988. *Change and Stability in Foreign Policy*. Princeton: Princeton University Press.

Goldstein, Joshua. 1992. "A Conflict-Cooperation Scale for WEIS Events Data." *Journal of Conflict Resolution* 36: 369–385.

Goldstein, Joshua and John Freeman. 1990. *Three-Way Street. Strategic Reciprocity in World Politics*. Chicago: The University of Chicago Press.

Goldstein, Judith. 1996. "International Law and Domestic Institutions: Reconciling North American 'Unfair' Trade Law." *International Organization* 50 (4): 541–564.

Goldstein, Judith and Robert O. Keohane, eds. 1993. *Ideas and Foreign Policy: Beliefs, Institutions, and Political Change*. Ithaca and London: Cornell University Press.

Gormley, Dennis. 1988. *Double Zero and Soviet Military Strategy: Implications for Western Security*. UK: Jane's.

Goshko, John. 1985. "Reagan Lashes Communism: Conciliatory Tone Dropped in Broadcast to Soviets, East Europeans." *Washington Post*, June 15, sec. A17.

Gould, Harry. 1998. "What *Is* at Stake in the Agent-Structure Debate?" In *International Relations in a Constructed World*. Eds. Vendulka Kubalkova, Nicholas Onuf, and Paul Kowert. New York: M.E. Sharpe, pp. 79–98.

Gourevitch, P.E. 1996. "Domestic Sources of International Cooperation." *International Organization* 50 (2): 301–324.

Greenstein, Fred. 1969. *Personality and Politics: Problems of Evidence, Inference and Conceptualization*. Chicago: Markham.

Gujarati, Damodar. 2003. *Basic Econometrics*. 4th Ed. New York: McGraw Hill.

Hagan, Joe. 2001. "Does Decision-Making Matter: Systemic Assumptions versus Historical Reality." In *Leaders, Groups, and Coalitions: Understanding the People and Processes in Foreign Policymaking*. Eds. Joe Hagan and Margaret Hermann. International Studies Review Presidential Series. London: Blackwell, pp. 5–41.

Hall, Rodney Bruce. 2003. "The Discursive Demolition of the Asian Development Model." *International Studies Quarterly* 47: 71–99.

Hastings, Max and Simon Jenkins. 1983. *The Battle for the Falklands*. New York: W.W. Norton.

Hays, Jude C., John Freeman, and Hans Nesseth. 2003. "Exchange Rate Volatility and Democratization in Emerging Market Countries." *International Studies Quarterly* 47 (2): 203–228.

Hedstrom, Peter and Richard Swedberg. 1998. *Social Mechanisms*. Cambridge: Cambridge University.

Heider, Fritz. 1958. *The Psychology of Interpersonal Relations*. New York: Wiley.

Heilbrunn, Jacob. 1999/2000. "Condoleezza Rice." *World Policy Journal* 16 (4): 49–54.

Hennessey, Paul. 1996. *Muddling Through: Power, Politics, and the Quality of Government in Postwar Britain*. London: Gollancz.

Hermann, Charles. 1971. "What Is a Foreign Policy Event?" In *Comparative Foreign Policy*. Ed. Wolfram Hanrieder. New York: David McKay, pp. 295–321.

Hermann, Charles, Maurice East, Margaret G. Hermann, Barbara Salmore, and Stephen Salmore. 1973. *CREON: A Foreign Events Data Set*. Beverly Hills, CA: Sage.

Hermann, Margaret G. 1974. "Leader Personality and Foreign Policy Behavior." In *Comparing Foreign Policies*. Ed. James Rosenau. New York: John Wiley, pp. 201–234.

———. 1980. "Explaining Foreign Policy Behavior Using the Personal Characteristics of Political Leaders." *International Studies Quarterly* 24 (1): 7–46.

———. 1984. "Personality and Foreign Policy Decision Making: A Study of 53 Heads of Government." In *Foreign Policy Decision Making: Perception, Cognition, and Artificial Intelligence*. Eds. Donald Sylvan and Steve Chan. New York: Praeger, pp. 53–80.

———. 1987. "Assessing the Foreign Policy Role Orientations of Sub-Saharan African Leaders." In *Role Theory and Foreign Policy Analysis*. Ed. S.G. Walker. Durham, NC: Duke University Press, pp. 161–198.

———. 2001. *Leaders, Groups, and Coalitions*. London: Blackwell.

———. 2002. *Leaders, Groups, and Coalitions: Understanding the People and Processes in Foreign Policymaking*. Special Issue of *International Studies Review*. London: Blackwell.

———. 2003. "Assessing Leadership Style: Trait Analysis." In *The Psychological Assessment of Political Leaders*. Ed. Jerrold Post. Ann Arbor: The University of Michigan Press, pp. 178–212.

———. 2004. *Political Psychology as a Perspective on Politics*. Advances in Political Psychology. Vol. 1. London: Elsevier.

Hermann, Margaret G. and Charles Hermann. 1989. "Who Makes Foreign Policy Decisions and How: An Empirical Inquiry." *International Studies Quarterly* 33: 361–387.

Herrmann, Richard K. 1984. "Perceptions and Foreign Policy Analysis." In *Foreign Policy Decision Making: Perception, Cognition, and Artificial Intelligence*. Eds. Donald A. Sylvan and Steve Chan. New York: Praeger, pp. 25–52.

————. 1985. *Perceptions and Behavior in Soviet Foreign Policy*. Pittsburgh: University of Pittsburgh Press.

Herrmann, Richard K. and Jonathan W. Keller. 2004. "Beliefs, Values, and Strategic Choice: U.S. Leaders' Decisions to Engage, Contain, and Use Force in an Era of Globalization." *The Journal of Politics* 66(2): 557–580.

Herrmann, Richard K. and Michael P. Fischerkeller. 1995. "Beyond the Enemy Image and Spiral Model: Cognitive Strategic Research after the Cold War." *International Organization* 49(3): 415–450.

Herrmann, Richard K., James Voss, Tanya Schooler, and Joseph Ciarrocci. 1997. "Images in International Relations: An Experimental Test of Cognitive Schemata." *International Studies Quarterly* 41: 403–433.

Hermann, Richard K., Phillip Tetlock, and Penny Visser. 1999. "Mass Public Decisions to Go to War: A Cognitive-Interactionist Framework." *American Political Science Review* 93: 553–573.

Hiscox, M.J. 1999. "The Magic Bullet? The RTAA, Institutional Reform, and Trade Liberalization." *International Organization* 53 (4): 669–698.

Hollis, Martin and Steve Smith. 1991. "Beware of Gurus: Structure and Action in International Relations." *Review of International Studies* 17: 393–410.

————. 1992. "Structure and Action: Further Comment." *Review of International Studies* 18: 187–188.

————. 1994. "Two Stories About Structure and Agency." *Review of International Studies* 20: 241–251.

Holsti, K.J. 1987. "National Role Conceptions in the Study of Foreign Policy." In *Role Theory and Foreign Policy Analysis*. Ed. Stephen Walker. Durham: Duke University Press, pp. 5–43.

Holsti, Ole. 1967. "Cognitive Dynamics and Images of the Enemy." *Journal of International Affairs* 21: 16–39.

————. 1970. "The Operational Code Approach to the Study of Political Leaders." *Canadian Journal of Political Science* 3: 123–157.

————. 1972. *Crisis, Escalation, and War*. Montreal: McGill-Queens University Press.

————. 1976. "Foreign Policy Viewed Cognitively." In *The Structure of Decision*. Ed. Robert Axelrod. Princeton: Princeton University Press, pp. 18–54.

————. 1977. *The 'Operational Code' as an Approach to the Analysis of Belief Systems. Final Report to the National Science Foundation*. Grant SOC 75–15368. Duke University.

Holsti, Ole and Alexander L. George. 1975. "The Effects of Stress on the Performance of Foreign Policy Makers." In *Political Science Annual*. Vol. 6. Ed. Cornelius P. Cotter. Indianapolis: Bobbs-Merrill, pp. 255–319.

Hopcraft, J.E. and J.D. Ullman. 1979. *An Introduction to Automata Theory, Languages and Computation*. Reading, MA: Addison-Wesley.

Howe, Geoffrey. 1994. *Conflict of Loyalty*. New York: St. Martin's.

Hufbauer, G. and J. Schott. 1985. *Economic Sanctions Reconsidered: History and Current Policy*. 1st Edition. Washington, DC: Institute for International Economics.

Hufbauer, G., J. Schott, and K. Elliott. 1990a. *Economic Sanctions Reconsidered: History and Current Policy*, 2nd Edition. Washington, DC: Institute for International Economics.

Hufbauer, G., J. Schott, and K. Elliott. 1990b. *Economic Sanctions Reconsidered: Supplemental Case Histories*. Washington, DC: Institute for International Economics.

Hufbauer, G., J. Schott, and K. Elliott. 2005. *Economic Sanctions Reconsidered. 3rd Ed*. Washington, DC: Institute for International Economics.

Jackson, Karl D., ed. 1999. *Asian Contagion: The Causes and Consequences of a Financial Crisis*. Boulder: Westview Press.

Janis, Irving. 1982. *Victims of Groupthink*. Boston: Houghton-Mifflin.

———. 1989. *Crucial Decisions: Leadership in Policymaking and Crisis Management*. New York: The Free Press.

Jervis, Robert. 1976. *Perceptions and Misperceptions in International Relations*. Princeton: Princeton University Press.

———. 1988. "Realism, Game Theory, and Cooperation." *World Politics* 40: 324–325.

———. 1994. "Leadership, Post-Cold War Politics, and Psychology." *Political Psychology* 15: 769–778.

———. 1997. *System Effects: Complexity in Political and Social Life*. Princeton: Princeton University Press.

———. 2003. "Understanding the Bush Doctrine." *Political Science Quarterly* 118 (3): 365–388.

Johnston, Alistair. 1995a. *Cultural Realism: Strategic Culture and Grand Strategy in Chinese History*. Princeton, NJ: Princeton University Press.

———. 1995b. "Thinking About Strategic Culture." *International Security* 19: 32–64.

Kaempfer, William H. and Anton D. Lowenberg. 1988. "The Theory of International Economic Sanctions: A Public Choice Perspective." *American Economic Review* 78 (4): 786–794.

———. 1989. "The Theory of International Economic Sanctions: A Public Choice Approach: Reply." *American Economic Review* 79 (5): 1304–1306.

Kane, Thomas. 2001. "China's Foundations: Guiding Principles of Chinese Foreign Policy," *Comparative Strategy* 20 (1): 45–55.

Kaplowitz, Noel. 1990. "National Self-Images, Perceptions of Enemies, and Conflict Strategies." *Political Psychology* 11: 39–82.

Kaplowitz, Stan. 1978. "Towards a Systematic Theory of Power Attribution." *Social Psychology* 41: 131–148.

Katzenstein, Peter, ed. 1996. *The Culture of National Security*. New York: Columbia University Press.

Keefer, Philip and David Stasavage. 2002. "Checks and Balances, Private Information, and the Credibility of Monetary Commitments." *International Organization* 56 (4): 751–774.

Keefer, Philip and David Stasavage. 2003. "The Limits of Delegation: Veto Players, Central Bank Independence, and the Credibility of Monetary Policy." *American Political Science Review* 97 (3): 407–423.

Keifer, Francine. 2002. "Backlash Grows Against White House Secrecy." *Christian Science Monitor* 94 (83): 3.

Kennan, George. 1984. *American Diplomacy*. Chicago: University of Chicago.

Keohane, Robert. 1983. "Theory of World Politics." In *Political Science*. Ed. Ada Finifter. Washington, DC: American Political Science Association, pp. 503–540.

———. 1984. *After Hegemony: Cooperation and Discord in the World Political Economy*. Princeton: Princeton University Press.

———. 1988. "International Institutions: Two Approaches." *International Studies Quarterly* 32: 379–396.

———. 2002. *Power and Governance in a Partially Globalized World*. London and New York: Routledge.

Keohane, Robert and Joseph Nye. 2001. *Power and Interdependence. 3rd Ed.* Boston: Little, Brown.

Keohane, Robert and Lisa Martin. 2003. "Institutional Theory as a Research Program." In *Progress in International Relations Theory: Appraising the Field*. Eds. Colin Elman and Miriam Fendius Elman. Cambridge, MA: The MIT Press, pp. 71–107.

Khong, Yuen. 1992. *Analogies at War*. Princeton: Princeton University Press.

Kissinger, Henry. 1982. *Years of Upheaval*. Boston: Little, Brown.

Koslowski, Rey and Friedrich Kratochwil. 1994. "Understanding Change in International Politics: The Soviet Empire's Demise and the International System." *International Organization* 48: 215–247.

Kowert, Paul and Jeffrey Legro. 1996. "Norms, Identity, and Their Limits." In *The Culture of National Security*. Ed. Peter Katzenstein. Ithaca: Cornell University Press, pp. 451–497.

Kratochwil, Friedrich. 1986. "Of Systems, Boundaries and Territoriality: An Inquiry into the Formation of the State System." *World Politics* 39: 27–52.

———. 2001. "Constructivism as an Approach to Interdisciplinary Study." In *Constructing International Relations*. Eds. Karin Fierke and Knud Erik Jorgensen. New York: M.E. Sharpe, pp. 13–36.

Krauthammer, Charles. 2002/2003. "The Unipolar Moment Revisited." *National Interest* 70: 5–18.

———. 2001. "The Bush Doctrine." *Time* 157 (9): 42.

Kugler, Jacek and Douglas Lemke. 1996. *Parity and War*. Ann Arbor: University of Michigan Press.

Kuhn, Thomas. 1970. *The Structure of Scientific Revolutions. 2nd Ed.* Chicago: University of Chicago Press.

Kupchan, Charles. 1994. *The Vulnerability of Empire*. Ithaca and London: Cornell.

Lacy, Dean and Emerson M.S. Niou. 2004. "A Theory of Economic Sanctions and Issue Linkage: The Roles of Preferences, Information, and Threats." *Journal of Politics* 66: 25–42.

Lakatos, Imre and Alan Musgrave, eds. 1970. *Criticism and the Growth of Knowledge.* Cambridge: Cambridge University Press.

Lake, David. 1988. *Power, Protection, and Free Trade: International Sources of U.S. Commercial Strategy, 1887–1939.* Ithaca: Cornell University Press.

Lake, David and Robert Powell. 1999a. *Strategic Choice and International Relations.* Princeton: Princeton University Press.

———. 1999b. "International Relations: A Strategic Choice Approach." In *Strategic Choice and International Relations.* Eds. D. Lake and R. Powell. Princeton, NJ: Princeton University Press, pp. 3–38.

Lampton, David M. 2004. "Cross-Strait Relations, the Present and Near Term, A Washington View." *The Nixon Center Publications Archive.* Accessed April 24, 2005. Available http://www.nixoncenter.org/publications/LamptonSpeech.pdf.

Langer, Ellen J. 1983. *The Psychology of Control.* Beverly Hills, CA: Sage.

Langlois, Catherine C. and Jean-Pierre Langlois. 1999. "Behavioral Issues of Rationality in International Interaction: An Empirical Appraisal." *Journal of Conflict Resolution* 43 (6): 818–839.

Lapid, Yosef. 1989. "The Third Debate: On the Prospects of International Theory in a Post-positivist Era." *International Studies Quarterly* 33: 235–254.

Larson, Deborah. 1985. *Origins of Containment: A Psychological Explanation.* Princeton: Princeton University Press.

———. 1986. "Game Theory and the Psychology of Reciprocity." Presented at the Annual Meeting of the American Political Science Association, Washington, DC.

———. 1994. "The Role of Belief Systems and Schemas in Foreign Policy Decision-Making." *Political Psychology* 15: 17–34.

Lasswell, Harold. 1958. *Politics: Who Gets What, When, How.* With Postscipt. New York: Meridian Books.

Laudan, Larry 1977 *Progress and Its Problems.* Berkeley, CA: University of California Press.

Leblang, David. 2003. "To Devalue or to Defend: The Political Economy of Exchange Rate Policy." *International Studies Quarterly* 47 (4): 533–559.

Lebow, Richard. 1994. "The Long Peace, the End of the Cold War, and the Failure of Realism." *International Organization* 48: 249–277.

Lebow, Richard and Thomas Risse-Kappen, eds. 1995. *International Relations Theory and the End of the Cold War.* New York: Columbia University Press.

LeDoux, Joseph. 2002. *Synaptic Self: How Our Brains Become Who We Are.* New York: Viking Penguin.

LeDoux, Joseph and William Hirst. 1986. *Mind and Brain: Dialogues in Cognitive Neuroscience.* Cambridge: Cambridge University Press.

Lee, Chung H., ed. 2003. *Financial Liberalization and the Economic Crisis in Asia.* London: Routledge.

Lefcourt, Herbert M. 1976. *Locus of Control.* Hillsdale, NJ: Lawrence Eribaum Associates.

Leites, Nathan. 1951. *The Operational Code of the Politburo.* New York: McGraw-Hill.

———. 1953. *A Study of Bolshevism.* New York: Free Press.

Lektzian, David and Mark Souva. 2001. "Institutions and International Cooperation: An Event History Analysis of the Effects of Economic Sanctions." *Journal of Conflict Resolution* 45 (February): 61–79.

———. 2003. "The Economic Peace Between Democracies: Economic Sanctions and Domestic Institutions." *Journal of Peace Research* 40 (6): 641–660.

Leng, Russell J. 1993. *Interstate Crisis Behavior, 1815–1980.* New York: Cambridge University Press.

Leng, Russell J. 2000. *Bargaining and Learning in Recurring Crises.* Ann Arbor, MI: University of Michigan Press.

Leng, Russell J. and Stephen Walker. 1982. "Comparing Two Studies of Crisis Bargaining." *Journal of Conflict Resolution* 26 (4): 571–591.

Lepgold, Joseph and Alan Lamborn. 2002. "Locating Bridges: Connecting Research Agendas on Cognition and Strategic Choice." *International Studies Review* 3: 3–30.

"Letters and Statements." 2005. *Project for the New American Century.* Accessed May 2005. Available http://www.newamericancentury.org/lettersstatements.htm.

Levi, Ariel and Philip Tetlock. 1980. "A Cognitive Analysis of Japan's 1941 Decision for War." *Journal of Conflict Resolution* 24: 195–211.

Levy, Jack S. 1989. "Diversionary Theory of War." In *Hand Book of War Studies.* Ed. Manus I. Midlarsky. Winchester, MA: Unwin Hyman, Inc., pp. 259–288.

———. 1994. "Learning and Foreign Policy: Sweeping a Conceptual Minefield." *International Organization* 48: 279–312.

———. 1997. "Prospect Theory, Rational Choice, and International Relations." *International Studies Quarterly* 41: 87–112.

Li, Yitan and A. Cooper Drury. 2004. "Granting MFN Status to China: Implications and Practices of Sanction Threats." *International Studies Perspectives* 5: 378–394.

Lijphart, Arend. 1971. "Comparative Politics and the Comparative Method." *American Political Science Review* 65: 682–693.

Lindsey, James M. 1986. "Trade Sanctions as Policy Instruments: A Re-examination." *International Studies Quarterly* 30: 153–173.

Little, Daniel. 1991. *Varieties of Social Explanation.* Boulder: Westview.

———. 1998. *Microfoundations, Method, and Causation.* New Brunswick: Transaction.

Lohmann, S. and S. O'Halloran. 1994. "Divided Government and U.S. Trade Policy: Theory and Evidence." *International Organization* 48 (4): 595–632.

Long, J. Scott and Jeremy Freese. 2001. *Regression Models for Categorical Dependent Variables Using Stata.* College Station, TX: Stata Press.

Luard, Tim. 2004. "Military Balance Goes Against Taiwan." *BBC News, March 9.* Accessed May 9, 2004. Available http://news.bbc.co.uk/2/hi/asia-pacific/3545361.stm.

MacIntyre, Andrew. 2001. "Institutions and Investors: The Politics of the Economic Crisis in Southeast Asia." *International Organization* 55 (1): 81–122.

Malici, Akan. 2004. "Reformers and Revolutionaries in the International System: Mikhail Gorbachev and Kim Il Sung." Ph.D. diss. Tempe, AZ: Arizona State University.

Malici, Akan. 2005. "Discord and Collaboration Between Allies: Managing External Threats and Internal Cohesion in Franco-British Relations During the 9/11 Era." *Journal of Conflict Resolution* 49: 90–119.

———. 2006. "Germans as Venutians: The Culture of German Foreign Policy Behavior." *Foreign Policy Analysis* 2 (1): 37–62.

Malici, Akan and Johnna Malici. 2005a. "The Operational Codes of Fidel Castro and Kim-Il Sung: The Last Cold Warriors?" *Political Psychology* 26 (3): 387–412.

Malici, Akan and Johnna Malici. 2005b. "When Will They Ever Learn? An Examination of Fidel Castro and Kim Jong-Il's Operational Code Beliefs." *Psicologia Politica* 31 (November): 7–22.

Mandelbaum, Michael and Strobe Talbott. 1987. *Reagan and Gorbachev*. New York: Vintage Books.

Mann, James. 2004. *Rise of the Vulcans*. New York: Penguin.

Mansfield, Edward and Marc Busch. 1995. "Political Economy of Nontariff Barriers." *International Organization* 49: 723–749.

Maoz, Zeev. 1990. *National Choices and International Processes*. New York: Cambridge University Press.

———. 1998. "Realist and Cultural Critiques of the Democratic Peace." *International Interactions* 24: 3–89.

Maoz, Zeev and Anat Shayer. 1987. "The Structure of Peace and War Argumentation." *Political Psychology* 8: 575–602.

Maoz, Zeev and Ben Mor. 2002. *Bound by Struggle*. Ann Arbor: University of Michigan Press.

Marfleet, B. Gregory. 2000. "The Operational Code of John F. Kennedy during the Cuban Missile Crisis: A Comparison of Public and Private Rhetoric." *Political Psychology* 21 (3): 545–558.

Marfleet, B. Gregory and Colleen Miller. 2005. "Failure after 1441: Bush and Chirac in the UN Security Council." *Foreign Policy Analysis* 1 (Fall): 333–359.

Marr, Andrew. 1995. *Ruling Britannia: The Failure and Future of British Democracy*. London: Michael Joseph.

Marshall, Monty and Keith Jaggers. 2000. "Polity IV Project: Political Regime Characteristics and Transitions, 1800–1999." *The Polity IV Project*. Accessed December 1, 2000. Available http://www.cidcm.umd.edu/inscr/polity/.

Maxfield, Sylvia. 1997. *Gatekeepers of Growth: The International Political Economy of Central Banking in Developing Countries*. Princeton: Princeton University Press.

McClelland, Charles A. 1966. *Theory and the International System*. New York: Macmillan.

———. 1968. "Access to Berlin: The Quantity and Variety of Events, 1948–1963." In *Quantitative International Politics: Insights and Evidence*. Ed. J. David Singer. New York, NY: The Free Press, pp. 159–186.

———. 1972. "The Beginning, Duration, and Abatement of International Crises." In *Internationl Crises*. Ed. C. Hermann. New York, NY: The Free Press, pp. 83–105.

———. 1983. "Let the User Beware." *International Studies Quarterly* 27: 169–177.

McClelland, Charles A. and Gary Hoggard. 1969. "Conflict Patterns in the Interactions Among Nations." In *International Politics and Foreign Policy, Revised Edition*. Ed. J.N. Rosenau. New York, NY: The Free Press, pp. 711–724.

McGeary, Johanna, Jay Branegan, Mark Thompson, Bruce Dickerson, John F. McAllister, and Paul Quinn-Judge. 2001. "A Salesman on the Road." *Time Europe* 158 (5): 18–19.

Mearsheimer, John. 2001. *The Tragedy of Great Power Politics*. New York: W.W. Norton.

Meernik, James. 1994. "Presidential Decision Making and the Political Use of Force." *International Studies Quarterly* 38: 121–138.

Meernik, James and Peter Waterman. 1996. "The Myth of the Diversionary Use of Force by American Presidents." *Political Research Quarterly* 49: 573–590.

Merton, Robert. 1996. *On Social Structure and Science*. Chicago: University of Chicago Press.

Miers, Anne C. and T. Clifton Morgan. 2002. "Multilateral Sanctions and Foreign Policy Success: Can Too Many Cooks Spoil the Broth?" *International Interactions* 28: 117–136.

Milbank, Dana. 1999. "What the 'W' Stands For." *New Republic* 220 (17/18): 66–71.

Milburn, T. and R. Billings. 1976. "Decision-Making Perspectives from Psychology: Dealing with Risk and Uncertainty." *American Behavioral Scientist* 20: 111–126.

Milner, H.V. and D.B. Yoffie. 1989. "Between Free Trade and Protectionism: Strategic Trade Policy and a Theory of Corporate Trade Demands." *International Organization* 43 (2): 241–272.

Minnick, Wendell. 2004. "The year to fear for Taiwan: 2006." *Asia Times Online*. Accessed April 24, 2005. Available http://www.atimes.com/atimes/China/FD10Ad02.html.

Mintz, Alex, ed. 2003. *Integrating Cognitive and Rational Theories of Foreign Policy Decision Making*. New York: Palgrave Macmillan.

———. 2004. "How Do Individuals Make Decisions: A Polyheuristic Perspective." *Journal of Conflict Resolution* 48: 3–13.

———, ed. N.d. *Advances in Foreign Policy Analysis*. New York: Palgrave. Forthcoming.

Monroe, Kristen R., James Hankin, and Renee B.V. Vechten. 2000. "The Psychological Foundations of Identity Politics." *Annual Review of Political Science* 3 (1): 419–448.

Moravcsik, Andrew. 2003. "Liberal International Relations Theory." In *Progress in International Relations Theory*, ed. Colin Elman and Miriam Fendius Elman. Cambridge: MIT Press, 149–204.

Morgan, T. Clifton. 1990. "Power, Resolve and Bargaining In International Crises: A Spatial Theory." *International Interactions* 15: 279–302.

———. 1994. *Untying the Knot of War: A Bargaining Theory of International Crises*. Ann Arbor: The University of Michigan Press.

Morgan, T. Clifton and Anne Miers. 1999. "When Threats Succeed: A Formal Model of Threat and Use of Economic Sanctions." Presented at the Annual Meeting of the American Political Science Association, Atlanta, GA.

Morgan, T. Clifton and Kenneth N. Bickers. 1992. "Domestic discontent and the External Use of Force." *Journal of Conflict Resolution* 36 (1): 25–52.

Morgenthau, Hans. 1985. *Politics Among Nations*. 6th Ed. New York: Alfred A. Knopf.

Morrow, James. 1987. "On the Theoretical Basis of a Measure of National Risk Attitudes." *International Studies Quarterly* 31: 423–439.

———. 1997. "A Rational Choice Approach to International Conflict." In *Decisionmaking in War and Peace: The Cognitive-Rational Debate*. Eds. Alex Mintz and Nehemia Geva. Boulder, CO: Lynn-Rienner, pp. 11–31.

Mulvenon, James. 2004. "Anticipation Is Making Me Wait: The "Inevitability of War" and Deadlines in Cross-Strait Relations." *China Leadership Monitor* 12. Accessed April 25, 2005. Available http://www.chinaleadershipmonitor. org/default.htm.

Noble, Gregory W. and John Ravenhill, eds. 2000. *The Asian Financial Crisis and the Architecture of Global Finance*. Cambridge: Cambridge University Press.

Nye, Joseph. 1987. "Nuclear Learning and U.S.-Soviet Security Regimes." *International Organization* 41: 371–402.

Oberdorfer, Don. 1986. "U.S. Is 'No Longer Bound' By Salt II, Weinberger Says." *Washington Post*, 28 May: A1.

———. 1991. *From the Cold War to A New Era. The United States and The Soviet Union, 1983–1991*. New York: Poseidon Press.

———. 1998. *From the Cold War to A New Era. The United States and The Soviet Union, 1983–1991*. Updated Ed. Baltimore: The Johns Hopkins University Press.

Olson, Richard Stuart. 1979. "Economic Coercion in World Politics: With a Focus on North-South Relations." *World Politics* 31: 471–494.

Onuf, Nicholas. 1989. *World of Our Making: Rules and Rule in Social Theory and International Relations*. Columbia, SC: University of South Carolina Press.

Organski, Kenneth and Jacek Kugler. 1980. *The War Ledger*. Chicago: University of Chicago Press.

Osgood, Charles E. 1960. "Cognitive Dynamics in the Conduct of Human Affairs." *Public Opinion Quarterly* 24: 341–365.

Osgood, Charles E., George J. Suci, and Percy H. Tannenbaum. 1957. *The Measurement of Meaning*. Champaign, IL: University of Illinois Press.

Ostrom, Charles and Brian Job, 1986. "The President and the Political Use of Force." *American Political Science Review* 80 (2): 541–566.

Papers of the U.S. Presidents. 1989–2002. Washington, DC: U.S. Government Printing Office.

Parunak, H. Van Dyke, Robert Savit, and Rick Riolo. 1998. "Agent-Based Modeling vs. Equation-Based Modeling: A Case Study and Users' Guide." In *Multi-Agent Systems and Agent-Based Simulation: First International Workshop, MABS '98, Paris, France, July 4–6, 1998, Proceedings*. Eds. Jaime S. Sichman, Rosario Conte, and Nigel Gilbert. Springer, LNAI 1534, pp. 10–25.

Pempel, T.J., ed. 1999. *The Politics of the Asian Economic Crisis*. Ithaca: Cornell University Press.

Peterson, Christopher, Steven F. Maire, and Martin E.P. Seligman. 1993. *Learned Helplessness: A Theory for the Age of Personal Control.* New York: Oxford University Press.

Phares, E. Jerry. 1976. *Locus of Control in Personality.* Morristown, NJ: General Learning Press.

Post, Jerrold. 1979. "Personality Profiles in Support of the Camp David Summit." *Studies in Intelligence* (Spring): 1–5.

———. 1980. "The Seasons of a Leader's Life: Influences of the Life Cycle on Political Behavior." *Political Psychology* 2 (3/4): 35–49.

———. 2003. *The Psychological Assessment of Political Leaders with Profiles of Saddam Hussein and Bill Clinton.* Ann Arbor: University of Michigan.

Powell, Colin. 2004. "Search Secretary of State Remarks." *U.S. State Department.* Accessed September 12, 2004. Available http://www.state.gov/search/search_sec_rem.cfm.

Prestowitz, Clyde. 2003. *Rogue Nation: American Unilateralism and the Failure of Good Intentions.* Cambridge, MA: Basic Books.

Przeworski, Adam. 1985. "Marxism and Rational Choice." *Politics and Society* 14: 379–409.

Purkitt, Helen. 1998. "Problem Representation and Political Expertise: Evidence from 'Think Aloud' Protocols of South African Elite." In *Problem Representation in Foreign Policy Decision Making.* Eds. D.A. Sylvan and J.F. Voss. Cambridge: Cambridge University Press, pp. 147–186.

Putnam, Robert. 1988. "Diplomacy and Domestic Politics: The Logic of Two-Level Games." *International Organization* 42 (3): 427–459.

Rapoport, A. and Melvin Guyer. 1966. "A Taxonomy of 2 × 2 Games." *General Systems: Yearbook for the Society of General Systems Research* 11: 203–214.

Raub, Werner. 1990. "A General Game-Theoretic Model of Preference Adaptations in Problematic Social Situations." *Rationality and Society* 2: 67–93.

Rawls, John. 1955. "Two Concepts of Justice." *Philosophical Review* 64: 3–33.

Reagan, Ronald. 1987a. "Remarks on Soviet-United States Relations at the Town Hall of California Meeting in Los Angeles." *Ronald Reagan Presidential Library Archives.* Accessed September 25, 2005. Available: http://www.reagan.utexas.edu/archives/speeches/1987/082687a.htm.

———. 1987b. "Joint Statement on the Soviet-United States Summit Meeting." *Ronald Reagan Presidential Library Archives.* Accessed September 25, 2005. Available http://www.reagan.utexas.edu/archives/speeches/1987/ 121087a.htm.

———. 1987c. "Remarks at INF Treaty Signing Ceremony." *Department of State Bulletin.* Accessed September 25, 2005. Available http://www.findarticles.com/p/articles/mi_m1079/is_n2131_v88/ai_6456505.

Renshon, Stanley. 1996. *High Hopes: The Clinton Presidency and the Politics of Ambition.* New York: New York University Press.

Rice, Condoleezza. 2004. "National Security Counsel-News Releases and Speeches." *The White House Online.* Accessed September 17, 2004. Available http://www.whitehouse.gov/nsc/archive.html.

Risse-Kappen, Thomas. 1994. "Ideas Do Not Float Freely: Transnational Coalitions, Domestic Structures, and the End of the Cold War." *International Organization* 48: 185–214.

Rosati, Jerel. 1981. "Developing a Systematic Decision-Making Framework: Bureaucratic Politics in Perspective." *World Politics* 33: 234–252.

———. 1987. *The Carter Administration's Quest for Global Community: Beliefs and Their Impact on Behavior.* Columbia, SC: University of South Carolina Press.

Rothkopf, David J. 2005. "Inside the Committee that Runs the World." *Foreign Policy* 147 (March/April): 30–40.

Ruggie, John. 1998. "What Makes the World Hang Together? Neo-Utilitarianism and the Social Constructivist Challenge." *International Organization* 52: 855–885.

———. 1999. "What Makes the World Hang Together? Neo-Utilitarianism and the Social Constructivist Challenge." In *Exploration and Contestation in World Politics.* Eds. P. Katzenstein, R. Keohane, and S. Krasner. Cambridge, MA: The MIT Press, pp. 215–246.

Rumsfeld, Donald. 2004. "DOD News and Press Resources." U.S. Department of Defense. Accessed September 16, 2004. Available http://www.defense. gov/search/.

Runyon, W. 1983. "Idiographic Goals and Methods in the Study of Lives." *Journal of Personality* 51: 413–437.

Russett, Bruce and Harvey Starr. 2000. "From Democratic Peace to Kantian Peace: Democracy and Conflict in the International System. In *Handbook of War Studies II.* Ed. Manus I. Midlarsky. Ann Arbor, MI: University of Michigan Press, pp. 93–128.

Sakwa, Richard. 1990. *Gorbachev and His Reforms 1985–1990.* New York: Philip Allan.

Sanger, Donald. "The Lambasting of Clinton that Didn't Last Long." *New York Times* September 16, 1999 sec. A0.

Sarbin, T.R. and V.L. Allen. 1968. "Role Theory." In *Handbook of Social Psychology.* Eds. G. Lindzey and E. Aronson. Reading, MA: Addison-Wesley, pp. 488–567.

Schafer, Mark. 1996. "Altering Conflict Attitudes Through Prenegotiation Contact." *International Interactions* 22: 89–104.

———. 1997. "Cooperation in an Objective Conflict of Interest: Testing Two Psychological Approaches." *Journal of Politics* 59: 729–750.

———. 1999. "Explaining Groupthink: Do the Psychological Characteristics of Leaders Matter?" *International Interactions* 25: 1–31.

———. 2000. "Issues in Assessing Psychological Characteristics at a Distance." *Political Psychology* 21: 511–528.

Schafer, Mark and April Glasser. 2000. "Sadat Takes Control: A Quantitative Analysis of Anwar Sadat's Operational Code Before and After the October War of 1973." *The Political Psychologist* 5: 10–16.

Schafer, Mark and Scott Crichlow. 1996. "Antecedents of Groupthink." *Journal of Conflict Resolution* 40: 415–435.

Schafer, Mark and Scott Crichlow. 2000. "Bill Clinton's Operational Code: Assessing Source Material Bias." *Political Psychology* 21 (3): 559–571.

———. 2002. "The Process-Outcome Connection in Foreign Policy Decision Making: A Quantitative Study Building on Groupthink." *International Studies Quarterly* 46: 45–68.

Schafer, Mark and Stephen G. Walker. 2001a. "The Operational Code of Vladimir Putin: Analyzing a New Global Leader with a New Automated Coding System." Presented at the Annual Meeting of the International Studies Association. Chicago, IL, February 21–24.

———. 2001b. "Political Leadership and the Democratic Peace: The Operational Code of Prime Minister Tony Blair." In *Profiling Political Leaders and the Analysis of Political Leadership: The Cross-National Study of Personality and Behavior*. Eds. Ofer Feldman and Linda Valenty. Westport, CT: Greenwood Press, pp. 21–35.

———. 2006. "Democratic Leaders and the Democratic Peace: The Operational Codes of Tony Blair and Bill Clinton." *International Studies Quarterly* 50(3).

Schafer, Mark, Michael Young, and Stephen G. Walker. 2002. "U.S. Presidents as Conflict Managers: The Operational Codes of George H.W. Bush and Bill Clinton." In *Political Leadership for the New Century: Lessons from the Study of Personality and Behavior Among American Leaders*. Eds. Ofer Feldman and Linda Valenty. Westport, CT: Praeger, pp. 51–63.

Schafer, Mark, Sam Robison, and Bradley Aldrich. 2006. "Operational Codes and the 1916 Easter Rising in Ireland: A Test of the Frustration-Aggression Hypothesis." *Foreign Policy Analysis* 2 (1): 65–84.

Schattschneider, Elmer E. 1935. *Politics, Pressures, and the Tariff*. New York: Arno Press.

Schrodt, Philip A., Shannon G. Davis, and Judith L. Weddle. 1994. "Political Science: KEDS-A Program for the Machine Coding of Event Data." *Social Science Computer Review* 12 (3): 561–588.

Schultz, George P. and Ronald Reagan. 1988. "Agreements on Afghanistan." *U.S. Department of State Bulletin*. Accessed September 25, 2005. Available http://www.findarticles.com/p/articles/mi_m1079/is_n2135_v88/ai_6495654.

Schwalbe, Michael. 1988. "Role Taking Reconsidered: Linking Competence and Performance to Social Structure." *Journal for the Theory of Social Behavior* 18: 411–436.

Schweller, Randall. 2003. "The Progressiveness of Neoclassical Realism." In *Progress in International Relations Theory: Appraising the Field*. Eds. Colin Elman and Miriam Elman. Cambridge: MIT, pp. 311–348.

Scobell, Andrew. 2001. "The Chinese Cult of Defense." *Issues and Studies* 37 (5): 100–127.

———. 2002. "China and Strategic Culture." *Strategic Studies Institute*. Occasional paper. Accessed May 2002. Available http://www.carlisle.army.mil/ssi/pubs/2002/culture/culture.htm.

Searle, John. 1995. *The Construction of Social Reality*. New York: Free Press.

Seldon, Anthony and Daniel Collings. 2000. *Britain Under Thatcher*. Harlow: Longman.

Seymour, Richard. 2005. "Are the Neocons Slipping Into Extinction?" *Middle East* 354: 26–27.

Shambaugh, David. 2002. *Modernizing China's Military: Progress, Problems, and Prospects*. Berkeley: University of California Press.

Sharp, Paul. 1991. "Thatcher's Wholly British Foreign Policy." *Orbis* 35: 395–410.

———. 1997. *Thatcher's Diplomacy: The Revival of British Foreign Policy*. New York: Palgrave Macmillan.

Shlapak, David A., David T. Orletsky, and Barry A. Wilson. 2000. "Dire Strait? Military Aspects of the China-Taiwan Confrontation and Options for U.S. Policy." *Rand Corporation*. Accessed March 2004. Available http://www.rand.org/publications/MR/MR1217/.

"Shock and Awe." 2005. *The Economist* 374 (8411): 31.

Signorino, Curtis. 1999. "Strategic Interaction and the Statistical Analysis of International Conflict." *American Political Science Review* 93: 279–298.

Simon, Dan and Keith J. Holyoak. 2002. "Structural Dynamics of Cognition: From Consistency Theories to Constraint Satisfaction." *Personality and Social Psychology Review* 6 (4): 283–295.

Simon, Herbert. 1957. *Models of Man*. New York: John Wiley.

———. 1985. "Human Nature in Politics: The Dialogue of Psychology with Political Science." *American Political Science Review* 79: 293–304.

Simon, Mark V. 1996. "When Sanctions Can Work: Economic Sanctions and the Theory of Moves." *International Interactions* 21: 203–228.

Sislin, John. 1994. "Arms as Influence: The Determinants of Successful Influence." *Journal of Conflict Resolution* 38 (4): 665–689.

Smith, Charles. 1992. *Motivation and Personality: Handbook of Thematic Content Analysis*. New York: Cambridge University Press.

Smith, Steve. 1988. "Belief Systems and the Study of International Relations." In *Belief Systems and International Relations*. Eds. Richard Little and Steve Smith. New York: Basil Blackwell, 11–36.

———. 2001. "Social Constructivism and European Studies." In *The Social Construction of Europe*. Eds. Thomas Christiansen, Knud Erik Jorgensen, and Antje Wiener. London: Sage, pp. 189–198.

———. 2004. "Policy Preferences and Bureaucratic Position: The Case of the American Hostage Rescue Mission." In *The Domestic Sources of American Foreign Policy*. Eds. Eugene Wittkopf and James McCormick. Lanham, MD: Rowman and Littlefield, pp. 303–318.

Snyder, G. and P. Diesing. 1977. *Conflict Among Nations*. Princeton: Princeton University Press.

Snyder, Richard C., Howard W. Bruck, and Burton Sapin. 1954. *Foreign Policy Decision-Making as an Approach to the Study of International Politics*. Foreign Policy Analysis Project Series, No. 3. Princeton: Princeton University Press.

———. 1962. *Foreign Policy Decision-Making: An Approach to the Study of International Politics*. New York: Free Press of Glencoe.

Starr, Harvey. 1984. *Henry Kissinger*. Lexington: University Press of Kentucky.

StataCorp. 2004. *Stata Statistical Software: Release 8.2.* College Station, TX: Stata Corporation.

"Stealth Foreign Policy." 2001. *Commonweal* 128 (7): 5–6.

Stein, A. 1990. *Why Nations Cooperate.* Ithaca, NY: Cornell University Press.

Stein, Janice. 1988. "Building Politics in Psychology." *Political Psychology* 9: 245–272.

———. 1994. "Political Learning by Doing: Gorbachev as an Uncommitted Thinker and Motivated Learner." *International Organization* 48: 155–183.

Steinbrunner, John. 1974. *The Cybernetic Theory of Decision.* Princeton, NJ: Princeton University Press.

Stephen, Andrew. 1999. "Will the Next President be a Killer?" *New Statesman* 128 (4453): 20.

Sternthal, Susanne. 1997. *Gorbachev's Reforms. De-Stalinization through Demilitarization.* Westport, CO: Praeger.

Stevenson, Matthew. 1999. "Separated by a Common Purpose: Regional and Domestic Factors in NAFTA Trade Dispute Initiation." Ph.D. diss. Tempe, AZ: Arizona State University.

Stiglitz, Joseph. 2003. *The Roaring Nineties: A New History of the World's Most Prosperous Decade.* New York: W.W. Norton.

Stoessinger, John. 1979. *Crusaders and Pragmatists.* New York: W.W. Norton.

Stryker, Sheldon. 1987. "The Vitalization of Symbolic Interactionism." *Social Psychology Quarterly* 50: 83–94.

Suedfeld, P. and Philip Tetlock. 1977. "Integrative Complexity of Communications in International Crises." *Journal of Conflict Resolution* 21: 169–184.

Suettinger, Robert L. 2004. "Leadership Policy toward Taiwan and the United States in the Wake of Chen Shui-Bian's Reelection." *China Leadership Monitor* 11. Available http://www.chinaleadershipmonitor.org/default.htm.

"Taiwan Strait IV: How an Ultimate Political Settlement Might Look." 2004. *International Crisis Group, ICG Asia Report N. 75.* Accessed May 2005. Available http://www.crisisgroup.org/home/index.cfm?id=2524&1=1.

"Taiwan's Elections, Seen from the Mainland." 2004. *The Economist,* March 18.

Taylor, Michael. 1976. *Anarchy and Cooperation.* New York: Wiley.

Tetlock, Philip. 1983. "Accountability and Complexity of Thought." *Journal of Personality and Social Psychology* 41:74–83.

———. 1985. "Integrative Complexity of American and Soviet Foreign Policy Rhetoric: A Time-Series Analysis." *Journal of Personality and Social Psychology* 49: 565–585.

———. 1991. "Learning in U.S. and Soviet Foreign Policy. In Search of an Elusive Concept." In *Learning in U.S. and Soviet Foreign Policy.* Eds. George Breslauer and Philip Tetlock. Boulder, CO: Westview Press, pp. 20–61.

———. 1998. "Social Psychology and World Politics." In *Handbook of Social Psychology.* Eds. Daniel Gilbert, Susan Fiske, and Gardner Lindzey. New York: McGraw-Hill, pp. 869–912.

Tetlock, Philip and Antony S.R. Manstead. 1985. "Impression Management Versus Intrapsychic Explanations in Social Psychology: A Useful Dichotomy?" *Psychological Review* 92: 59–77.

Thatcher, Margaret. 1993. *The Downing Street Years*. New York: HarperCollins.

Thies, Cameron G. 2004. "Individuals, Institutions, and Inflation: Conceptual Complexity, Central Bank Independence, and the Asian Crisis." *International Studies Quarterly* 48 (3): 579–602.

Tsebelis, George. 1990. *Nested Games: Rational Choice in Comparative Politics*. Berkeley: University of California Press.

Tsurumi, Masayoshi, ed. 2001. *Financial Big Bang in Asia*. Aldershot: Ashgate.

Tucker, Robert. 1965. "The Dictator and Totalitarianism." *World Politics* 17: 55–83.

Tufte, Edward R. 1978. *Political Control of the Economy*. Princeton: Princeton University Press.

Turner, Ralph. 1956. "Role-taking, Role Standpoint, and Reference Group Behavior." *American Journal of Sociology* 60: 316–328.

United States Department of State. 2003. *Patterns of Global Terrorism*. Accessed February 7, 2005. Available http://www.state.gov/s/ct/rls/pgtrpt/2003/.

Valenty, Linda and Ofer Feldman. 2002. *Political Leadership for the New Century: Personality and Behavior Among American Leaders*. Westport: Praeger.

Van Hoa, Tran and Charles Harvie. 2000. *The Causes and Impact of the Asian Financial Crisis*. New York: St. Martin's.

Vertzberger, Yaacov. 1990. *The World in Their Minds: Information Processing, Cognition, and Perception in Foreign Policy Decisionmaking*. Stanford, CA: Stanford University Press

———. 1997. "The Antinomies of Collective Political Trauma: A Pre-Theory." *Political Psychology* 18 (4): 863–874.

Walker, Stephen G. 1977, "The Interface Between Beliefs and Behavior: Henry Kissinger's Operational Code and the Vietnam War." *Journal of Conflict Resolution* 21: 129–168.

———. 1983. "The Motivational Foundations of Political Belief Systems: A Re-Analysis of the Operational Code Construct." *International Studies Quarterly* 27: 179–201.

———. 1990. "The Evolution of Operational Code Analysis. *Political Psychology* 11: 403–418.

———. 1991. "Game Theory and Foreign Policy Decisions: Solution Strategies and Restructuring Strategies in the Vietnam Conflict." Presented at the Annual Meeting of the American Political Science Association, Washington, DC.

———. 1995. "Psychodynamic Processes and Framing Effects in Foreign Policy Decision-Making." *Political Psychology* 16: 697–717.

———. 2000. "Assessing Psychological Characteristics at a Distance: Symposium Lessons and Future Directions." *Political Psychology* 21: 597–603.

———. 2002. "Beliefs and Foreign Policy Analysis in the New Millenium." In *Conflict, Security, Foreign Policy, and International Political Economy*. Eds. Michael Brecher and Frank Harvey. Ann Arbor: University of Michigan, pp. 56–71.

Walker, Stephen G. 2003. "Operational Code Analysis as a Scientific Research Program: A Cautionary Tale." In *Progress in International Relations Theory: Appraising the Field*. Eds. Colin Elman and Miriam Fendius Elman. Cambridge, MA: MIT, pp. 245–276.

———. 2004a. "The Management and Resolution of Conflict in a 'Single' Case." In *Multiple Paths to Knowledge in International Relations*. Eds. Z. Maoz, G. Mintz, T. Morgan, G. Palmer, and R. Stoll. Lanham, MD: Lexington Books, pp. 287–308.

———. 2004b. "Role Identities and the Operational Codes of Political Leaders." In *Political Psychology as a Perspective on Politics*. Vol. 1. Advances in Political Psychology. Ed. Margaret Hermann. London: Elsevier, pp. 71–106.

Walker, Stephen G. and George Watson. 1989. "Groupthink and Integrative Complexity in British Foreign Policy-Making: the Munich Case." *Cooperation and Conflict* 24: 199–212.

———. 1992. "The Cognitive Maps of British Leaders, 1938–1939: The Case of Chamberlain-in-Cabinet." In *Political Psychology and Foreign Policy*. Eds. Valerie Hudson and Eric Singer. Boulder: Westview, pp. 31–58.

———. 1994. "Integrative Complexity and British Decisions During the Munich and Polish Crises." *Journal of Conflict Resolution* 38: 3–23.

Walker, Stephen G. and Mark Schafer. 2000. "The Political Universe of Lyndon B. Johnson and His Advisors." *Political Psychology* 21: 529–544.

———. 2003. "Theodore Roosevelt and Woodrow Wilson: Realist and Idealist Archetypes?" Presented at the Annual Meeting of the International Society of Political Psychology, Boston, MA, July 5–9.

———. 2004. "Dueling with Dictators: Explaining Strategic Interaction Patterns Between the United States and Rogue Leaders." Presented at the Annual Meeting of the American Political Science Association, Chicago, IL.

———. N.d. "Operational Code Analysis and Foreign Policy Decision-Making." In *Advances in Foreign Policy Analysis*. Ed. Alex Mintz. New York: Palgrave-Macmillan. Forthcoming.

Walker, Stephen G., Mark Schafer, and Greg Marfleet. 2001. "The British Strategy of Appeasement: Why did Britain Persist in the Face of Negative Feedback?" Paper presented at the annual meeting of the American Political Science Association, San Francisco, CA.

Walker, Stephen G., Mark Schafer, and Michael Young. 1998. "Systemic Procedures for Operational Code Analysis: Measuring and Modeling Jimmy Carter's Operational Code." *International Studies Quarterly* 42: 175–190.

———. 1999. "Presidential Operational Codes and the Management of Foreign Policy Conflicts in the Post-Cold War World." *Journal of Conflict Resolution* 43: 610–625.

———. 2003. "Profiling the Operational Codes of Political Leaders." In *The Psychological Assessment of Political Leaders*. Ed. Jerrold M. Post. Ann Arbor: The University of Michigan Press, pp. 215–245.

Walt, Stephen. 1987. *The Origins of Alliances*. Ithaca, NY: Cornell University Press.

Walters, Glenn D. 2005. "Mapping the Criminal Mind: Idiographic Assessment of Criminal Belief Systems." *International Journal of Offender Therapy & Comparative Criminology* 49 (1): 5–24.

Waltz, Kenneth. 1959. *Man, the State, and War*. New York: Columbia University Press.

———. 1967. *Foreign Policy and Democratic Politics*. Boston: Little, Brown.

———. 1979. *Theory of International Politics*. New York: McGraw-Hill.

———. 1999. "Comments as a Discussant." Panel on Evaluating Progress in International Relations Theory at the Annual Meeting of the American Political Science Association, Atlanta, GA, September 2–5.

Wang, Yuan-kang. 2002. "Culture and Foreign Policy: What Imperial China Tells Us?" Paper prepared for the 2002 APSA Annual Conference.

Watson, George and Dickinson McGaw. 1980. *Statistical Inquiry*. New York, NY: John Wiley & Sons.

Watson, Russel, Roy Gutman, Martha Brant, Alan Zarembo, Christopher Dickey, and Adam Piore. 2001. "Bush vs. Iraq: The Rematch." *Newsweek* 137 (9): 38–40.

Weinstein, Eugene and Paul Deutschberger. 1963. "Some Dimensions of Altercasting." *Sociometry* 26: 454–466.

Weintraub, Walter. 1986. "Personality Profiles of American Presidents as Revealed in Their Public Statements: The Presidential News Conferences of Jimmy Carter and Ronald Reagan." *Political Psychology* 7: 85–95.

Wendt, Alexander. 1987. "The Agent-Structure Problem in International Relations Theory." *International Organization* 41 (3): 335–370.

———. 1992. "Anarchy is What States Make of it: The Social Construction of Power Politics." *International Organization* 46: 391–425.

———. 1999. *Social Theory of International Politics*. Cambridge: Cambridge University Press.

White, Stephen. 1990. *Gorbachev in Power*. Cambridge: Cambridge University Press.

Whiting, Allen. 2005. "China Versus Taiwan: Balance of Power or of Will?" *UCLA International Institute*. Accessed May 2005. Available http://www.international.ucla.edu/article.asp?parentid=6671.

Widmaier, Wesley W. 2004. "The Social Construction of the 'Impossible Trinity': The Intersubjective Bases of Monetary Cooperation." *International Studies Quarterly* 48: 433–453.

Willing, Richard. 2003. "Airport anti-terror systems flub tests." *USA Today*. Accessed May 5, 2005. Available http://www.usatoday.com/news/nation/2003-09-01-faces-usat_x.htm.

Winter, David G. 1980. "Measuring the Motives of Southern Africa Political Leaders at a Distance." *Political Psychology* 2 (2): 75–85.

———. 1987. "Leader Appeal, Leader Performance, and the Motive Profile of Leaders and Followers: A Study of American Presidents and Elections." *Journal of Personality and Social Psychology* 52: 196–202.

Winter, David G. 1991. "Measuring Personality at a Distance: Development of an Integrated System for Scoring Motives in Running Text." In *Perspectives in Personality: Approaches to Understanding Lives*. Eds. A.J. Stewart, J.M. Healy Jr., and D. Ozer. London: Jessica Kingsley, pp. 59–89.

———. 1993. "Power, Affiliation, and War: Three Tests of a Motivational Model." *Journal of Personality and Social Psychology* 65: 532–545.

Winger, David G. and A.J. Stewart. 1977. "Content Analysis as a Method of Studying Political Leaders." In *A Psychological Examination of Political Leaders*. Ed. M.G. Hermann. New York: Free Press, pp. 27–61.

Winter, David G., Margaret G. Hermann, Walter Weintraub, and Stephen G. Walker. 1991. "The Personalities of Bush and Gorbechev Measured at a Distance: Procedures, Portraits, and Policy." *Political Psychology* 12: 215–245.

Wohlforth, William. 1994/1995. "Realism and the End of the Cold War." *International Security* 19: 91–129.

———. 1998. "Reality Check: Revising Theories of International Politics in Response to the End of the Cold War." *World Politics* 50: 650–680.

Wolfowitz, Paul. 2004. "DOD News and Press Releases." U.S. Department of Defense. Accessed September 19, 2004. Available http://www.defense.gov/search/.

Woodward, Bob. 2004. *Plan of Attack*. New York: Simon and Schuster.

"A World Transformed: Foreign Policy Attitudes of the U.S. Public After September 11." *The Chicago Council on Foreign Relations: Worldviews*. Accessed April 26, 2005. Available http://www.worldviews.org/key_findings/us_911_ report.htm.

Wu, Guoguang. 2004. "Passions, Politics, and Politicians: Beijing between Taipei and Washington." *The Pacific Review* 17 (2): 179–198.

Young, Hugo. 1989. *The Iron Lady*. New York: Farrar Straus Giroux.

Young, Michael. 1996. "Cognitive Mapping Meets Semantic Networks." *Journal of Conflict Resolution* 40: 395–414.

———. 2001. "Building World Views with Profiler+." In *Progress in Communication Sciences: Applications of Computer Content Analysis*. Vol. 17. Ed. Mark D. West. Westport, CT: Ablex Publishing, pp. 17–32.

Zajonc, Robert. 1960. "The Concept of Balance, Congruity, and Dissonance." *Public Opinion Quarterly* 24: 280–296.

Zemtsov, Ilya and John Farrar. 1989. *Gorbachev. The Man and the System*. New Brunswick: Transaction.

Zhang, Tiejun. 2002. "Chinese Strategic Culture: Traditional and Present Features." *Comparative Strategy* 21 (2): 73–90.

NOTES ON EDITORS AND CONTRIBUTORS

Editors

Mark Schafer is associate professor of political science at Louisiana State University. He received a dissertation fellowship from the National Science Foundation and won the Erik Erikson Award for Early Career Achievement in 2003 from the International Society of Political Psychology. He is on the editorial board of *Political Psychology* and has published in *Journal of Conflict Resolution, International Studies Quarterly, Journal of Politics, International Interactions, Political Psychology*, and elsewhere. His research areas include the operational code, groupthink, psychological traits of leaders, and identity-based conflict and conflict resolution.

Stephen G. Walker is professor emeritus of political science at Arizona State University. He received the Distinguished Scholar Award in 2003 from the Foreign Policy Section of the International Studies Association. He has served as an editor of *International Studies Quarterly* and is on the editorial boards of *Political Psychology, Foreign Policy Analysis*, and *International Interactions*. He has published in *Journal of Conflict Resolution, International Studies Quarterly, Political Psychology, Journal of Peace Research, Journal of Politics*, and *World Politics*. He is a past vice president of the International Studies Association and the International Society of Political Psychology.

Contributors

Scott Crichlow is assistant professor of political science at West Virginia University. His research focuses on the intersection of foreign policy decision making and political psychology. His work has appeared in *International Studies Quarterly, Journal of Conflict Resolution, Cooperation and Conflict*, and *Political Psychology*.

A. Cooper Drury is assistant professor of political science at University of Missouri, Columbia. He is the author of *Economic Sanctions and Presidential Decisions:*

Models of Political Rationality (Palgrave, 2005). His most recent articles appear in *Journal of Politics, Journal of Peace Research*, and *International Political Science Review*. He has served as the president of both the Foreign Policy Analysis Section and the Midwest Region of the International Studies Association.

Huiyun Feng is assistant professor of political science at Utah State University. She has published an article in *Security Studies* based on her dissertation research on China's foreign policy, which was funded by a Jennings Randolph Fellowship from the United States Institute of Peace. She also received a Millennium Interdisciplinary dissertation fellowship from Arizona State University. Her research focuses on the security situation in the Asia-Pacific region, China's foreign policy decision making, and U.S.–China relations. Formerly she worked in the China Center for International Studies and the China Institute of International Studies.

Elena Lazarevska is currently pursuing a career with the State of Ohio. After completing her MA in international relations at Syracuse University, Ms. Lazarevska worked on a variety of research projects with Social Science Automation, Inc.

Akan Malici is a visiting assistant professor at Furman University in South Carolina. He teaches and publishes in the field of international relations with concentrations in conflict processes, political psychology, and foreign policy decision making. His empirical focus is on superpower relations, rogue states, and the European Union. His work has been published in *Political Psychology, Foreign Policy Analysis, Psicologia Politica*, and *Journal of Conflict Resolution*. He is currently engaged in a book project addressing questions of European foreign and security policy integration.

B. Gregory Marfleet is assistant professor of political science at Carleton College. He was awarded a Harry Frank Guggenheim Foundation Dissertation Fellowship and has published in *Political Psychology, Foreign Policy Analysis*, and the *Journal of Political Science Education*. His teaching and research interests include political psychology, elite foreign-policy decision making, complex systems, and agent-based modeling.

Sam Robison is a Ph.D. student in the department of political science at Louisiana State University. His current research interests include the operational code, psychological influences on U.S. foreign policy decision making, and media framing. His work has been published in *Foreign Policy Analysis* and elsewhere.

Jayne M. Sholl is currently pursuing a career in marketing. While completing her BA at The Ohio State University and thereafter Ms. Sholl worked on a variety of research projects with Social Science Automation, Inc.

Matthew Stevenson is a consultant with the Mercer Consulting Group. He currently works in the Strategy and Metrics practice in Washington, DC. He received his Ph.D. from Arizona State University in 1999.

Cameron G. Thies is associate professor in the department of political science at University of Missouri, Columbia. He has published in outlets such as the *American Journal of Political Science, Comparative Political Studies, International Studies Quarterly,* and *Political Psychology.* His current research focuses on expanding the study of individual central bankers and the institutional features of central banks in the developing world.

Michael D. Young received his Ph.D. from The Ohio State University in 1994. In 1997 he and Margaret Hermann founded Social Science Automation, Inc. to commercialize his software for general-purpose text analysis and for the creation and use of cognitive maps to forecast political behavior. He has published on these topics and on approaches to cognitive analysis more broadly. Beginning in 1998 Dr. Young has worked continuously with various federal agencies on a range of projects that seek to improve remote assessment capabilities.

INDEX

NOTE: **BOLD** indicates that a term is found in a figure or table.

.